(Continued from previous page)

Sir Harbottle Grimston, Bt. m. Mary, dau. of Sir C
b. 1602 d. 1685

George   Mary   m. Sir Capel Luckyn,   Samuel   m. (
Grimston   Grimston   Kt. and Bart.,   Grimston
b. 1631   b. 1632   b. 1621 d. 1680   b. 1643
d. 1655   d, 1718   d. 1700   d.

                                                    Elizabeth m. Wm. Savile   Edward   Mary
                                                               2nd Marquess   b. 1647   b. 1675
                                                               of Halifax   c. 1674   d. 1684

Many children, including:
Sir William Luckyn   m. Jane Cooke   Anne   m. Lord Bruce, eld. son
5th Baronet   b. 1706   Savile   & heir apparent of
b. c. 1663. Succ\ :sup:`d`. his grt-   d. 1765   Thomas, Earl of
uncle Sir Samuel Grimston   Ailesbury
1700, took name of
Grimston 1719   living issue
crtd. Visct. Grimston
d. 1756

James, 2nd   m.   Mary Bucknall   19 children
Viscount   b. 1717, d. 1778
Grimston   m. 1746
b. 1711 d. 1773

        James Bucknall   m.   Harriot Walter   5 daughters   2 sons
        3rd Viscount Grimston
        b. 1747 d. 1806

James Walter Grimston
1st Earl of Verulam   2 daughters
b. 26.9.1775
d. 17.11.1845

James Walter Grimston m.   Elizabeth Joanna Weyland   4 sons   5 daughters
2nd Earl of Verulam   d. 1886
b. 1809 d. 1895

        James Walter Grimston m. Margaret Francis Graham   3 sisters   2 brothers
        3rd Earl of Verulam   b. 1852 d. 1927
        b. 1859 d. 1924

6 sisters   James Walter Grimston m.   Lady Violet Brabazon
             4th Earl of Verulam   d. 1936
             b. 1880 d. 1949

2 brothers   James Brabazon   John   m.   Marjorie Duncan
             5th Earl of Verulam 6th Earl of Verulam   b. 1918
             b. 1910 d. 1960   b. 1912 d. 1973
             unmarried

                4 sisters   John Duncan   m.   Dione Smith
                              7th Earl of Verulam   b. 1954
                              b. 1951

THE GRIMSTONS OF GORHAMBURY

The
GRIMSTONS
of
GORHAMBURY

Norah King

PHILLIMORE

Edward Grimston, 'the Ambassador',
oil painting by Petrus Christus, 1446.

The GRIMSTONS of GORHAMBURY

Norah King

PHILLIMORE

1983

Published by
PHILLIMORE AND CO. LTD.
Shopwyke Hall, Chichester, Sussex

ISBN 0 85033 474 8

Printed and bound in Great Britain by
THE CAMELOT PRESS LTD.
Southampton, England

CONTENTS

List of Plates

Monochrome Plates
(between pages 82 and 83)

(between pages 114 and 115)

List of Text Illustrations and Family Trees

'The historical sense involves a perception, not only of the pastness of the past, but of its presence'.

T.S. Eliot, *Tradition and the Individual Talent*

Acknowledgements

My thanks go to John, 7th Earl of Verulam, for allowing me to tell the story of his family from letters, documents and diaries, and to reproduce pictures from Gorhambury in this book. Thanks also go to his wife, Dione, for encouragement during my struggles with the writing of it; many times her enthusiasm to learn more of her husband's family has spurred me on.

I do not overlook the research on pictures and papers by Violet, 4th Countess of Verulam, and her sister-in-law, Lady Sibyl Fraser (née Grimston), in the early years of this century. Violet Verulam died in 1936 a few months before I first came to Gorhambury. She had used the expertise of a kinsman genealogist, Charles Moor (d. 1943), to research very early Grimstons, and he should also be remembered, for he it was who quashed the myth that the first named Grimston, Sylvester, was standard bearer to William I at the time of the Conquest.

My thanks go to others now dead: to James, 5th Earl of Verulam, who in my younger days instilled in me a love for Gorhambury, and a thirst to learn more about it; to his brother John the 6th Earl, whose understanding personality enabled me to continue the work I loved on family diaries and letters, amid a veritable multitude of other duties. In regard to the Gorhambury portraits, I have benefited from the researches of Pamela Tudor-Craig (Lady Wedgwood).

Words of gratitude go to Robin Harcourt-Williams, Librarian at Hatfield, for his very generous help; to Frances Robson, my genealogist friend, who with obvious delight motored me to visit Grimston churches in Suffolk and Essex; to Beryl Carrington of the *Herts Advertiser*, a cheerful friend to the Grimstons and to me over the years; to Peter Walne and his staff at the Hertfordshire County Record Office who gave untold assistance, as did K.C. Newton, former County Archivist of Essex, and Joyce Wells at the St Albans Library. I wish to thank Jonathan Scott, John Wilton-Ely, and Marcus Binney for their discussions with me about Giambattista Piranesi and Robert Taylor. Elizabeth McCutcheon of the University of Hawaii at Manoa, and the publishers of the *English Renaissance Supplements* helped me with Sir Nicholas Bacon's 'sentences'. And then there is Sally Downes of the Jockey Club; Percy Birchnell, the expert on Berkhamsted; and my special friends, Pamela Kidd, Hermione Cassel, Josephine Pugh, and Mavis Silber, who have all helped in various ways. Special thanks go to Rebecca Lomax for great skill in typing out the family pedigrees for me. The staff at Heath Print, St Albans, copied old documents for me with undisguised pleasure. My publishers, Phillimore and Co., were welcoming and charming and particular thanks for her great help goes to Frances Condick.

I am indebted to my nephew, James Salmon, whose generosity has made the reproduction of so many colour plates possible.

Last of all I should record my gratitude in no small measure to my husband, who not only made most of the illustrations for the book, but whose constant encouragement kept me keeping on with it; he has, through the years, shared my fascination for Gorhambury and admiration for the Grimstons.

Note

All photographs in this book are by Basil King, husband of the author, with the exception of that of Miss Mary Grimston, photographed for the Paul Mellon Centre.

Preface

The root of the tree of Grimston was well established in Yorkshire long before the Norman Conquest. Through the centuries, a branch of the family moved south, via Suffolk and Essex, to a place in Hertfordshire known since medieval times as Gorhambury. The first Grimston to make Gorhambury his home was Sir Harbottle Grimston, who came to live there in 1652. Within the space of two years, he had lost his wife, his parents, and, in 1648, part of his home at Bradfield in Essex had been plundered and occupied by Parliamentary troops. The death of his wife Mary left him bereft. He had married her when she was fifteen; she had borne him nine children, and now at 35 she was dead.

With Mary gone, his home plundered, Sir Harbottle's former happiness at Bradfield was gone for ever. He decided he should move nearer to London, both for his own convenience and for the sake of his children. Thus he passed from the Essex scene, although Bradfield remained in his possession.

In 1651 he married again: his new bride was a young widow, Anne Meautys, whose late husband, Sir Thomas Meautys, had acquired the estate of Gorhambury from the executors of Sir Francis Bacon, Gorhambury's former owner. By 1652 Sir Harbottle Grimston had settled at Gorhambury, having bought the property from Sir Thomas's heirs. Thus began the long association between the Grimstons and Gorhambury, which has now lasted for more than 300 years. This book will trace the history of that family through good times and bad.

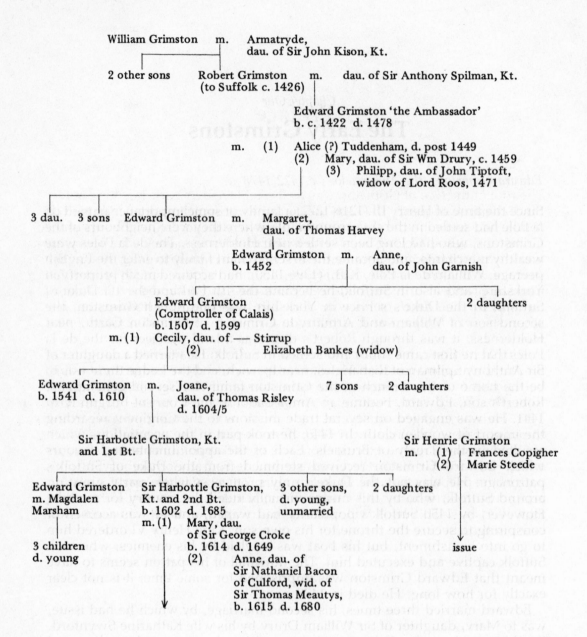

William Grimston   m.   Armatryde,
dau. of Sir John Kison, Kt.

2 other sons   Robert Grimston   m.   dau. of Sir Anthony Spilman, Kt.
(to Suffolk c. 1426)

Edward Grimston 'the Ambassador'
b. c. 1422 d. 1478

m.   (1)   Alice (?) Tuddenham, d. post 1449
(2)   Mary, dau. of Sir Wm Drury, c. 1459
(3)   Philipp, dau. of John Tiptoft,
widow of Lord Roos, 1471

3 dau.   3 sons   Edward Grimston   m.   Margaret,
dau. of Thomas Harvey

Edward Grimston   m.   Anne,
b. 1452   dau. of John Garnish

Edward Grimston   2 daughters
(Comptroller of Calais)
b. 1507 d. 1599

m. (1)   Cecily, dau. of —— Stirrup
(2)   Elizabeth Bankes (widow)

Edward Grimston   m.   Joane,   7 sons   2 daughters
b. 1541 d. 1610   dau. of Thomas Risley
d. 1604/5

Sir Harbottle Grimston, Kt.   Sir Henrie Grimston
and 1st Bt.   m.   (1) | Frances Copigher
                                                (2) | Marie Steede

Edward Grimston   Sir Harbottle Grimston,   3 other sons,   2 daughters
m. Magdalen   Kt. and 2nd Bt.   d. young,
Marsham   b. 1602 d. 1685   unmarried
                 m. (1)   Mary, dau.
3 children   of Sir George Croke
d. young   b. 1614 d. 1649   issue
                 (2)   Anne, dau. of
                 Sir Nathaniel Bacon
                 of Culford, wid. of
                 Sir Thomas Meautys,
                 b. 1615 d. 1680

Grimston Pedigree 1: The Early Grimstons

Chapter One

The Early Grimstons

Edward Grimston, 'the Ambassador', c.1422-1478

Since the time of Henry III (1216-1272) a family of some importance named de la Pole had settled in the area around Hull, where they were neighbours of the Grimstons, who had long been settled near Holderness. The de la Poles were wealthy merchants, and became the first merchant family to enter the English peerage. William de la Pole, K.B., (1396-1450), had acquired much property in Yorkshire, and also in Suffolk; he became the 4th Earl and the 1st Duke of Suffolk. In the Duke's service in Yorkshire was one Robert Grimston, the second son of William and Armatryde Grimston of Grimston Garth, near Holderness; it was through Robert's duties as a land overseer for the de la Poles that he first came south and settled in Suffolk. He married a daughter of Sir Anthony Spilman of Rishangles, near Ipswich, and the Lodge there was to be the home of this branch of the Grimston family for several generations. Robert's son, Edward, became an Ambassador at the Court of Burgundy in 1441. He was engaged on several trade missions to the Continent regarding the import of woollen cloth. In 1446, he took part in the negotiations which resulted in the Treaty of Brussels. Each of the appointments and favours which Edward Grimston received stemmed from the Duke of Suffolk's patronage. He was not the Duke's only protégé; a whole party grew up around Suffolk, who by this means virtually ruled the country for a while. However, by 1450 Suffolk's popularity had waned, and he was accused of conspiring to secure the throne for his own son. King Henry VI ordered him to go into banishment, but his boat was waylaid by his enemies, who took Suffolk captive and executed him. The downfall of his patron seems to have meant that Edward Grimston was imprisoned for some time; it is not clear exactly for how long. He died in 1478.

Edward married three times; his second marriage, by which he had issue, was to Mary, daughter of Sir William Drury by his wife Katharine Swynford. By this marriage the Grimstons became distantly connected to the royal House of Lancaster (see Appendix One for more details).

Edward's role in the foreign policy of his country is forgotten today; he has, however, another claim to fame for his contribution to the history of art. Whilst in Brussels in 1446 he did a remarkable thing; he had his portrait painted and had the good taste to sit to Petrus Christus (c.1410-1472), a rare artist of the post-Van Eyck tradition. Edward's portrait is the earliest known

1

portrait of an Englishman where the name of the sitter, the name of the artist, and the date are all authenticated. His portrait represents one of the highest pinnacles in the art annals of this country, a unique work for the 15th century. The painting is on a small panel, 12½″ x 9⅛″. It shows a youngish man with a serious expression, facing quarter-left. He is clean-shaven and wears a black cap from which a silken appendage falls over his shoulder. His doublet is green, open on the shoulders to show tight-fitting long red sleeves. His red collar is caught together over a white shirt by a gold chain and narrow bands of red. In his right hand he holds the collar of 'SS'. This livery collar was established by John of Gaunt during the reign of Edward III and it denotes royal service. The origin of the device was the motto *Souvente me souvene* in Old French, which can be translated as either 'often me remember' or 'often I recall'. Edward Grimston sits in a raftered room with a small round lattice window to the right. On the lower panelling of the wall, on either side, are two Grimston shields. On the reverse of the panel, which is painted in dark green, the Grimston coat-of-arms is repeated, with a badge representing a heart transfixed by the escapement of a clock. There is an inscription which reads *Petrus Xti me fecit a.1446*. The portrait, which is still mounted in its original frame of black wood with gilded scrolls at the corners, alternating with gilded shields bearing the Grimston arms, hangs today in the National Gallery in London, where it is on loan.

In the library at Gorhambury there is another relic of Edward Grimston, 'the Ambassador'. It is a fine 15th century manuscript, written in French on vellum. From an inscription inside the book it is evident that this rare manuscript belonged to Edward Grimston, and came into his possession on the death of his patron, William de la Pole. The volume measures 15″ by 10½″; it contains 113 folio pages, with 48 superbly painted miniatures, some of such a quality as to suggest it is the work of a master artist. The manuscript is entitled *Le Fait des Romains*. It begins delightfully with an illuminated page to show the Creation, with God carefully placing a fish into the waters, and continues with stories from the Old Testament – Noah, Abraham, Isaac and Jacob. It also includes stories of such legendary figures as Helen of Troy, Achilles, Romulus and Remus. Each story is exquisitely illuminated by the miniature paintings, which are lavishly gilded.

It is satisfying and exciting to find on an endpaper of the manuscript a reference in a poem to a 'treaty' then in progress, which could refer to the Treaty of Brussels (1446).

Sir Edward Grimston, Kt; Comptroller of Calais, 1507-1599

By the end of the 15th century, with their growing wealth and status, the Grimstons had moved from the Lodge at Rishangles to the Manor House. At this period, the Christian name of Edward was borne by many members of the family. To the recorder of their history, the repetition of this name tangles the whole thread, for not only did the eldest son in each successive generation bear the name, but several other children would also be baptised Edward, in the hope of ensuring that one child would survive to manhood to perpetuate it. It was the fame of that earlier Edward, the ambassador, that made the name important to them.

The second Grimston of merit called Edward was a great-grandson of the ambassador, born in 1507. He was a very remarkable man who lived to the age of 92. Although he suffered many hardships, he remained active until late in life. This Edward served in several Parliaments for the borough of Ipswich: he also gave service in a military capacity in the Bodyguard of Spears in 1539. In 1553 he was appointed Comptroller of Calais, and reported back to England on the defences of the town in very unfavourable terms.

These defences were soon to be put to the test, for in 1558 the French forces laid siege to the town, and Edward Grimston was one of the leaders of the beleaguered garrison. A report on the state of the defences in Calais sent to London noted that 'my Lord [Grey] commanded the soldiers of his garrison to keep their ordinary wards, and Master Grimston to the breach with the residue of the best soldiers'. As soon as it became clear that a siege was inevitable, Edward had sent his wife Elizabeth and his children back home to Rishangles Manor, by ship. The English garrison, inadequate and ill-equipped, as Edward had earlier reported, consisted of 800 men: for seven days they put up a gallant but ultimately useless resistance to the 30,000-strong forces of the Duc de Guise. On 7 January , 1558, 'Thomas, Lord Wentworth, Sir Ralph Chamberlain, Edward Grimston and Nicholas Alexander sent a herald and trumpeter to the Duc de Guise to surrender the town of Calais, with all its goods, worth £20,000, to the King of France, after which the four admitted a captain and 30 of the enemy's army by the Boulogne Gate that they might seize the city'.

Edward Grimston was now a French prisoner; the ransom set upon him was very high. Having now lost the great estate which he had acquired around Calais, he felt that he could put no further financial burden on his family by gaining his liberty at the high price of 10,000 crowns. He determined that he would either remain a prisoner, or make a bid to escape. For 19 months he was a prisoner in the Bastille. Then he made a dramatic and exciting escape. The way in which he achieved this is described in his own narrative, the manuscript of which, written in his own handwriting, still survives. The story was intended for his family, perhaps for a favourite daughter, for on the back of the first sheet are these words: 'to my daughter Grimston at Bradfield give this'.

[1558]. At the earnest request of my friends I am moved to call to mind and to set down in writing my being taken prisoner at the loss of Calais, my continuance in prison and my delivery by the great favour, aid and assistance of Almighty God. First Calais was yielded to the Duke of Guise in the Christmas the 4th and 5th year of King Philip and Queen Mary; the Lord Wentworth (being Deputy), Sir Ralph Chamberleyne, Captain of the Castle, Sir Anthony Ager, marshal, being slain, with all the rest of the council there being taken prisoners. I, Edward Grimston, being then Controller of the said town and marches, with all the garrisons and fortresses of that side of the seas, after the town was yielded, was taken and carried out of the town of Calais by one Monsieur de Suasse [sic] to the French camp, lying at Sandgate and remaining there two nights and being then carried back to Calais. After two days remaining there I was given and delivered as prisoner to Monsieur Sopyer [sic] who committed me to the charge and custody of an Italian, being a farrier or smith, and to four Frenchmen, harquebusiers, who carried me in the first day from Calais to Boulogne in my nightgown without any boots, and the next day to Hardlowe [sic], where I and they remained until the King returned and had dissolved his camp: from thence I was carried to Abbeville, where I had a new pair of boots, and from thence to Bewoyss [sic]: from thence to St Denis to dinner, where they procured me the sight of all the shrines and the jewels of the house, and so that night to Paris to the house of one Gavaston, an Italian and captain of the watch of horsemen in Paris, where I was kept close prisoner until Ash Wednesday, and then carried from thence to the Bastille, where I remained 19 months; and being there I was often solicited...to yield to the payment of 10,000 crowns, for my ransom, being a sum much more than I was any way able to pay.

Edward decided to try to file through the bars of his prison window, and persuaded Sir Nicholas Throckmorton, the English ambassador in Paris, to procure files for him and to arrange for their secret delivery to him.

I was 21 days in filing; I cut two bars of irons, either of them the bigness of mine arm, and one cross-bar twice cut; to cover the cinder of the filing was somewhat troublesome, but I did it with water and ashes; and to make the bars to stand fast after the filing, I did it with wet brown paper...The days before my coming-forth, I prepared something in readiness as by ripping of some of my canvas curtains, putting my shirts, handkerchiefs, and books into a canvas wallet, and in the pockets of my nightgown I did put my bag and certain monies, in it also my boots and spurs.

At last, one dark night, after he had supped and the keeper of the keys had left, Edward took out one of the bars (which he says weighed about 40 lbs) from his window, and laid it in the straw, beneath his bed. He threw his gown, wallet and boots out of the window, and then replaced the bar. As usual, soldiers then searched the room before one of them was locked in with Edward for the night. Edward then offered wine liberally to his guard, who became drunk and eventually fell into a heavy sleep. To make sure that the soldier was oblivious of everything, Edward 'feigned occasion to go to the privy', as he had often done before, since he was suffering from 'some looseness'. The soldier did not stir. Edward then tore up his sheets and curtains, and fastened them together to make a rope, which he estimated to be about 16 yards long. One end was tied to the remaining bar in the cell window, and then Edward slid down the rope to freedom. On reaching the ground, however, an unpleasant surprise awaited him: his wallet, books and gown, which he had thrown out earlier, had been stolen. Worse still, Hans, an accomplice, who was meant to be meeting him, was nowhere to be seen.

In a heap of great free stones I did draw on my boots, and with a half-kerchief did bind up my beard, after the Scottish manner, then ensued and did take my wallet upon my shoulder and (at a breach in the wall) I did go into the city (for I durst not go [by] the fields nor woods, for I had no clothes to cover me from cold, nor weapons to defend me from the wolves or any other thing) and walk[ed] all that night up and down in the city.

Edward made his way to the house occupied by the English peer, Lord Grey, only to find that he and his people had left two days earlier. He tried to find a lodging, but was refused several times because he had no horse, a sufficiently unusual circumstance to arouse suspicion. However, eventually Edward found a widow, with two daughters, who took him in and gave him a breakfast of sheep's feet and white wine, which he described as 'a pleasant breakfast after a cold night's travel'. After dinner, while Edward was resting, officials came to search the widow's house, for Protestant fugitives (who were opposed to the dominance of the Catholic Guise family). Edward managed to convince these inquisitors that he was a Scot, come to serve in the French King's Scottish Guard; they left him in peace, but warned him to be gone from the city in the morning. The widow gave Edward some of her dead husband's clothes and clad in these, he set off again to search the city for help. After a long search in the university area, he found Hans, and with his help procured horses for them both. Together Edward and Hans travelled towards the coast, going via Nantes and Caen.

On the coast of Brittany they hired a sailing boat and set out for England; but after only one night afloat, the bad weather drove them back to Brittany: 'where the seas rose very high; and being all the night and day sore tormented, and our foremast and sail blown over the board, our mainsail torn through'. Fortunately the storm at last abated, and after 'amending' their sails, the two set off again. When they sighted land, they thought their troubles were at an end, for it was the island of Guernsey, then as now English territory. However, the rough seas drove them too near the rocks, and they had to anchor for the night in a position of extreme danger. In the morning, they saw men on shore, and having attracted their attention by signals, were aided to safety, jumping from rock to rock. When Edward was safely on dry land, he 'knelt down and made a cross, and did kiss it, giving God thanks that we were upon English ground'.

Edward's escape was by no means the end of his troubles. He ultimately reached London, only to be arrested and held as a traitor for his part in the surrender of Calais. His trial took place on 1 December 1559, and the indictment and record of it still exist. He pleaded not guilty, and eventually the court passed a verdict in his favour and released him. 'I did weep full bitterly', he wrote, 'for in truth in hearing and answering what was said and vehemently objected against me, I did sweat as if I had travelled in a hot summer's day'. On 14 December, Queen Elizabeth I (newly come to the throne in succession to her sister Mary) exonerated Edward Grimston from charges of treason and restored his property to him.

After his return to England, he continued to play an important part in public life. He represented the constituencies of Ipswich and Eye, and finally that of Oxford, in various Parliaments; he was still an MP in 1593 when he was 86. This wonderful old man was still employed in diplomatic work in France in the 1580s and 1590s, so it would appear that his daring escape had not permanently soured his relationship with the French.

Edward died in 1599, aged 92, after a life of immense distinction and activity. He was buried in the old Saxon church at Rishangles. He is immortalised in a brass on the south wall, which bears the following inscription:

> By twice two Kings and Queens his life was graced
> Yet one religion held from first to last
> Justice and truth he loved and common good
> No less than the issue of his private blood,
> His years more than himself did others please
> For counsel and discourse of war and peace
> His life was rule to lives, his death a mirror
> One felt no vain care nor the other terror.

Although this epitaph states that 'by twice two Kings and Queens his life was graced', (ie Henry VIII, Edward VI, Mary I and Elizabeth I), Edward was actually born in the reign of Henry VII, and thus lived through five reigns, not four.

There are two pictures of him at Gorhambury: the first shows him as a middle-aged man with a reddish brown beard and moustache, blue eyes and dark eyebrows. He wears a small black velvet cap, a tight-fitting black doublet and full breeches. His sleeves are close-fitting, slightly puffed at the shoulders. At his neck and wrists are narrow frills. In his right hand he holds a leather bag. On the slate-coloured background to his right are the Arms of the Guild of the Wool Staple of Calais. From this shield it may be concluded that Edward Grimston was a member of this Guild. The Staple was a town or place appointed by royal authority, in which was a body of merchants having the exclusive right of purchase of certain classes of goods destined for export.

The second portrait, a half-length, represents an aged man with blue eyes and a long thin white beard. It is attributed to the brush of Robert Peake. The subject wears a high-crowned hat, black doublet and a close white ruff. Both hands are gloved and in the left he holds a skull. The Grimston arms appear in the top right-hand corner, with the motto *Gratia dei Grata*. This latter portrait is mentioned by Pennant as 'in the dining parlour' at Gorhambury. This refers to its position in the Tudor house at Gorhambury.

Edward Grimston, 'The Lawyer', (1541-1610)

The founder of the legal tradition in the Grimston family was yet another Edward, the eldest son of the Comptroller of Calais by his second wife, Cecily Styrrope of Ipswich. Edward was admitted to Gray's Inn in 1559. As well as being a practising lawyer, Edward was a man of letters. He made translations into English of several hefty historical works. In their brown leather bindings, these volumes sit together today on a shelf in the Library at Gorhambury. Such impressive titles – *The Estates, Empires and Principalities of the World*, *A Generall Historie of the Netherlands*, *A General Inventorie of the History of France*, and *The Generall History of Spaine*.

This was the Grimston who, by his marriage, brought to the family what must be considered an extremely unusual Christian name. And yet, strange though it may be, for a time it ends that repetitive 'Edward'. Edward 'the Lawyer's' wife was Joan Risby of Lavenham, one of two granddaughters of a gentleman called John Harbottel (or Harbottle), of Crowfield in Suffolk. Mr. Harbottel, a man of substance, left property in his will chiefly in Suffolk, but also in Norfolk, to his two granddaughters. His bequest to one of them, Joan Grimston, thus considerably enlarged the total acreage of Grimston land. Mr. Harbottel owned no property in Essex, and presumably lived with Joan and Edward Grimston at their home in Bradfield Hall, near Manningtree in that county, for in his will he is described as 'of Bradfield'. How surprised Mr. Harbottel would have been if he could have known that the result of his bequest was to be the introduction of his surname as a Grimston Christian name. His great-grandson was christened 'Harbottle' in the year of his death, and this name has occasionally recurred in the family ever since.

In the Great Hall at Gorhambury today, a most remarkable carpet stands framed on public exhibition. It is thought to be the earliest English hand-made woollen pile carpet in existence; the date 1570 is knotted into it, above the armorial achievement of Queen Elizabeth I. To the right of the royal arms appear those of the family of Harbottel, and the arms of the borough of Ipswich are on the left - it is probable that this was where the carpet was made. Unfortunately there is no documentation on the history of the carpet, but it is valid to assume that it was John Harbottel (who died in 1578) who had the carpet made, and that it was from him that his granddaughter Joan Grimston inherited it. Later, in 1652, the carpet came to Gorhambury with all the other family possessions from Bradfield with Sir Harbottle Grimston, the 2nd baronet.

This ancient carpet, perhaps originally made for a dais or to cover a long table, was at one point actually laid on the floor and later still mounted on hooks and runners. Despite its vicissitudes, it still remains beautiful. Four hundred years have hardly dimmed the main blue background, nor has the sunlight faded its repeated design of red carnations. It has a border of stylised yellow honeysuckle and around its outer border a pattern of acorns was doubtless intended as a reference to the carpet's English origins. During the First World War, with the shortage of household servants, it was neglected and moths found their way into it for the first time. On the orders of Violet, the 4th Countess of Verulam, it was repaired by D.J. Martin, one of the staff of the Textile Department of the Victoria and Albert Museum, in 1923-4. No new wool was added to it. At the suggestion of the Museum, the carpet was framed for protection. This type of carpet may have been peculiar to Suffolk.

An inventory of Hengrave Hall, Suffolk, in 1603 includes four carpets very similar to the Gorhambury one by their description:

> Item: one carpet of English work, with Sir Thomas Kyston's arms in the midst of it;
> Item: one square bordered carpet cloth, very large, the work aforesaid, with Sir Thomas Kyston and the Cornwallis [family] their arms in the midst of it

Edward Grimston 'the Lawyer' died in 1610 and was buried where he had requested, 'near unto my good father', in the parish church of Rishangles. On a stone in the chancel he is recorded thus:

> The son paid to his father's parts increase
> Witty and wise he was, used lawe for peace
> What first he choosed for good he changed never
> His care was temperate, his zeal fervent ever
> And those fair gifts wherein his powers did give
> Did make the father in the son to live.
> Where truth hath writ, that envy cannot blot
> The name of Grimston cannot be forgot.

Chapter Two
The Family in the Seventeenth Century

Sir Harbottle Grimston, the 1st Baronet: 1578-1648

Harbottle Grimston, the 1st baronet, lived the life of a country gentleman at the Grimston home at Rishangles, where his elder children were baptised. He came to live at Bradfield Hall only after the death of his father, Edward 'the Lawyer'. He and his brother Henry received the bulk of their father's goods and lands by his will. Henry was to have the use of part of his father's lodgings at Gray's Inn 'to make him more desirous to study common law, on condition he allows my son Harbottle to lodge there, together with his effects and books of law'. There was a bequest of £500 to his daughter, Mrs. Cornwallis, 'in consideration of her care and government of my house and household at Bradfield since the death of my wife, her mother'.

Harbottle and his brother Henry were good friends; they married two sisters from the Coppinger family. Both were to be awarded knighthoods. Henry carried on the family's legal tradition and never lived at Bradfield, which became the home of Harbottle and his wife Elizabeth. Harbottle was knighted in 1603 and received a baronetcy in 1612. Harbottle had Puritan inclinations in religion, and a taste for public affairs. He was MP for Essex in 1625 and in 1627 was imprisoned for refusing to contribute to the Forced Loan which Charles I demanded from many gentlemen that year as one of the desperate expedients resorted to in an attempt to improve the government's financial position. By 1628 Sir Harbottle had been released and was once more a member of Parliament: already three successive Grimston generations had served in the House of Commons.

In 1640, now M.P. for Harwich, he was concerned about the lack of fortifications of the port there, and afraid that an attempt might be made by foreign forces to seize the place. He tried to persuade Parliament to supply arms and men to guard it. The presence of Danish ships and pirates was causing him considerable concern; he thought it would take only 50 men to take the town, and requested that money should be provided to allow bullets and swords to be manufactured at Ipswich. He appealed to his son, the second Harbottle, who was by now M.P. for Colchester, for assistance, and with his support in the House of Commons the 1st baronet was successful in obtaining 60 muskets and sufficient powder to put in them for the defence of Harwich.

9

Sir Harbottle Grimston died in 1647, and was the only member of his family to be buried at Bradfield. His ghost is said to haunt the churchyard, riding on a white horse. The story is that the horse was interred in the churchyard on the death of his master. A stone on the north side of the altar in the chancel at Bradfield bears the Grimston arms and records Sir Harbottle's epitaph: *'Hic iacet corpus Harbotelli Grimston militis et baronetti: Deo aeque et hominibus carus. Animam creatori reddidit 19 Februarij Anno Domini: 1647 et aetatis suae 70'*. This can be translated as 'Here lies the body of Harbottle Grimston, Knight and Baronet: beloved of God and men. He rendered up his soul to his Creator on 19 February in the year of our Lord 1647, and he was 70 years old'.

To recall Sir Harbottle today there is a dismally bad portrait at Gorhambury which shows him in middle age. It is far below the standard of the other family portraits of that period. He is shown as having a bright complexion and merry eyes, with well-defined eyebrows. His high, pleated ruff is edged with lace and his turned-back cuffs have a similar edging to them. He wears a black satin figured doublet with black velvet sleeves. His hands are particularly badly painted. The artist is unknown. In the top left-hand corner is written 'Sir Harbottle Grimston, Knt. and Baronet, Father to Sir Harbottle Grimston, Master of the Rolls, Aetatis suae 56 1625'. There is a coat of arms with nine quarterings.

By contrast, the pale beauty of the companion portrait of his wife Elizabeth is delightful. It shows her in middle-age, with dark eyes and an unusually pallid complexion. Her dark hair is ornamented with jewels on the left-hand side. She wears pearl drop earrings, and a black and gold dress slashed with white. Her 'Medici' collar is trimmed with lace which matches that on her husband's cuffs. On her shoulders and her bodice are three large rosettes. Her deep lawn cuffs are also edged with lace, and she wears a pearl and coral bracelet. Round her shoulders is a double chain of figures of eight shaped links, joined by jewels. Her right hand holds against her heart a jewelled ring tied with a red ribbon. She was 46 in 1625, when the portrait was painted by an unknown artist, as a pendant to that of her husband.

Sir Harbottle Grimston, 2nd Baronet,1602-1685: Early Life

High infant mortality in the 17th century, even in wealthy families, often meant that it was the second son who actually inherited. Such was the case in this generation of the Grimston family. Harbottle, the second son of the 1st Baronet, succeeded his father in 1647. He had been born at Bradfield in 1602. He received an education 'in all piety and good learning but especially in sacred and theological learning' at Emmanuel College, Cambridge, as ordained by its Puritan founder Sir Walter Mildmay in the statutes he composed for the college in 1584.

From Emmanuel, Harbottle went on to Lincoln's Inn and began to study for the bar, but when George, his older brother, died unexpectedly, Harbottle gave up the idea of the law. However, he had fallen in love with Mary, daughter of Sir George Croke, one of the Justices of the Court of Common Pleas. Sir George refused to bestow Mary's hand on Harbottle unless he returned to his law studies. For this reason, Harbottle returned to the law and later became an eminent advocate. He married his Mary on 16 April 1629 at St Dunstan's in the West, London. He was 27; she was 15.

Eleven years later, Harbottle was elected to Parliament, and represented Colchester in the Long Parliament. A convinced Puritan, Harbottle's oratory was pompous and heavy in style, but this does not seem to have stopped him becoming a leading member of the House of Commons. As a member of the Committee which enquired into the new religious canons established under Archbishop William Laud, there was a motion for the impeachment of Laud, on which Harbottle spoke with great vehemence:

> We are now fallen on that great man, the Archbishop of Canterbury; Look upon him as he is in his highness, and he is the sty of all pestilential filth that hath infected the state and government of the Commonwealth. Look upon him in his dependencies, and he is the man, the only man, that hath raised and advanced all those that together with himself, have been the authors and the rouses of our ruins, miseries and calamities which we are now under...Who is it, Mr. Speaker, but he only that hath advanced all our popish bishops?...and there is scarce any grievance or complaint come before us in this place, where we do not find him mentioned and as it were twined with it: like a busy angry wasp his sting is in the tail of everything.

These were biting words from the mouth of someone described as 'so mild a family man'! Laud was condemmed to death, but his end on the scaffold did not come until he had been held in prison in the Tower for over four years. According to Bishop Gilbert Burnet, who knew Sir Harbottle well, he was 'much sharpened against popery', and incurred the displeasure of the government of Charles I 'on account of his dislike to the Roman Catholic religion. He was troubled when preachers asserted a divine right or regal government'. Harbottle once said 'the judges have overthrown the law, and the bishops the Gospel'.

However, by 1647, when the Parliamentary forces had defeated the Royalists and men began to wonder what sort of government should be formed in place of that of the King, Sir Harbottle had become more worried by the radical thinkers on his own side than by the idea of the King returning to power. He feared that the Parliamentary Army, under the leadership of Oliver Cromwell, was plotting to seize power from the hands of the Parliament, and openly accused Cromwell of having this intention. On hearing this, Cromwell fell to his knees and vowed before God that no man was more faithful to Parliament than he. Cromwell's dramatic protestation convinced the House of his sincerity, and Harbottle Grimston and others who thought likewise were silenced. And yet, in just over a year, Harbottle was to see his fears become reality.

He presided over the Committee which investigated the King's escape from Hampton Court in November 1648, and was then appointed one of the 15 Parliamentary commissioners who negotiated with Charles during his subsequent imprisonment in Carisbrooke Castle on the Isle of Wight.

Grimston, so Burnet says, was upon his knees before the King, begging him yield with all possible haste to the terms suggested by Parliament, for he feared that if the Army grew impatient with protracted negotiations, they would attempt to seize control of the situation. Sir Harbottle's persuasive powers proved inadequate to induce Charles to do this, however, and he refused Parliament's terms. This was a trying time for Sir Harbottle in more ways than one, for troops from the forces commanded by the Earl of Warwick, angered by his hostility to the Parliamentary Army, occupied and plundered Harbottle's home at Bradfield, and turned his wife Mary out of doors.

On his return to Parliament, Harbottle urged that the King's own terms should be accepted. It seems that Charles was well disposed to him as can be seen by the letter Harbottle wrote to Sir Robert Harley on 21 October 1648:

> We have sent you up the King's second final answer to the Church. It is somewhat better than the first, and the mending of it hath not much works, and yet we fear it will not give full satisfaction to the Houses, but if we break with the King about this, having condescended so far in this particular and almost fully satisfied in all other matters, I cannot tell you how we shall be able to answer to God, the world, or our own consciences ... Believe it, there is not a man amongst us that think it worth the endangering the Kingdom for, and if more cannot be gotten, I hope some expedient will be found out for an accommodation ... I suppose it may pass for a good bargain ... Pray desire all our friends to attend the house diligently and let not a ship richly laden after a long voyage full of hazards, be cast away within sight of land'.

Harbottle's efforts were in vain. Parliament and the King might have eventually reached some kind of agreement, but the Parliamentary Army, dissatisfied with the terms suggested, intervened directly in politics. In December 1648, Colonel Pride and a troop of soldiers blocked the entrance to the House of Commons and prevented those members known to be unsympathetic to the Army's views from entering. These members - including Sir Harbottle - were kept under guard, unable to prevent the remaining members of Parliament - now known as the 'Rump Parliament' - from agreeing to the trial of King Charles for treason.

Throughout the trial, which took place in January 1649, Sir Harbottle remained a virtual prisoner, in order that he could not influence events. He was only released on the day of the King's execution, 30 January, having given an undertaking that he would 'do nothing to the disservice of Parliament or of the Army'.

This was an unhappy period for Sir Harbottle. His political opponents seemed to have triumphed, and he was forced to retire into private life, where he had recently had the double blow of losing both his wife and his parents. He decided to leave his plundered house at Bradfield, and began, as will be described later, to negotiate for the purchase of Gorhambury. He devoted a good deal of time to the education of his children, and also found time to translate and edit the law reports of his father-in-law, Sir George Croke. He also travelled on the Continent.

However, Sir Harbottle had not lost his interest in national affairs. When the time seemed to him to be appropriate, he returned once more to the political arena. He maintained his strong opposition to Cromwell and to the political and religious Independent parties. When Cromwell summoned a Parliament in 1656, Sir Harbottle was elected as one of the 16 members for the County of Essex, but he was not permitted to take his seat. He protested that an assembly which excluded men of his own way of thinking was not representative of the country, but the government refused to change its mind, and Sir Harbottle once more returned to his quiet country life. Secretly, he began to establish contact with those who sought the restoration of the exiled King Charles II.

After Cromwell's death in 1658, and Richard Cromwell's 'abdication' in the following year, Sir Harbottle was appointed a member of the committee set up to summon a new Parliament in 1660. A contemporary source informs us that on 25 April, 'the House of Commons this day met at St Margaret's Church, Westminster … After sermon they came to the House, the General [General Monck, who was the major figure in bringing about Charles II's restoration] being accompanied by the Lord Fairfax and many honourable Members of Parliament, the Mace being carried before them … When being assembled the House chose Sir Harbottle Grimston to be Speaker of the House'. On 3 May 1660, Sir Harbottle received a letter in his capacity as Speaker from the King, delivered by Sir John Grenville. Harbottle read his reply to this letter aloud to the assembled House:

'I need not tell you with what grateful and thankful hearts the Commons now assembled in Parliament have his Majesty's gracious letter, *res ipsa loquitur*, you yourself have been *auricularis et ocularis testis de rei veritate*. Our bells and bonfires have already begun the proclamation of His Majesty's goodness and of our joys. We have told the people that our King, the glory of England, is coming home again, and they have resounded it back again in our ears, that they are ready and their hearts are open to receive him: both Parliament and people have cried aloud in their prayers to the King of Kings - long live King Charles II'

On 11 May, Sir Harbottle sailed to Holland to wait on the King at his place of exile in Breda, and to escort him back to England. During his visit, he wrote what he called 'observations of the States Countries, especially Holland'. His style was expressive and vivid, and his analogies always striking and often gastronomic! The area was, he wrote, 'a general sea-land, there is not such another marsh in the world, that's flat. They are an universal quagmire epitomised, a green cheese in pickle … They are the ingredients of a black pudding and want only stirring together … The soil is all flat, though wanting both colour and heat. Tis the buttock of the world, full of veins and blood, but no bone in it'. On 25 May, Charles II landed at Dover, and proceeded through cheering masses of people to London. John Evelyn, the diarist, described how the King was greeted with 'a triumph of above twenty thousand horse and foot, brandishing their swords and shouting with inexpressible joy; the ways strew'd with flowers, the bells ringing, the streets hung with tapestry; fountains running with wine; the Mayor, Aldermen, all the Companies in their liveries, [with] chains of gold, & banners; Lords and Nobles, cloth of silver, gold and velvet everybody clad in; the windows and balconies all set with ladies; trumpets, music, and [myriads] of people flocking ... I stood in the Strand, & beheld it, and & blessed God. And all this was done without one drop of blood, & by that very Army which rebell'd against him: but it was the Lord's doing, *et mirabile in oculum nostris*: for such a Restoration was never seen in the mention of any history, ancient or modern ...'

Sir Harbottle, as Speaker, played a key role in all the ceremonies and celebrations surrounding the Restoration, and four days after the King's arrival, made a somewhat fulsome speech of welcome to the King. His activities did not go unrewarded. 'For his great merit to restore' the King, he was 'worthily advanced on the third day of November in the same year, to be Master of the Rolls of the Court of Chancery, which Office he executed with great justice and equity, to the satisfaction of his Prince and all good people, for the space of six and twenty years'. As an enduring reminder of those days, the Grimston family possesses a very fine portrait of Charles II painted by Sir Peter Lely. It is the finest remaining version of this brilliant study of a King who was to become perhaps England's most popular monarch. Family tradition claims that it was Charles himself who gave the portrait to Sir Harbottle, in gratitude for his services, and as a token of the friendship which existed between them. This is not unlikely, for Sir Henry Chauncy recorded that King Charles paid a gracious compliment to Sir Harbottle by taking supper at the latter's house in Lincoln's Inn on 25 June 1660, when Harbottle laid on a 'great entertainment' for the monarch.

Sir Harbottle was a collector of portraits, sometimes originals, more often copies, of famous personages of the day. In the 17th century it was extremely fashionable amongst gentlemen of wealth to form such collections. Four of these were known as the 'Galleries of the Great': they were those of Sir Edward Nicholas (Secretary of State under Charles II); John Evelyn; Lord Clarendon (for many years the King's principal advisor); and Sir Harbottle Grimston. The latter appears to be the only one of the four which survives intact today. It is interesting to note that amongst his other portraits, Sir Harbottle had one of Charles II's 'gentleman of the backstairs', the discreet William Chiffinch. The backstairs had a very special function in the King's private life, and Chiffinch was an extremely useful man to know. Under his eye, priests, politicians, whores and whomsoever Chiffinch thought fit, were admitted into the King's presence for private audiences. Chiffinch's portrait hangs at Gorhambury today, together with Charles himself, his Queen, Catherine of Braganza, General Monck, Lord Fairfax, Sir Harbottle himself, and many others.

There are, in fact, four likenesses of Sir Harbottle at Gorhambury. The earliest, a companion portrait to one of his wife Mary, affords us a glimpse of a more romantic, even 'Cavalier', Sir Harbottle, before his arrival at Gorhambury. The second is a quaintly clumsy full-length portrait against a background of baroque columns, dated 1665, and by an unknown artist. To one side of the figure, a book lies on a pedestal, inscribed with the words *Aetatis suae 52. Anno 1655. Nec pudet vivere, nec piget mori.* ('He was aged 52 in the year 1655. Neither afraid to live, nor affeared to die'). This portrait is followed chronologically by one by John Riley, which shows Sir Harbottle as an elderly man wearing his robes as Master of the Rolls, seated in a red armchair with a gold fringe. A fourth likeness is by Mary Beale, and may afford us the best likeness.

Chapter Three

Tudor Gorhambury and the Bacons

Hidden from sight beneath Gorhambury's grassy parkland and green fields lies evidence of very early civilizations. Excavations show the existence of an Iron Age farm of about 50 B.C. In the period after the Roman conquest, a Roman villa was built outside the walls of Roman Verulamium. It was important, if small in size. The ancillary buildings which surrounded it show that it was the heart of a community, and although by the middle of the fourth century, it was reduced to a working farm, clearly there was still the nucleus of a settlement here. In Saxon times the area was known as 'Westwick', a name still borne by a nearby farm. In A.D. 996 the manor of Westwick came into the possession of the Abbey of St Albans, when King Ethelred 'the Unready' granted it to Abbot Aelfric, the eleventh abbot.

The name 'Gorham-bury' derives from the man who built the first documented house on the site, in 1130. He was Geoffrey de Gorham, who had come from Maine in France at the invitation of Richard de Albini, Abbot of St Albans, to take charge of the school attached to the monastery. Geoffrey did not arrive on time, and the post intended for him was filled by another. Instead, he journeyed 12 miles north to Dunstable where he taught at another school, afterwards returning to St Albans where he became the sixteenth abbot in 1120. The chronicler Matthew Paris states that Westwick was illegally conveyed to relatives of Abbot Geoffrey, and it remained in the de Gorham family until about 1310.

A survey of 1307 shows that the de Gorham house was of considerable size for its period. The buildings consisted of 'a hall with chambers; a chapel with a certain chamber; a storied edifice beyond the gate with a chamber; a kitchen, a bakehouse, a dairy and a larder, with a certain chamber; a granary with a chamber for the bailiff; a dwelling for the servants of the manor; two cow houses; two sheep houses; a pig-sty and gardens'. Shortly afterwards the manor passed into the possession of the de Veres, and upon the attainder of Robert de Vere, 9th Earl of Oxford, in 1388, the property escheated to the Crown. In 1395 the manor again became the property of the Abbey of St Albans through the payment to the Crown of 900 marks (a mark was a weight of 8 ounces of gold or silver, valued at 20 pennies to the ounce). And so Gorhambury remained in the hands of the Abbey until the Dissolution of the Monasteries in 1539.

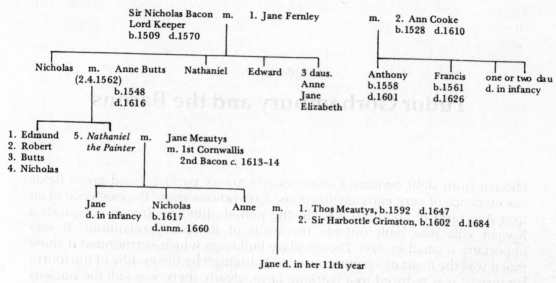

Sir Nicholas Bacon m. 1. Jane Fernley   m.   2. Ann Cooke
Lord Keeper   b.1528   d.1610
b.1509 d.1570

Nicholas   m.   Anne Butts   Nathaniel   Edward   3 daus.   Anthony   Francis   one or two dau
(2.4.1562)   Anne   b.1558   b.1561   d. in infancy
b.1548   Jane   d.1601   d.1626
d.1616   Elizabeth

1. Edmund   5. *Nathaniel*   m.   Jane Meautys
2. Robert   *the Painter*   m. 1st Cornwallis
3. Butts   2nd Bacon *c.* 1613–14
4. Nicholas

Jane   Nicholas   Anne   m.   1. Thos Meautys, b.1592 d.1647
d. in infancy   b.1617   2. Sir Harbottle Grimston, b.1602   d.1684
             d.unm. 1660

Jane d. in her 11th year

Sir Nicholas Bacon at Gorhambury   *Bacon Pedigree*

In 1541, Henry VIII granted the manor of Gorhambury to Ralph Rowlett, a merchant of the Staple at Calais. Descending to his sons, it was then purchased 20 years later by Sir Nicholas Bacon, head of an ancient Suffolk yeoman family, who had risen to the important office of Lord Keeper of the Great Seal of England.

By the time that Nicholas Bacon enters the story of Gorhambury, he had already suffered the death of his first wife, Jane Fernley: she had given him three sons and three daughters. By now, Sir Nicholas, though over 50, had remarried. His choice was a girl 19 years his junior, called Anne Cooke. Her considerable academic attainments proved the belief of her father, Sir Anthony Cooke, that women were as capable of learning as men. Anne could read Greek, Latin and French, and took delight in translating sermons from Italian into English. By his marriage, however, Sir Nicholas acquired not only a most erudite bride, but also the entry into prestigious circles. Her father, Sir Anthony, was a man of vast learning who was tutor to the boy-king Edward VI, and a close friend of Queen Catherine Parr, another lover of learning. Anne's four sisters had all married important men, whose friendship was of the greatest value to Sir Nicholas. Mildred became Lady Burghley; Elizabeth became Lady Hoby; Katherine became Lady Killigrew; and Margaret married Ralph Rowlett of Gorhambury, a merchant and fashionable London goldsmith. It was from this brother-in-law that Sir Nicholas was to purchase Gorhambury with its medieval manor house in 1561. He already knew the area, for the previous year he had bought a farm called 'Pleydells' in the nearby parish of St Michael's from Sir Richard Lee. By 1560 the rotund and jolly Sir Nicholas, and his scholarly wife Anne, had a two year old son -

Anthony - and Anne was again pregnant with Francis, who was born at York House in the Strand in the same year in which his father purchased Gorhambury, 1561.

The fine undulating wooded landscape of Hertfordshire appealed to Sir Nicholas, and Gorhambury's proximity to London and the court seemed convenient. However, he found the de Gorham house old-fashioned, and decided he would build a new house in keeping with modern taste, to the west of the old medieval manor, where the prospect of the landscape was even lovelier. There is some evidence of Sir Nicholas's previous interest in architecture, for he had earlier had a house built to his design at Redgrave in Suffolk, and he had been involved in the rebuilding of the library at Gray's Inn.

In the construction of his new country seat, he used the services of local workmen, allowing them to follow their own traditions and only introducing outside specialists at key points. He made use of materials from the de Gorham house, and also from the old Abbey buildings at St Albans, then in process of demolition. Building work started in 1563, but records of it are meagre: only a single sheet of accounts for the period 1563-8 survives amongst the papers at Lambeth Palace Library. This gives us the names of the men who were in charge - Nicholas Bourdeman in the first year and Thomas Wytherhead in the following four years. It also notes the cost of artisan labour - of carpenters, joiners, bricklayers and plasterers - for each year; it ends with a note that 'there is not accounted for in this brief any timber felled within any [of] your Lordship's woods nor otherwise of any person, neither is there valued any free stone brought from the Abbey of St Albans, lime, sand, nor the profits that might have accrued of burning and making of brick within the time above mentioned'. The total cost, excluding these stated exceptions, comes to £3,177 11s 9¼d. It shows that in addition to the reuse of materials in the form of stone and flint, Sir Nicholas also made use of a large quantity of brick made on the estate, where the clay soil is ideal for brick-making.

Because Sir Nicholas used the de Gorham house as a quarry, recent excavations have revealed no trace of it, although deep wells in the area indicate the existence of post-Roman buildings there. During the very many years of David Neal's excavations in the 1970s, there was always a hope that evidence of the medieval manor might be revealed. In the 19th century, Charlotte Grimston, sister of the 1st Earl of Verulam, made a sketch plan indicating the position where family tradition believed the manor to have been. David Neal and his team found no post-medieval pottery on this site, and clearly the manor must have been sited elsewhere: some archaeologists consider the site to have been adjacent to that of the Tudor house.

Bacon's house remained in use until the late 18th century, when, because of the state of disrepair into which it had fallen, it was abandoned. Although today there is little to be seen apart from the roofless remains of the hall, and the remnants of the fine Italianate portico, it is now a preserved site under the

Sir Nathaniel Bacon of Culford; self portrait.

Some details of the enamelled glass from Sir Nicholas Bacon's Gorhambury and from Francis Bacon's Verulam House: II an Eskimo; III Juno and her peacock; IV animals and a flower; V A fighting man, based on a plate in a fencing manual of 1570.

supervision of the Department of the Environment, and remains a rare example of English Renaissance architecture.

Sir Nicholas Bacon planned his house four-square, enclosing a quadrangle or court measuring 80′ by 72′. It was a normal domestic building of the period, according to a plan made long after the erection of the house, in respect of the positioning of the various rooms and offices (see below). Strikingly, it had a white plastered face on all the external wall surfaces. Some of the plaster can still be seen adhering to the brick and flint.

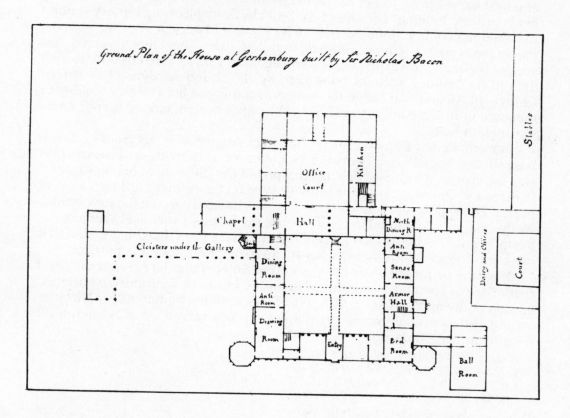

2. *Ground plan of the Tudor Gorhambury, the house built by Sir Nicholas Bacon.*

It is surprising, but true, to find that the house had an ample piped water supply. Small pieces of lead piping, wooden-clad, have been found amongst the ruins. Dr. Rawley, who was Sir Francis Bacon's chaplain, made this remarkable statement on the subject: 'When Sir Nicholas Bacon the Lord Keeper lived, every room at Gorhambury was served with a pipe of water from the ponds, distant of about a mile off. In the lifetime of Mr. Anthony Bacon, the water ceased; after whose death, his Lordship coming into the inheritance, could not recover the water without infinite charge'. It was an elaborate system, using windmills and a donkey wheel to give force to bring water to all parts of the house.

In her progresses with her Court through the kingdom, Queen Elizabeth often visited the Bacons at Gorhambury. These royal progresses did much to warm and cheer the majority of her subjects, who were delighted by the chance to see their sovereign in person. On the other hand, the cost of feeding and entertaining Her Majesty and her Court was said to be calculated as a means of impoverishing the most wealthy - and hence most powerful - men amongst her subjects, under colour of granting them the high favour of giving her board and lodging! The church bells of Hertfordshire rang out many times to herald her coming. John Nichols, who wrote a history of *The Progresses and Public Processions of Queen Elizabeth*, recalled that 'The Queen visited this ancient borough [St Albans] in 1565 and again in 1573'. He referred to the first item in the tattered account book kept by the churchwardens of St Peter's Church, St Albans: 'Paid unto the ringers at coming of the Queen's Majesty in the town unto Gorhambury, 1572...'. The paper is torn and we do not know the amount paid.

Elizabeth signed a royal charter, dated 25 August 1568, as from Gorhambury. (It appointed Lord Hunsdon as Governor of Berwick-on-Tweed). 1568 was the year in which Sir Nicholas completed the building of his new house. Perhaps the Queen was staying with Sir William Cecil, later Lord Burghley, at nearby Theobalds, and had come over to Gorhambury to see the new house. As the charter is amended in Cecil's hand, this seems a very likely conjecture. In any event, in August 1568 Elizabeth would have been delighted to find that her Lord Keeper had honoured her by an inscription upon his portico.

Above the pediment, over the main door, Sir Nicholas had placed the royal coat of arms, spendidly sculptured in stone, but with a curiously shortened version of the motto - *DIU.E.MO.DROIT*. Beneath the pediment, Sir Nicholas set out his own attainments. In Roman capitals carved on grey marble, it remains in place today:

HAEC CUM PERFECIT NICOLAUS TECTA BACONUS,
ELIZABETH REGNI LUSTRA FUERE DUO.
FACTUS EQUES, MAGNI CUSTOS FUIT IPSA SIGILLI,
GLORIA SIT SOLI TOTA TRIBUTA DEO

This has been translated as follows:

'When Nicholas Bacon brought these buildings to completion
Two lustrums of Elizabeth's reign had passed.
He had been knighted and made Keeper of the Great Seal,
May all glory be ascribed to God alone'.

A 'lustrum' was a period of five years

On one of the Queen's visits, as she alighted from her carriage and her portly Lord Keeper stepped out from his portico to greet her, she remarked jokingly to him 'My Lord Keeper, what a little house you have gotten yourself'. To which Sir Nicholas replied, with the proper humility of one whose motto was *MEDIOCRIA FIRMA*, 'All is well with mine house, Ma'am, but you have made me too great for it'. However, it would seem that he heeded the Queen's comments as to the size of the house, for before her next visit, he built on a long gallery, projecting westwards, the better to accommodate her. It was finely panelled, 120' long by 18' wide, and was at first-floor level over an open loggia. It was built of lath and plaster. In the centre of the rear wall a niche was provided, which formed the setting for a life-size figure of the Queen's father, in gilded armour.

* * * * *

The 17th-century writer John Aubrey found Bacon's long gallery 'stately'; a hundred or more years later Horace Walpole called it 'pleasing' and Thomas Pennant found it 'noble and magnificent'. There was a large fireplace on the north side, and large windows of painted glass on the south or long garden side, and also on the west end. These windows were very beautiful, 'every pane with several figures of beast, bird or flower' as John Aubrey noted. The ceiling, barrel-vaulted in shape, was 'painted in genteel grotesque, but spoiled by bad heads upon it' according to the fastidious Walpole. On the other hand, Aubrey, like Pennant after him, admired the burnished gold and shadowed 'umbre' of the 'heads and busts of Greek and Roman Emperors and heroes'. The Grimston family's own historian, Charlotte Grimston, recorded in the 19th century that the walls of the gallery were wainscotted or panelled in oak, 'gilt in compartments' was her wording. To decorate and animate these, Sir Nicholas Bacon turned to a form he had used elsewhere at Gorhambury – on his porch, in his hall, in the little banqueting house in his orchard, and on the doorway opening into his oak wood – painted inscriptions. These inscriptions were moral maxims or inspiring and thought-provoking sentences by the great men of the past, and they were painted on all four sides of the compartments of the wainscotting. One can but speculate as to the beauty of their appearance; executed in Roman capitals and richly gilded, decorated like the lettering of a medieval illuminated manuscript, they were put there both to please the eye and to inform the mind.

On one of Queen Elizabeth's visits to Gorhambury, she was accompanied by Jane, Lady Lumley (daughter of Henry Fitzalan, Earl of Arundel, and first wife of John, Lord Lumley), who was a Lady of Honour to the Queen. Lady Lumley was a classicist, and her husband was also a scholar and a wealthy collector of art treasures. Sir Nicholas's 'sentences' appealed to the aesthetic sense of this lady: she recognised them as a reflection of the character and needs of the person who had chosen them. She asked the Lord Keeper to allow her to have a copy of them. Bacon, flattered, sent them to her 'at her desire', not in simple note form, but as an exceptionally fine illuminated manuscript, which today is in the royal collection of manuscripts housed in the British Library. The small volume, 6½" by 9½", is of exquisite beauty. The 37 sentences are written on 14 oblong leaves of vellum, in gold lettering upon various coloured backgrounds - pink, green and orange. The pages are enriched by elegant tasselled frames of gold and delicate golden foliage. The first page contains an illumination of the arms of Lady Lumley. The next page tells us that these were the sentences 'painted in the Lord Keeper's gallery at Gorhambury: and selected by him out of divers authors and sent to the good Lady Lumley at her desire'. The lettering and decoration are not signed. Here, as in the architecture of his porch, his sculpture, or the design of his decorative windows, Sir Nicholas's choice was superb, a fact also apparent to contemporaries: a century after his death, the writer David Lloyd asserted that Sir Nicholas's 'use of learned artists was continual'.

It is apparent that Sir Nicholas chose phrases perceived as 'short directions for life and action' from his favourite philosophers - Seneca, Cicero, and other ancient writers, as well as more modern figures such as Erasmus and Elyot. Sir Nicholas chose to decorate his house in this way not only for the delight of his guests and friends, but assuredly for the education and upbringing of his sons Anthony and Francis, and his other older children. The full text of these sentences, with translations, is given by Professor Elizabeth McCutcheon in *Sir Nicholas Bacon's Great House Sententiae*. Professor McCutcheon also identifies the sources of the sentences in each case.

In 1577 Queen Elizabeth arrived at Gorhambury with her entourage on Sunday, 18 May, and left on the following Wednesday. The total expenditure over these four days was a staggering £577 6s 7¼d – about one-third of the cost of the building of Bacon's house! The 'brief' or account for that weekend is preserved in Lambeth Palace Library. It includes 'in beef, 8 oxen, £31 3s 7d. In mutton 60 carcasses £27. In veals, 18 carcasses, £9 6s 3d, in lambs 34 carcasses £7 15s 4d. Capons of all kinds 206 ... chickens 31 dozen and 8 ...Geese 10 dozen, herons 12 dozen and 8, bitterns 8 dozen and 7 ...' and so on through birds of the nest to 'godwits, pheasants, partridges, quails (16 dozen) and ... mallards, teals, curlews, sea fish ... bacon, tongues, cows' udders and calves' feet ...'.

When Sir Nicholas was made Lord Keeper, the seal of the preceding reign was broken up and presented to him, as was the custom. From this – the great seal of Philip and Mary – Bacon had three cups made, one for each of his houses, Redgrave, Stiffkey, and Gorhambury. The silver-gilt cup which was made for his 'house of Redgrave, 1574', is in the British Museum. A similar cup made for Stiffkey is in the Victoria and Albert Museum. The present whereabouts of the cup made for Gorhambury are unknown. Yet another memorial to Sir Nicholas and his unerringly excellent taste survives in the form of his printed armorial bookplate, said to be the earliest surviving example of its kind. It dates from 1574, and records Sir Nicholas's bequest to aid the rebuilding of Cambridge University Library.

At Gorhambury today there are three painted terracotta busts made from life in 1568 of Sir Nicholas, his wife, and a boy of about ten years old. The bust of Sir Nicholas shows him with a merry look about the eyes, and indeed there are stories which testify to his sense of humour. When he was judge for the

Northern Circuit, he was on one occasion about to pass sentence, when the prisoner begged for mercy on account of his 'kinship' with him.

"'Prithee", said my Lord Judge, "how came that in?"
"Why, if it please you, my lord, your name is Bacon, and mine is Hog, and in all ages Hog and Bacon have been so near kindred, that they are not to be separated".
"Ay, but", replied Judge Bacon, "you and I cannot be kindred, except you be hanged; for Hog is not Bacon until it be *well* hanged".

The second bust is of Anne, Sir Nicholas's second wife, the mother of Anthony and Francis. She was a woman of great piety and ability. She felt that she must admonish her sons continually about their friendships with Catholics and theatre people, and demand that they shun the mumming and revels for which Gray's Inn was well-known. It is said that during the annual revelry known as 'Call Night' at Gray's Inn, Lady Anne's ghost may be seen to 'come down as an opiate from the catalpha tree [that] Francis Bacon planted. Gliding along the grass, alone and palely loitering, she wrings her lily-white hands and mops her magnolia-like brow. "Alas, they mum! They sinfully revel!" she moans, and then disappears'.

The third bust represents a boy of about ten years of age with a fine brow and well-shaped head. Tradition identifies the child as Francis, but if the busts are contemporary with each other and were all made in 1568, this one must surely represent not Francis but his elder brother Anthony, who in that year would indeed have been ten years old.

A little less than two years after the Queen's visit to Gorhambury in 1577, when such enormous quantities of food had been consumed, Sir Nicholas Bacon was dead. Sir William Rawley wrote in his *Commonplace Book*: 'Old Lord Sir Nicholas Bacon had a barber rubbing his head. Because it was very hot, the window was opened to let in the fresh wind. The Lord Keeper fell asleep and awakened all distempered and in a great sweat. Said he to his barber, "Why did you let me sleep?" "Why, my lord, I durst not wake your lordship". "Why, then," said my Lord, "you have killed me with kindness". So moved he to his bed and within a few days died'.

Sir Nicholas was buried in the classical tomb in old St Paul's Cathedral which he had prepared for himself three years earlier. Only a fragment of his effigy remains in the crypt of the cathedral today, all that was saved from the Great Fire of London in 1666.

Apart from the terracotta.bust, Gorhambury also has an unattractive painting of Sir Nicholas, in which he looks gross and humourless. It is a copy of a painting at Raveningham made by a 'Mr. Wright' in 1675, who charged £10 for the job. Perhaps this was John Michael Wright, sometimes called the 'King's Painter'. There is also a painting of Anne, showing her as a widow, aged 51. In her hand she holds her translation of Bishop Jewel's *Apologia pro Ecclesia Anglicana*, for which she was much praised by her husband's old friend from university days, Matthew Parker, now Archbishop of Canterbury. Perhaps Anne Bacon was not as unbending and unattractive as she is sometimes thought to have been. There is a charming poem written to her by her husband, in which he delightfully recalls long afternoons they spent together, perhaps at Gorhambury, when he was troubled by an attack of gout:

'The idle times which irksome be
You have made short through your good skill
In reading pleasant things to me.
As witness can if they could speak
Both your Tully and my Senecke'. [sic: Seneca]

Sir Francis Bacon at Gorhambury

With the death of Sir Nicholas, those almost biennial visits of the Queen to Gorhambury came to an end. By his will, Sir Nicholas had appointed his wife to look after their two sons, 'that are now left poor orphans without a father'. Anthony, the elder son, shy and brilliant, was now twenty, and it was to him that Sir Nicholas had willed the reversion of Gorhambury after his mother's death. However, for the most part Anthony lived abroad on diplomatic missions, with his friend and patron, the unfortunate Earl of Essex, and as Lady Bacon outlived him, Gorhambury never became his.

There is much evidence of the conscientious way in which Lady Bacon carried out her husband's last wishes. She feared that Anthony might forsake the Protestant faith, and on one occasion when she had asked him to dismiss a Roman Catholic servant, and begged him to return home, only to meet with refusal on both counts, she called him a traitor to his God and country.

The other 'poor orphan', Francis, received nothing on his father's sudden death. When the news reached him, he was in France, serving as secretary to Sir Amyas Paulet, Queen Elizabeth's ambassador there. Sir Amyas thought Francis to be endowed with 'many good and singular parts' and 'likely to do the Queen good and acceptable service'. Francis returned to England, read law at Gray's Inn, and five years later entered Parliament. He was eager for office, but although his powerful uncle Lord Burghley did not lack goodwill towards him, he gave him little positive aid in furthering his career. This may have been because Francis was unwise enough to offend Elizabeth by an outspoken speech in the House of Commons in which he spoke against the granting of a triple subsidy to the Queen in 1593. Francis then attached himself to the Earl of Essex, who at that time was high in the royal favour, and Essex tried unsuccessfully to secure Francis's appointment as Attorney General – which went, however, to Sir Edward Coke.

Francis Bacon did not become embittered by repeated disappointment, for he found consolation in literary composition at home in Gorhambury. In 1601 his elder brother Anthony died, and soon after Lady Bacon surrendered her life interest in Gorhambury to Francis. She lived on there herself, but her mind began to fail with advancing years. Godfrey Goodman, Bishop of Gloucester, wrote of her that 'she was little better than frantic in her old age'.

When Queen Elizabeth died in 1603, and King James became king, Francis once more began to have hopes of winning a high office. He was increasingly employed in Parliamentary business, and played an important part in the negotiations over the joint kingship of England and Scotland. At the time of the coronation, Bacon wrote to his cousin Robert Cecil, who had followed his father and assumed the position of the Crown's chief minister, concerning the possibility of his being granted a knighthood: 'I should be content to have it,' he wrote, 'because I have found out an Alderman's daughter, an handsome maiden and to my liking'. Francis was knighted, but only in a crowd with 237 other gentlemen! On 11 May 1606 we read that 'Sir Francis Bacon was married ... to his young wench in Marylebone Chapel. He was clad from top to toe in purple, and his wife had such a store of fine raiments of cloth of silver and gold that it draws deep into her portion'. His 'young wench' was Alice Barnham, the daughter, as he said, of an Alderman of London. Her marriage portion amounted to £1,000. On the day of their wedding Francis was 45 and Alice was 14.

It was not until the following year that Francis received tangible rewards for his years of service, when he was given the post of Solicitor-General, and a year later became Clerk of the Star Chamber. He had waited nearly 30 years for advancement, and now his delayed success seems to have shaken him. 'I have found' he wrote, 'now twice upon amendment of my fortunes, disposition to melancholy and distaste'. He recognised his own failings and found the knowledge tragic. 'My soul hath been a stranger in the course of my pilgrimage'.

As he walked amongst Gorhambury's oak groves, through stately walks of elm and the beautiful gardens, he felt refreshed by the pure country air. On rainy days in springtime, he would sometimes travel in an open coach 'to receive the benefit of irrigation, which was very wholesome because of the nitre in the air'. Sir Francis was very fond of Gorhambury, which remained his only country seat, and it was his residence for most of his life. He spent a good deal of money on the property, both inside and out; painters, carvers and sculptors embellished the buildings, whilst gardeners laboured to interpret the owner's own designs for the gardens.

In October 1616, Sir Francis bought back some land which had formerly been in his family's possession, but which had been sold by his brother Anthony to the Marston family of Hill End, St Michael's. The land was situated upon the London highway and amounted to 28 acres of arable land and pasture. On this site, in 1621, Sir Francis built a new house; it has been suggested that he did this because the water supply to his father's house failed one summer and he decided to establish a new one on the banks of the River Ver. There might, however, be another reason: it could be that he wanted a chance to test his own theories about architecture by building a house which would incorporate his ideas. He had written in his *Essay on Buildings* that as a man should wear different clothing in winter from that worn in summer, so he should have 'one house for winter and another for summer-living'.

Whatever the reason, the new house was built. Francis called it Verulam House, for he had now become Baron Verulam and also Lord Chancellor of

England. By any standards, the house was architecturally advanced. 'It was', wrote Aubrey, that indefatigable recorder of vivid detail, 'the most ingeniously contrived little pile that ever I saw. No question but that his lordship was the chiefest architect'. If Aubrey had not described the house, and left a sketch of it, the very fact of its existence might be doubted, for not a visible trace of it remains today. Aubrey's evidence, however, is supported by a Gorhambury estate map of 1634 which positions it for us, and also shows the area of Bacon's famous water gardens with a 'dovehouse' and 'orchard' shown lying to the north-east. The drawing of it on the map compares well with Aubrey's rough sketch.

3. *Verulam House as sketched by John Aubrey. This house, built by Sir Francis Bacon was demolished by order of Sir Harbottle Grimston.*

It was a gem of a house, with fine lofty rooms, all wainscotted and with fine chimney pieces. There were two bathrooms, and 'on the dome of the upper story on the outside (which was painted a dark umber) were figures of the gods of the Gentiles, viz. on the south door, second story, was Apollo, on another, was Jupiter with his thunderbolt, etc., bigger than life, and done by an ancient hand; the heightenings were of hatchings of gold, which when the sun shone on them made a most glorious show'. Mirror doors were placed strategically, so that as one approached, one could see the prospect of Bacon's 'long walks with trees and of the park, reflected in them', thus creating an amazing *trompe d'oeil*. 'All the tunnels of the chimneys were carried to the middle of the house' and in the flat space thus left seats were placed; from this lofty viewpoint, one could look down on to the 'beauty of the variegated greens of the tree tops', a spectacle which Aubrey likened to 'a tapestry of Irish stitch-work'.

And from the roof to the east could be seen Bacon's water gardens. He constructed a series of geometrically-shaped ponds covering altogether about four acres of ground, and called them his 'pondyards'. 'The figures of the ponds were thus: they were pitched at the bottom with pebbles of several colours which were worked into several figures, as of fishes, etc, which in his lordship's time were plainly to be seen through the clear water, now overgrown with flags and rushes. If a poor body had brought his lordship half a dozen pebbles of a curious colour, he would give them a shilling, so curious was he in perfecting his fishponds ... In the middle of the middlemost pond, in the island, is a curious banqueting house of Roman architecture, paved with black and white marble, covered with Cornish slate and neatly wainscotted'.

4. *Sketch of the summerhouse 'on the middlemost island' of Sir Francis Bacon's Pondyards. Artist unknown.*

Between the two houses of Gorhambury and Verulam, Bacon built three parallel roads, running straight and wide so that seven coaches could roll abreast. Throngs of noblemen and knights came up these roads, to ask Bacon for his favour or the gift of a place. 'When his lordship was at his country house at Gorhambury, St Albans seemed as if the court was there, so nobly did he live'. Bacon's servants wore a livery with his crest, the boar. He employed more watermen to row him along the river than did King James himself. His servants had their own coaches, and some even kept racehorses. Bacon lived on a princely scale, displaying his magnificence with such gestures as rewarding the servant who brought him a buck as a present from the King with the enormous sum of £50.

The surroundings he created for himself at Gorhambury were full of beauty and refinement. The elegance that we find in his *Essays* was reflected in his house, his gardens and his woodlands. He loved music, and liked to have musicians playing whilst he meditated in an adjoining room. He also loved flowers, and designed his gardens so that 'the breath of flowers, blowing freely or crushed underfoot, should come and go like the warbling of music'. All the year round he had his table strewn with sweet herbs and flowers, to 'refresh his spirit and his memory'.

These years were the zenith of his career. Disappointment and disaster lay in store for him. Although his marriage to Alice had been placid enough for 15 years, it remained barren, and he now described her as having a 'cow-like countenance'. In January 1621 as Lord Chancellor, and now also as Viscount St Alban, Francis sat by the King's side as the royal coach bore him through the streets of London to open Parliament. Only three months later, the new Viscount's career was shattered: he was impeached for taking bribes. Always short of money, on his own admission he had borrowed even from those whose cases were to come before him. He had many enemies, who seized upon the chance to destroy him. He pleaded that everyone in public life took bribes - which was no more than the truth - but he was sentenced to pay the enormous fine of £40,000 and sent to prison. In the event, King James remitted the fine and Bacon's imprisonment lasted only a token few days, but never again could he play any part in public life.

He found refuge at his beloved Gorhambury, and despite his desperate shortage of money he refused to sell Gorhambury's magnificent oak woods for timber, which he called his 'feathers'. He went on writing, and we may imagine him walking and meditating in the gardens and woods of his beautiful country seat. In Prae Wood, at one particularly lofty point, he built a temple of retreat, where he studied the stars and made scientific experiments. As he walked through his 'delicate groves', he would have one of his secretaries at his side to jot down his thoughts as they occurred to him. According to Aubrey, the secretary he preferred above all others for this role was Thomas Hobbes, later to become famous as the author of the work of political theory, *Leviathan*. In 1622 Bacon produced his *History of the Reign of King Henry VII*, particularly remarkable for its vivid characterisation. Once again he revised and added to his essays. Was it at Gorhambury that he wrote his *Essay on Gardens*, for Aubrey tells us that 'under every tree there he planted some fine flower – peonies, tulips, violets'? We shall never know how deeply he regretted not having a child of his own who could inherit his beloved Gorhambury; in his *Essay on Parents and Children*, he used the very words of his grandfather Sir Anthony Cooke when he wrote 'the joys of parents are secret, and so are their griefs and fears. Children sweeten labours but make misfortunes more bitter; they increase the cares of life, but mitigate the remembrance of death'.

In 1624 the whole of his sentence was remitted by a warrant, stating that 'calling to mind the former good services of Lord St Alban and how well and profitably he hath spent his time since his trouble we are pleased to remove from him that blot of ignominy which yet remaineth on him of incapacity and disablement and to remit to him all penalties whatsoever inflicted by that sentence'.

The manner of his death, two years later, was characteristic. He caught a chill whilst stuffing a chicken with snow 'in order to observe the effect of cold on the preservation of flesh'. In his will he wrote 'For my burial it may be in St Michael's Church. There was my mother buried, and it is the parish church of my mansion house at Gorhambury, and it is the only Christian church within the walls of old Verulam'. His friend, the poet George Herbert, wrote of him:

> While thou dost groan 'neath weight of sickness slow
> And wasting life with doubtful step doth go,
> What wise fates sought I see at last fulfilled:
> Thou needs must die in April – so they willed,
> That here the flowers their tears might weep forlorn,
> And there the nightingales melodious mourn,
> Such dirges only fitting for thy tongue,
> Wherein all eloquence most surely hung.

Bacon's death in 1626 brought to an end the career of one of the great figures of the Elizabethan epoch. A man of extraordinary ability, his *Essays* alone would have assured him a place in the history of English literature. His scientific writings reflected a mind which ranged far beyond the boundaries of conventional thinking in his day; his hypotheses were often wrong but his methods were new. His activities as lawyer, politician and statesman will stimulate controversy as long as English history is read and studied.

Chapter Four

Sir Harbottle Grimston at Gorhambury

Francis Bacon cut his wife Alice out of his will by a codicil dated 19 December 1625. She was having an affair with her husband's gentleman-usher, John Underhill, whom she married within a few months of Bacon's death. Her dead husband's financial affairs were in a sorry state, and it was left to his friends to sort them out. Sir Thomas Meautys, who had been Bacon's friend and secretary, bore the brunt of the lengthy proceedings and eventually acquired Gorhambury in June 1632. However, it was not until 1646 that he was able to move to the house with his wife and daughter. In the interim, Gorhambury was leased to the Countess of Sussex, and Sir Thomas himself lived at St Germain's, a house in St Michael's parish. At about this time Sir Thomas erected a fine marble statue to the memory of Francis Bacon in St Michael's church, and left instructions that he himself should be buried at the foot of the statue*.

In 1649 two deaths took place. Sir Thomas Meautys died, leaving a young widow; and Sir Harbottle Grimston's wife Mary also died. Before her marriage (at the age of 12) Anne Meautys had been Anne Bacon, daughter of Sir Nathaniel Bacon of Culford, a grandson of Sir Nicholas Bacon (the builder of Gorhambury) and his first wife Jane Fernley. (An account of Sir Nathaniel Bacon, a gifted artist, will be found in Appendix Two.) Sir Thomas left his wife a life interest in Gorhambury, with the reversion of the property left to their little daughter Jane. Anne Meautys and Sir Harbottle Grimston, then aged 36 and 49 respectively, fell in love and married. The marriage seems to have met with the approval of Anne's mother, and with that of her little daughter, for just before the wedding Anne wrote to her future husband (on 3 April 1651), to say that 'my mother continues her resolution of meeting you at London next week. Little Janey presents her humble love to her dear Sir Harreby and says the wedding gown *shall* be ready'. Sadly, the next year, 'little Janey' was dead; Sir Harbottle purchased the reversion of the manors of

---

*In December 1827 Bacon's monument was moved 'to make more room for officiating at the altar', since it stood out into the chancel. In 1981 the monument was removed for cleaning and restoration and then replaced. Between 1886 and 1900 at the request of certain Baconians an investigation was carried out beneath the monument; nothing was found. In 1958 a vault was discovered in the north aisle, partly of Roman construction. It had nothing in it, nor any concealed exit of any kind.

Gorhambury and Kingsbury for £10,000 from Henry Meautys, who was Sir Thomas's elder brother and now his heir.

This, then, is how the Grimstons came to Gorhambury; there is no blood relationship between them and the Bacons, but through Sir Harbottle's marriage with Anne Meautys much remains at Gorhambury today which recalls the Tudor Gorhambury's first owners.

Harbottle and Anne: Family Life at Gorhambury

We are fortunate in having many different types of document which together give us some idea of the kind of life the first Grimstons led at Gorhambury. For instance, we discover that they survived outbreaks of the plague because of – or perhaps in spite of – Sir Harbottle's special recipe for a preventative medicine, which his daughter wrote out. The concoction was thought to be not only proof against plague, but also for other diseases:

'Against plague take 3 pints of the best malmsey or sack. Boil therein one handful of rue, as much sage, till one pint is boiled away. Then strain it and add to that liquor long pepper, ginger, nutmegs, of each 3 drams, bruised; boil it a while, then take it off the fire and dissolve in it 1 ounce of mithridate and 2 ounces of the best treacle and a quarter of a pint of angelica water or strong aquavitae. Keep this above all medicines and use it as follows: If you think yourself infected, each morning take one spoonful of it; next unto God trust to this remedy, if the heart be not clean mortified and drowned with the poison so long before the drink comes. It is not only good against the plague, but the sweating sickness, surfeits, measles and small pox, take one spoonful of this when they first take and at all other times as need requires. This will keep 6 months, very good, or longer: proved by Sir Harbottle Grimston's family, during the time of the plague'.

A very different document which throws much light on Sir Harbottle's personality and ideas is a small book which he wrote in Latin, and originally intended as a guide to the proper conduct of life for his eldest son George. It was written in 1644 and printed when George was 13. Sir Harbottle entitled it *Strena Christiana: A Christian New Year's Gift*, and dedicated it 'to his beloved son and heir, George Grimston'. It contained 15 chapters of advice and exhortation dealing with such topics as 'Faith', 'Charity towards our Neighbours', and 'Temperance'. When George died soon after the book was published, Harbottle rededicated it to his second son Samuel, and inserted the following preface:

'Dear Son,
    This book being dedicated formerly to your brother (who was snatched hence by an overhasty death), appeared first in public without my knowledge or approbation. And now I have exposed it to open view myself thought I could not finish it (as I intended) being diverted by public employment; nevertheless I have added one chapter more, viz., concerning travelling, because I designed you should see some foreign nations which though you have not yet accomplished (by reason of some occurences that happened) yet I made that small addition that if ever your inclinations should bend that way, you might have some directions, not altogether incommodious. And I shall think it a sufficient recompense for my labour if you diligently observe these precepts which are chiefly intended for your welfare; and if any others are benefited or grow better thereby, I shall account that as clear gain. And seeing we live in an age that cries up virtue and still acts it down that exclaims against all vice and yet will admit of no remedy; I will not, nay, I

cannot be silent, and suffer my own bowels to perish. Son, it is in your power, to beautify and adorn this token of your father's love; by living up to the rules thereof; and if you would recommend it to others, be sure to study and practise it first yourself; that so, when God shall have multiplied, and blessed you with a numerous offspring, they may read and imitate, not so much this book, as yourself; and both you and they become venerable to posterity; which is as earnestly desired and hoped for, by your most loving father, Harbottle Grimston'.

The advice on travelling abroad which Sir Harbottle gave his son seems very sound. He recommended that Samuel 'might at least have one good associate and faithful guide in your journey ... you must seriously propose to your thoughts the end, advantage and ultimate design of travelling and ... be sure to consult with and to take the advice of your wisest friends. Use all diligence to inform your understanding and to get a critical and true notion of things; and so you may rightly distinguish between good and evil; but be most in your consultations with others, and be not ashamed to be taught by any. Speak but sparingly of yourself and yours; and that but amongst some few particular persons. Avoid all kinds of rash and over-prying curiosity lest the consequences of it prove dangerous. Remember that to be seemingly mute and deaf are no imperfections in a strange country. Yet carry yourself friendly and civilly with a courteous affability to strangers, and all persons that you meet with and casting aside the morose kind of rustic bashfulness, accustom yourself to a free modesty in all your behaviour, not too lavish in laughing at others, or making them to object of your derision. Present your commendations often, and pay your duty frequently to your friends either by letters or messengers ... Pass away the tediousness of travelling with the harmless mirth of pleasant stories, and innocent discourses, without any sort of scurrility, either in words or deeds; and intersperse and season your journey with holy meditations, religious talk and pious hymns'.

'As for your abode in any place', Sir Harbottle went on, 'be sure to make a diligent and cautious enquiry into the ecclesiastical rites and ceremonies; with the political government and into the usual manners and civil customs of the same. Entertain not the vanity of priding yourself with the shew of much money or jewels; for that will be a means only to invite robbers, and prove a snare to your own safety. Do not gaze at, or admire anything with astonishment, for that will rebound to the discredit of your country, and be an argument that you never saw the like at home; and on the other side do not decry, or fastidiously detract from anything that is truly worthy of admiration: lest thereby you betray yourself to infamy and seem both injurious and indiscreet. If you have obtained a familiarity, and promptness in the Latin tongue, then into what strange parts soever you go, you will not be a stranger'.

Sir Harbottle believed that 'the wisdom and ingenuity of most nations lies couched under their proverbs; therefore it behoves you to acquire the knowledge of their language. Do not shun the society of your own countrymen lest you should seem to slight and despise them; and yet be not over greedily ambitious of their company, for 'tis altogether unprofitable and beside your present purpose. Every nation is famous for some things and infamous for others; so that it has both a badge of honour and a mark of disgrace. Whatever you meet with that deserves to be remembered commit it to writing, for it may be afterwards both advantageous and delightful. Be always mindful that you never do, nor suffer anything, unworthy of your country. Abstain from that which you cannot endure; yet do not disgracefully decline dangers or rashly invite them. But behave yourself so in all things, that you give a good account both to God and your friends'.

The author even had advice for when the actual journey was completed. 'As for your return, when you come back to your native country, do not indulge yourself in telling strange stories, and prattling beyond belief, lest you should become famous only for lying. And do not now despise your own possessions, and domestic concerns, though you have seen many greater, nobler and more pleasant elsewhere ... Endeavour to return better and wiser; and not seem so much to have changed the heavens, as your intellects, for he returns in the greatest poverty imaginable, that has lost himself abroad. Be willing to inform the ignorant in those things which they ask; and though their questions may perhaps be somewhat ridiculous and erroneous, yet expose them not, but modestly correct their errors. And when you have performed your duty to God, and your friends, be not a stranger now at home too; but look over the face of things and enquire whether your country (in your absence) hath added, altered or diminished anything.. Lastly, at this, and all other times, you owe many things to yourself, more to your friends, and all to God. These things your most loving earthly father had to give you in his commands; who does recommend you, both at home and abroad, to the protection and conduct of the Father of Light, Lord of Heaven and Earth; who will illuminate and guide you in the ways of righteousness'.

As the tone of this extract makes clear, Sir Harbottle, like most 17th century gentlemen, was extremely religious. His beliefs were shared by his wife Anne. They spent at least an hour in the morning and again at night in prayer and meditation. Even when Sir Harbottle had to rise especially early to fulfil his duties as a Judge, he took care to allow enough time to carry out his devotions. His friend, Bishop Gilbert Burnet, wrote of Anne Grimston:

'She had all the high notions of the Church and the Crown, in which she had been bred, but was the humblest, the devoutest and best-tempered person I ever knew of that sort. It was really a pleasure to hear her talk of religion. She did it with so much elevation and force. She was always very plain in her clothes and went oft to jails, to consider the wants of the prisoners and relieve or discharge them, and by the meanness of her dress she passed but for a servant trusted with the charities of others. When she was in the country, as she drew near a village, she often ordered her coach to stay behind until she had walked about it, giving orders for the instruction of the children and leaving liberally for that end'.

Sir Harbottle Grimston and Verulam House

Many generations of Grimstons have speculated as to why it was that Sir Harbottle should have sold Verulam House for demolition, and destroyed Sir Francis Bacon's famous architectural creation. Letters recently found at Gorhambury throw a new light on an incident which might appear as an act of insensitive destruction. Harbottle's eldest son, George, was born at Bradfield in 1631. At 21 he fell in love with a doctor's daughter, from a neighbouring Suffolk family, whose name was Sarah Alston. A marriage was arranged by 'a tripartite Indenture made on November 1st 1652 between Sir Harbottle Grimston, his wife Dame Anne (née Bacon) of the first part ... Edward Alston ... doctor in physic of the second part ... and George Grimston Esq., son and heir apparent of Sir Harbottle Grimston and Sarah Alston, younger daughter of Edward Alston of the third part'. The deed settled Grimston land in Essex on George, and Dr. Alston contributed 'six thousand pounds of lawful English money for their jointure' while Sir Harbottle was to provide Verulam House for the young couple's home.

At the time that this transaction was being set in motion, Verulam House was occupied by Mathew Bigg, a lawyer of Gray's Inn. There is a document leasing to Bigg 'all that capital messuage or tenement called or known by the name of Verulam House ... together with the Dove House, Pond House, etc ... the close pasture containing 12 acres in which the house stands, Pond Close or Pond Meadow containing eight acres wherein the fishponds are'. A letter from Bigg, written from Verulam House, asks permission to hunt at Gorhambury, and also for a new 21-year lease on the house. Both requests were refused. In April 1656, Bigg wrote again from 'Colney Chappell, concerning damage done to Verulam House, allegedly during his tenancy. He insisted that the 'pales, ponds, sluices, fish and dwelling house' were left in good condition, and added that he had had the leads and windows repaired before his departure. Whilst on the subject of this tenancy, there is also a strange note in existence addressed to Harbottle which contains the following extraordinary sentence: 'Mr. Bigg for Verulam House was to give you yearly a tearce [sic] of claret and for your grounds was the agreement between you and Mr. Bigg when you let him the house and if there be occasion I must witness as much'. This document, written in June 1656, has a completely illegible signature appended. Should we take it as implying that Bigg's rent for Verulam House was merely 'a tearce of claret'?

Both Gorhambury and Verulam House were in need of considerable repair work when Sir Harbottle acquired them. Sir Francis, when 'bringing his house to the water', may have chosen too low-lying a location in the water-meadows. It may have been that the River Ver burst its banks and flooded the cellars, causing the house to be affected by damp. Was that leaded roof, so well described by John Aubrey, also defective?

Although the intention was that George and Sarah Grimston should make Verulam House their home, they never did so, for their married life was too short. Two sons were born, but both died in infancy, and George himself died in 1655, leaving poor Sarah a childless widow at barely 22. A well-polished black marble slab in the central aisle of St Michael's church records George's life and death: 'Here lieth the body of George Grimston, Esq., son and heir apparent of the honourable Sir Harbottle Grimston, Baronet, Master of the Rolls, a gentleman full of piety and humility, dutiful to his parents, loving and beloved, his person and comportment both worthy of conservation, of a comely shape and most persuasive behaviour but death put a period to his growing hopes in the 25th year of his age'. By the 20th century, the feet of worshippers had worn away the inscription, but fortunately, not long after the stone had been placed in position, the antiquary Elias Ashmole had noted down the inscription. In 1957, on the instructions of the 5th Earl of Verulam, George's stone, and that of Sir Thomas Meautys, were recut with their original inscriptions.

But for George's death, Verulam House would have stood longer than it did. Shortly after he died, his sister Mary (wife of Sir Capel Luckyn) went to look over the house on behalf of her father. She reported back to him that 'upon examination I find the lead work very defective ... They were all cast and laid out not above eight or nine years since. There are also other defects, whereof your man hath a note in writing, which I suppose he will give order for the mending ...'. Mary suggested that a lawyer, 'Mr Francis Lowe of Gray's Inn should determine the business and I shall desire to know your resolution therein ... for till the difference between us be ended, I cannot tell well how to conclude with any other, for as it is 'tis fit for nobody'.

The story may be traced further in a series of letters from Sarah Grimston to her father-in-law, written during the early days of her widowhood. The letters are models of correct composition and calligraphy. She was an intelligent, well-brought-up young woman with a mind of her own. The letters cover the period from May 1656 to September 1657 and are charmingly addressed 'for my ever honoured father, Sir Harbottle Grimston, Baronet, at Gorhambury in Hertfordshire, these'. The letters begin 'Most honoured Sir' and close 'Sir, I am, Your most obedient daughter-in-law: Sarah Grimston'.

Sarah indicated that she did not wish Sir Harbottle to prosecute Mr. Bigg for something for her gain which might prejudice his own interests in any way. On the other hand, she felt it would be hard if she had to pay to put Verulam House into repair, and to keep it so, when at her death it would revert to the Grimston estate. She would have been most willing to repair it, had God spared her a son, who should have received it after her death. The vault beneath the house had been opened, and she would 'take care for the emptying of it, or if that cannot be done, I shall be content that what part of the £18 you designed me for that work, shall be left after the repair of Verulam House go towards the making of the vault, for the paling you mention to be necessary, I am willing it should be done'.

It did seem hard that Sir Harbottle should expect his daughter-in-law to contribute to the cost of a house in which she had never actually lived, but

Sarah appreciated that he had considerable expenses himself to consider. In her next letter she condoled with him as to the amount which he had had to expend to maintain the estate, but reminded him of his promise to help her: 'seeing you have been pleased, more than once, to intimate, by your letters, your desire ... after my humble thanks to you, for what you have already done for me ... and your often promises gave me the expectation of your more continued assistance of me in my business'. She thought 'Verulam House, worth the keeping in repair', and was willing to do what he thought to be necessary to it, for 'although I have no use for it for the present, yet because it was one of those possessions, which was made for me, upon my marriage to my most dear husband, I shall keep it in memory of him, and it is also some content to me, that I have a house to go to, when either my mind, or conditions, shall require it'. This letter was written in June, 1656.

A month later another letter from Sarah reveals that Sir Harbottle had re-let Verulam House. Sarah apologises for her reluctance to go there herself 'yet I hope you will excuse me, if I cannot bring my mind to the going thither, where I shall have often[er] occasion than in other places to remember my dear husband ... Sir, as for Verulam's rent, I am willing that Mr. Smith, who as Mr. Lowe now tells me now rents it, should hold it, unless I should dispose of the house and land together ...'. That August Sarah sent 'a workman to view the house ... and shall accordingly give order for the doing of it'.

The last letter from Sarah in the series is dated over a year later. In it she expressed the feeling that her father-in-law had treated her a little unjustly. 'There hath been a great failing as to me, of that which is my right, which you Sir cannot have forgotten, the revenue of the lands I enjoy being far less than what in the particular you gave at my marriage ... And if those promises fall short ... it should afterwards be made good to me, I cannot find it yet performed'. For her part, Sarah would ever 'harbour ... a most cordial affection and service to you ... none can more truly desire and rejoice in your happiness than myself. That love which my most dear husband did bear to me, was so great as I can express ... which kindness of his I shall not forget, neither can time wear it out of my memory, so long as I live in this world'. There is no doubt that George's death affected his father with equal force. To a friend, whose son also died young, Sir Harbottle wrote these telling words:

> 'My heart is with you, though not myself: to visit now were to trouble, not to ease. I know you cannot at present but be a man of sorrows. I have trodden in the same steps, and it is some ease in sorrow to have liberty to sorrow. God hath now put you upon your trial, whether, with Abraham, you can be contented to part with a dear and hopeful child, as he was with the son of his blessings. I confess it is one of the greatest trials ...'.

Ten years after George's death the house where he and his wife should have lived a happy family life was sold. John Aubrey's account of its end makes sad reading. 'This house ... was sold about 1665 or 1666 by Sir Harbottle Grimston to two carpenters for £400, of which they made £800 ... I little suspected it would be pulled down for the sake of the materials ...'. Six years later, Sarah Grimston married for the second time. Her second husband was John Seymour, 4th Duke of Somerset, and she lived to have a third husband, Henry, Lord Coleraine. She died in 1692, aged 61. George Grimston's brother Samuel was an executor of his former sister-in-law's will, and Sarah left him '120 shilling pieces of broad gold'. Among other legacies, Sarah also left £500 for George's sister Mary – Lady Luckyn – and the same amount for another of his sisters, Elizabeth, Lady Grubham Howe. Sarah was a great character, and an important benefactress. Among her many endowments was one of a scholarship to Brasenose College, Oxford. This, surely, was in memory of her first husband, George, who was admitted there on 1 May 1649 when he was 18.

Chapter Five

Sir Harbottle Grimston's Contributions to Gorhambury

When Sir Harbottle came to Gorhambury, the house built by Sir Nicholas Bacon was already 100 years old. What were his actions there? During his first years, he carried out little more than necessary repairs. It is likely that he wished to adopt new fashions in interior decoration brought from the Continent by Charles II and his court. There was a taste for bright colours in materials for hangings, and for walnut furniture. Blue and white oriental porcelain was extremely popular.

However, given Sir Harbottle's deep religious convictions, it is not surprising to discover that he made alterations and improvements to the chapel a priority. The first repairs to it were done in 1668. In April and May of that year, we find the following entries in the account books: 2s 6d 'to Mr. Smyth for mending the ironwork of the chapel window'; £13 10s 'to Mr. Marshall upon bill for the chapel window'; £1 17s 11d 'to the glazier for glassing the chapel window'. There are also agreements for alterations to be made to the chapel with a bricklayer, Thomas Evans, who was 'to take down the end of the chapel and to build a new wall 20 foot in length from the old wall'; this was to be a new west end wall, projecting 20 feet from the rear wall of the old Long Gallery. The foundations were to be 'as thick as it was before and from the water table to the roof a foot and a half thick. The height and the breadth within according to the old chapel'. Evans was also to raise the roof next to the chaplain's chamber level with the new building and to lath, tile and seal it. In the same year, Thomas Ednee was appointed to 'build a new window to the chapel, containing 14 foot wide in transom, and 18 foot in the clear, with a pier in the middle and three lights in each side of the pier. The first light to be seven foot high with transom, the second six feet high, arched on the top'.

For this work as much stone as was useful and necessary was to come from Sopwell, the ancient nunnery, and its land, a property lying on the other side of St Albans which now belonged to the Gorhambury estate. The remainder was to come from the 'store in the barn at Gorhambury' and 'the said Thomas Ednee is to find lime for the said work, and to let in all the iron bars fit for the glazier, and do all other freemason's work to the finishing of the said window, which is to be done and finished before Midsummer Day next ensuing, in good and workmanlike manner. And he is to have and receive for the said work the sum of £19, that is to say £5 for the first day he begins the work, and £10 more when the work is half done and £4 when he has finished the said work'.

There is, however, little evidence that this work was ever carried out, for at this point Captain Richard Ryder, who had done repairs at Cranborne Manor and elsewhere for the Earl of Salisbury, and had worked with Inigo Jones, came on the scene. In April 1673 we find that Ednee was now instructed to 'make and set up one window in stone in the chapel belonging to Gorhambury in form and fashion according to the draft made thereof by Capt. Ryder, for which the said Sir Harbottle Grimston does agree to pay unto the said Ednee the sum of £10 and find stone, ironwork and the carrier of sand'. A subsequent memorandum notes that the window was to have been '18 foot and 20 foot' and is now to be '14 and 16 foot'. Was it Sir Harbottle's idea to put into this window some of the old coloured glass from the recently demolished Verulam House?

On 11 June 1675 Ednee agreed to 'lay the floor of the chapel at Gorhambury with good strong sound and well coloured white Purbeck stone and black marble, cornerwise, well polished' at the rate of 2s a foot 'which comes upon measure 443 feet'. Ednee also agreed to 'lay the floor of that part of the chapel where the communion table is to stand, with black and white marble, well polished and glazed, cornerwise' for which he was to have 3s 6d a foot, and to find the marble, lime and all other materials. He was also to work the step 'with an ostrigal mould, to polish, glaze and lay the same with the marble steps that are at Sopwell, finding all other matters' for which he was to have £3. The floor in the present Great Hall in the 18th century Gorhambury and on the east portico is the same Purbeck stone and 'cornerwise' black marble floor from Harbottle's chapel: the reuse of materials is an idea whose use was not confined to the 17th century at Gorhambury.

There are other reminders of Sir Harbottle's chapel still visible. The fine oak columns with Corinthian capitals (three free-standing and two pilasters) which are now in the stone passage in Gorhambury's Victorian north wing came from the chapel, but in a roundabout way. When the Tudor house was dismantled, some of the old oak panelling and balustrading was put into St Michael's Church, including these columns. A schoolmaster and antiquary called Pridmore, of Tewin, wrote in his notebook in 1797 that 'the pulpit stood on the north side of the nave, and a gallery, brought from Gorhambury, occupied the western end of the church. On it in gold capital letters was the inscription 'This gallery was the gift of Viscount Grimston, 1787'. It is supported by four elegant Corinthian columns of brown wood'. An entry in Sir Harbottle's account book for 29 June 1673 may refer to these columns, or at least to the men who probably carved them: it reads 'to John Nicholl and James Barnes in part of their contract for wainscotting the chapel at Gorhambury – £50'. St Michael's gallery was demolished at about the time that Gorhambury's north wing was being enlarged, and so the columns came back to Gorhambury and were incorporated into the 19th-century section of the house.

The fine Jacobean pulpit certainly also came to St. Michael's from Gorhambury. It dates from Francis Bacon's day, for this pulpit displays the complex symbolism in its design which he so delighted in. The design shows the altar becoming a Grail Chalice, and the Holy Grail arising from the Chalice as the royal rose, symbol of the Bride and the perfect human soul. The leaves and stem of the rose follow the pattern of the Tree of Life. Above this 'royal arch' is the winged Sun with a cherubic face, crowned with a rainbow. The heraldic glass in the chancel at St. Michael's also came from Sir Harbottle's chapel at Gorhambury.

Although Sir Harbottle made use of the ruins of Sopwell Nunnery in his new chapel, he was one of the benefactors of the Abbey of St Albans. In 1681 a brief was issued authorising the collection of money towards repairs and alterations to the Abbey, and among the list of those who contributed Sir Harbottle's name is to be found, as the donor of £100. Armorial shields of those who subscribed generously were placed in the presbytery: Sir Harbottle's shield is on the north side, and to the right of it is the shield of the notorious Judge Jeffreys.

Sir Harbottle brought many family treasures with him to Gorhambury, including the Harbottle armorial pile carpet, the splendid and important Petrus Christus portrait of his ancestor Edward Grimston, 'the ambassador', and the fine Robert Peake portrait of Edward Grimston, the Comptroller of Calais, together with many other less outstanding family portraits.

Harbottle and his wife Anne had only one child – a girl – who died young. Poor Anne, her first child had died in 1652 and now her second had also predeceased her. The succession rested, therefore, with Samuel, Sir Harbottle's surviving son by his first wife, Mary Croke. With Anne's death in 1680, this branch of the Bacon family came to an end. Was it for Anne's body, or in preparation for his own burial, that Sir Harbottle is said to have removed the coffin of Sir Francis Bacon from St Michael's Church? 'This October 1681', wrote John Aubrey, 'it rang all over St Albans that Harbottle Grimston, Master of the Rolls, had removed the coffin of this most renowned Lord Chancellor to make room for his own to lie in the vault there at St Michael's'. Sir Harbottle actually lived on for another four years after this affair. Luttrell gives the date of his death in his *Diary* as 2 January 1685:'The 2nd about 4 in the morning died that good old gentleman Sir Harbottle Grimston, Master of the Rolls, in the 82nd year of his age, after a sickness of 5 days'. Apparently he died of 'apoplexy'. The accounts for his funeral expenses are given in Appendix Three.

Bishop Gilbert Burnet, who lived for many years under Sir Harbottle's protection, and knew him well, offered this assessment of his character:

'I lived many years under the protection of Sir Harbottle Grimston, Master of the Rolls, who continued steady in his favour to me though the King sent Williamson to desire him to dismiss me. He said he was an old man, fitting himself to another world, and he found my ministry useful to him: so he prayed he might be excused in that. He was a long and very kind patron to me. I continued ten years in that post [settled preacher at the Rolls and sometimes lecturer at St Clement's], free from all necessities, and I thank God that was all I desired. But since I was so long happy, in so quiet a retreat, it seems but a just piece of gratitude that I should give some account of that venerable old man. He was descended from a long-lived family, for his grandfather lived till he was 98 and himself to 82. He had great soundness of health, of memory and judgment ... He ... was always looked upon as one who wished well to the ancient government of England. So he was chosen as Speaker of the House of Commons that called home the King; and had so great a merit in that whole affair that he was soon after, without any application of his own, made Master of the Rolls, in which post he continued until his death, with a high reputation as he well deserved. For he was a just judge; very slow and ready to hear everything that was offered without passion or partiality. I thought his only fault was that he was too rich. And yet he gave yearly great sums in charity, discharging many prisoners by paying their debts'.

Payments to Dr. Burnet can be found amongst Sir Harbottle's Steward's accounts. The following entry confirms Burnet's description of his master's kindness to him: '1682, to Dr. Burnet for Hilary term's salary, 1682, £20, and given him over by your order, £5'. Another contemporary of Sir Harbottle, Sir Henry Chauncy, said of him 'He was of free access, sociable in company, sincere to his friend, hospitable in his house, charitable to the poor, and an excellent master to his servants'.

Five of his six sons died before him; of his two daughters, Mary (of whom we will have more to say later) married Sir Capel Luckyn of Messing Hall, and Elizabeth married Sir George Grubham Howe, of Cold Berwick in Wiltshire.

Sir Samuel Grimston, 3rd Baronet, 1643-1700

Samuel was the sole survivor of six sons. Unlike his father, he did not play a significant role in national history. This may partly have been because James II considered Samuel to be 'obnoxious' to him, and during his reign the latter had no choice but to remain in private life. Under both Charles II and William III, however, Samuel served in several Parliaments, representing the borough of St Albans.

 Samuel's first marriage had a tragic end. In 1669 he married Elizabeth, the eldest of the 14 children of Heneage Finch, later to become the 1st Earl of Nottingham and Lord Chancellor of England. From Sir Peter Lely's painting of her, Elizabeth looks a demure, but homesick girl. Married at 16, she gave birth to a daughter the year after her marriage, who was named Elizabeth after her mother. Next year the young mother was dead; her daughter, however, survived to marry William Savile, 2nd Marquess of Halifax. It was this couple's daughter Anne whose inheritance from her grandfather was to bring so many problems later on (see pp. ooo-ooo below). Besides the painting of his wife, Samuel acquired a portrait of his wife's father, painted by Sir Godfrey Kneller, and another of her brother Daniel, painted by John Riley. All three Finches hang together in today's Gorhambury.

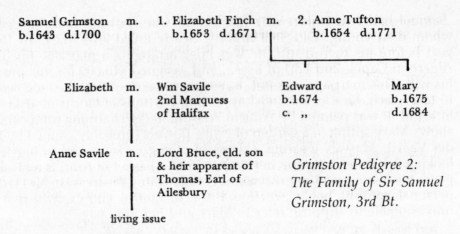

Samuel Grimston   m.   1. Elizabeth Finch m.   2. Anne Tufton
b.1643 d.1700   b.1653 d.1671   b.1654 d.1771

Elizabeth   m.   Wm Savile   Edward   Mary
                  2nd Marquess   b.1674   b.1675
                  of Halifax   c. „   d.1684

Anne Savile   m.   Lord Bruce, eld. son
                   & heir apparent of   *Grimston Pedigree 2:*
                   Thomas, Earl of   *The Family of Sir Samuel*
                   Ailesbury   *Grimston, 3rd Bt.*

living issue

Even at this early date, Samuel's financial affairs appear to have been extremely rocky, which seems strange when we remember what Bishop Burnet said of his father's great wealth. In a document relating to the marriage of his great-nephew, there is a paragraph which shows that Samuel had mortgaged vast areas of his estates in Suffolk and Essex at the time of his own marriage to Elizabeth. A couple of years after her death, he found himself a second bride – Anne Tufton, a girl little older than his first wife had been. She was an heiress, the daughter of the Earl of Thanet and a descendant of Margaret, Countess of Cumberland, whose portrait is at Gorhambury. Like Elizabeth before her, Anne Grimston was painted by Lely. She looks languid and beautiful, her golden dress complementing her golden hair. Her pose breathes serenity, and with her gentle features and fashionable curling hair, one can imagine her appeal to Samuel. However, her lovely face gave no indication of her true character, for she proved to be an extremely dominating woman. Samuel has been described by a later Grimston as 'a mild man of kindly disposition'. When he found himself married to this sultry, hot-tempered woman, it must have been a sorry day for him. She picked quarrels so often, nearly always over matters of religion, that Samuel finally felt he could take no more arguments, and resolved that by some means or another he must remove himself from her company for at least part of the day. He decided to build himself a place of refuge – a small room where he could have his books and writing materials, and a place quite inaccessible to his wife. He built a new room 'at the end of the billiard room', which could be approached only by a very narrow stairway, much too steep and far too narrow for the now corpulent Anne to climb. Samuel called this little retreat his 'Mount Pleasant'. Samuel's great-great grand daughter's comment on this was that 'anger as well as love could laugh at locksmiths'.

To Gorhambury's gain, Samuel sat not once but two or three times for his portrait to Sir Godfrey Kneller. There is a bill for one of them, dated 1694, for the sum of £22.

Samuel had two children by his second wife, Edward and Mary, both of whom died young. Old Sir Harbottle dearly loved little Mary. In 1684, the year before his own death, he was busy arranging a marriage for her with Algernon Capel, 2nd Earl of Essex, and assigned £10,000 for this purpose in his will. This marriage was not, however, to be, for Mary died too soon for it to take place. One of the most appealing portraits at Gorhambury is of this little girl. It was painted by William Wissing. It is a charming composition and shows Mary sitting in a garden of exotic flowers (probably painted by Jan van der Vaart). Mary is wearing a dress of blue-grey satin and to her left, and looking up at her, offering her grapes from a basket of fruit, is a blackamoor page, his own appeal as great as that of his young mistress. In Sir Harbottle's personal account books we find these delightful entries, which it is not unreasonable to suppose refer to Mary and her little page.

1683 January 22. Paid the page's master for a month's teaching		15	0
February 12. A play for Miss Mary		4	0
A pair of spurs for the page			6
February 26. For the page's coat		17	0
To Mr. Hall for a month's teaching him		15	0
Paid him for a fiddle and case	1	11	0
A quire of paper for Miss Grimston			7
For a music book for the page		1	0
March 26. Cutting the page's hair			6
April 31 [*sic*]Paid for the page's waistcoat, silk		13	0
The page's hat		8	6
For gloves for him		2	6
May 7. A shoulder knot and hat band for the page		4	8
Lace for the page's hat		5	0
June 25. Dr. Lower for corsets to Mistress Mary	6	9	0
July 2. A dancing book for the page		2	6
July 9. The page's stockings, with green tops		7	0
1694 January 21. Pair of shoes for the page		3	8
A sword for him		5	0
A belt for him		3	0
February 4. A music book for the page		2	6
For eleven tunes for the page			10
February 25. Four beagle puppies		2	6
May 25. For setting Mary's arm		10	0
July 14. Paid the coachmaker for the hire of a mourning coach this summer	10	0	0
August 24. Going to London for Dr. Burnett		1	0
November 3. Two quilted caps for the page		2	4
December 8. Paid for the page's peruke		16	0

From these items in Sir Harbottle's account book, it can be deduced that Mary's broken arm failed to mend properly, and that she died in the summer of 1684. We can but hope that the beagle puppies provided a happy diversion for her in her last weeks. Mary is referred to no more, and the entry of 14 July, 'for the hire of a mourning coach' makes sad reading. As late as March of that year William Luckyn wrote to his mother Mildred that 'Miss Mary is to [be] married to the Earl of Essex: there is as much done as possible to secure it until they come of age to give their consent'. Now the marriage had to be forgotten.

Chapter Six
The Luckyn Inheritance

On a cold grey January day in 1648, Samuel Grimston's 16-year-old sister Mary walked on the arm of her father, Sir Harbottle Grimston, from Bradfield Hall across the garden to Bradfield Church. It was her wedding day; she was marrying Capel Luckyn of Messing Hall. It was a Thursday, and Mr. Balls performed the ceremony. Mary's bridegroom was a Lincoln's Inn lawyer, heir to Sir William Luckyn of Great Baddow and Little Waltham, who was created a baronet in 1628. Capel, a florid-faced man with a very prominent nose, was 11 years older than Mary. He adored her and could not bear to be parted from her even for a day. If estate business made even a brief parting inevitable, he wrote her delicious love letters, addressing her as his 'dearest heart', his 'sweetest heart', his 'beloved heart'. He signed himself as 'thy most affectionate and ever loving husband', or 'thy ever loving and constant husband' and all manner of other permutations on this theme, to assure Mary of his love. 'Luckyn' is an old Essex surname, meaning 'love child'; it was appropriate for Capel Luckyn.

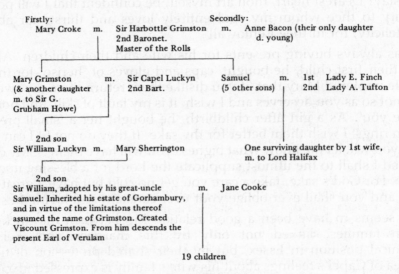

Grimston Pedigree 3: Table of Descent from Sir Harbottle Grimston

Capel's 'very soul longs in joy' for his 'wished for haven', his 'dearest heart'. When he was at the Luckyn estate at Hutton in Somerset in the autumn of 1649 he sent his 'dearest' a peck of long-keeping pears, called 'wardens', and explained that he had taken pains to put the worst at the top of the basket to discourage 'any that had a mind to steal the whole'. From Colchester, he sent her a box of 'ringoes', the candied 'eryngo' root for which Colchester was famous. In Tudor times the roots of sea holly – *eryngium maritimum* – were candied and eaten as sweetmeats. Shakespeare referred to them in *The Merry Wives of Windsor*, when Falstaff said in the Great Park at Windsor 'Let the sky rain potatoes; let it thunder to the tune of *Greensleeves*: hail kissing-comforts, and snow eringoes ...'. A Colchester confectioner, Robert Burton, started to market his eringo sweets on a large scale and became famous for them. They were thought to be excellent medicinal remedies for old people and for those suffering from cramp. Eringoes were also believed to be a diuretic, a restorative and an aphrodisiac – surely Capel and Mary had no need of them in this last capacity with their large brood! The herbalist Nicholas Culpepper, advised his readers to drink the distilled water from the roots of the sea holly as a restorative. Surely, it was for this purpose, to help his wife recover her strength after childbirth, that Capel obtained eringoes for Mary.

On another occasion we find Capel, after expressing his longing to 'embrace his sweetest heart', claiming that his 'rural pen' was wanting in expression for a 'heart so bounding in affection'. Despite his modesty, he became almost poetic as he went on, 'But oh methinks whilst I am thus musing I hear my beloved say Why comes he not himself away? Why does he so long stay? Dearest heart, thou art myself, be confident that I will post with all celerity to thee whom my soul entirely loves and thirsts for above all earthly felicity, for in thee I enjoy all'.

He was always buying presents for his wife and their children. After the birth of their first child, he bought 'caps and gloves of "heriso" for the child coats'. He implored Mary that 'if you dislike them return them my sweetest if they be not so as you deserves and I wish, it is my fault of skill, and not of will to please you'. As a gift after childbirth, he bought her a 'small present of cornelian rings: I wish them better for thy sake. If they do not fit I can change them, if you will let me know what bigness you will have them ... My dearest, be assured I shall to the utmost supplicate the Lord for a blessing upon your little one. For God's sake, take a care you get no cold but have a great care of yourself and you shall ever oblige your ever constant and loving husband'.

There seems to have been a good relationship between the Luckyn and Grimston families, linked not only by this marriage and their close geographical position in Essex, but by their shared profession of the law. Some idea of Capel's feelings about his wife's family is expressed in a letter of 1 November 1650. After enquiring of his 'only joy' what was her 'resolution as to what gown you would like to have for the winter and whether you hold your resolution to have it in the country or from Stockwells' and urging her to 'let it be very warm', he goes on to say:

> 'I pray God all things are likely to go on well: there is a very good understanding betwixt your father and my father. By my next you will hear that Messing is settled upon you and that Hutton is sold. My father wholly leaves himself to Sir Harbottle, and does nothing without his direction. Your father orders all. We are like to have 6,500 pounds for Hutton, your father gives you 300 pounds and my father besides the 500 pounds will settle St Osyth upon you wholly. Be you sure to give your father thanks in your next letter to him for £300 which he gives you. This good news will not please Lady Luckyn [his stepmother] who is in the country, so I am now in hopes we shall be settled in Messing and run not one penny more in debt. I am now going to carry these writings to the lawyer which is to convey the estate to Mr. Cory. I mean to settle Hutton upon him. Hardly a day but what I both dine and sup with Sir Harbottle and so does Sir William also, they are very merry'.

In the year that Capel and Mary married, Capel entered Parliament for Harwich. It had been the parliamentary seat of Mary's grandfather, the 1st Baronet, and became available for Capel because of the old man's death.

Capel Luckyn died in 1680, and according to the Messing Parish Church register, he was buried by torchlight. Mary survived her husband by 38 years.

Although Capel and Mary's marriage was prolific, their children were not strong. Of their seven daughters and six sons, only three survived their parents. The survivors were William, the fourth son, and two daughters, Mildred and Sarah. William was 'born on Monday morning 31st Jan. Anno Domini 1658, betwixt five and six of the clock. Messing Hall Clock went six in the morning he was born in Messing Hall Great Chamber'. This William was, in turn, to marry another Mary, Mary Sherrington. Of their two sons, the older, named Harbottle, was Cupbearer both to Queen Anne and to George I. In the Library at Gorhambury today, there is a Bible covered in a faded violet velvet cover, and inscribed 'Queen Anne to Sir Harbottle Luckyn, her Cupbearer'. Nearby hangs a portrait of Harbottle Luckyn, resplendent in a long blue velvet coat which he wears over a red waistcoat and breastplate. His breeches are embroidered in gold, and a white lawn shirt is visible at his neck and wrists. He wears a white wig and carries a three-cornered hat. To complete his uniform, that of the 1st Troop Horse Grenadier Guards, in which he served as a lieutenant, he wears a sword. This Harbottle Luckyn, the 4th Baronet, died in 1736. His younger brother William thus became the 5th Baronet Luckyn, and was the godson of his maternal great-uncle Samuel Grimston. Samuel, having no living issue of his own, had adopted William in his youth, and it was thus that William came to inherit all the Grimston estates at the early age of 17.

Among the many famous faces and the serious features of the religious Grimstons at Gorhambury, there is a refreshing portrait of a young boy dressed in a coat of pale blue velvet, with flame-coloured facings. One hand clasps the lead of an enormous Newfoundland dog, the other a shield emblazoned with a Union Jack. The frame is of interest, deeply carved with cupids and foliage. It is dated 1691. Incorporated in the picture is an oval marble relief, depicting Cupid wrestling with Pan; this repetition of the 'cupid motif' links portrait and frame and suggests that 1691 may be taken as the date of both. Formerly this portrait was thought to be a Grimston born in 1707, but the frame-dating suggests that we may regard it as a likeness of young William Grimston – perhaps even commissioned by his great-uncle, Sir Samuel. Another portrait of William, painted a few years later, shows him wearing his own hair, powdered and brushed back from his forehead. It hangs in the yellow drawing room at Gorhambury today, and has the fine feeling of Sir Godfrey Kneller's work. It is likely that it was painted at about the time that William inherited Gorhambury and took the name of Grimston.

Sir Samuel Grimston made two provisos in his will which William was obliged to accept in order to receive his inheritance. The first was that his great-nephew should change his name from Luckyn to Grimston, and the second was that William should pay £30,000 to Lady Anne Savile, Sir Samuel's only surviving grandchild. The first of these conditions was easily acceded to, but the second posed an enormous problem for the young heir. Many years later, Harriot Grimston (1776-1846) told the story as she had heard it from the 'elders' of her family, so that her 'dear nieces' should know of it.

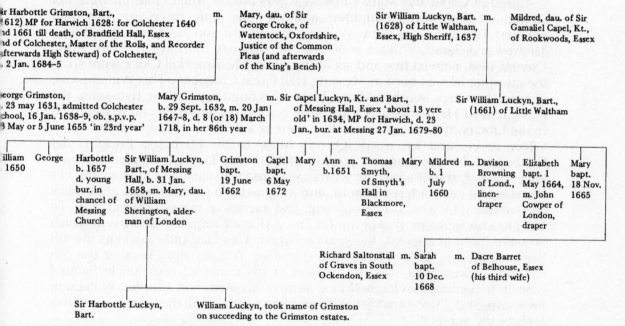

Grimston Pedigree 4: Grimston and Luckyn Connections

William Luckyn hesitated long, if he should accept the estate subject to such an encumbrance. His elder brother, Sir Harbottle Luckyn, strongly urged him to agree to the terms, and fortunately for our family his arguments proved effectual. You are therefore to fancy William Luckyn, now William Grimston, wandering through the immense suite of rooms at Gorhambury considering by what means he could liquidate this debt. The subject preyed upon his spirits, and, if these walls could speak, they would tell you how bitterly he lamented the acquisition of them, and how heartily he wished, like Sir Harbottle Grimston, his only fault was that of being too rich. I have seen innumerable letters from Mr. Grimston to Sir Harbottle Luckyn full of mournful details of his poverty, and expressions of regret at the necessity of keeping the house in repair, without the means adequate for the purpose. Sir Harbottle Luckyn could give nothing but his advice, for, poor himself, an immense number of younger brothers and sisters were to be provided for. There were Capel, Henry, Charles, Edward, Samuel, George, Sherington and James, besides Mary, Elizabeth, Sarah, Mildred and Martha, all hanging upon him for support. "Raise what money you can upon the estate, and marry an heiress: I can only wish you well", was the language of his answers. Mr. Grimston accordingly let half the house and lived himself in the remainder. He likewise made the axe to sound throughout the park at Gorhambury. The wood called Broke, and the cluster of trees named the Rookery, were in those days united, and fine timber grew where at present not one stick remains. Oak Wood was likewise cleared of every tree which had grown to its full size, and a screen of young elms, now still growing, were planted on the outside of the wood, in order to conceal the deficiencies of the inside'.

Harriot asked the new Grimston generation not to 'abuse' their great-great-grandfather 'for having made this havoc in the park', because 'it was an act of necessity. He mourned the loss of the trees more than you can do, and only consented to their removal because it was impossible otherwise to pay the debt upon the estate'.

By the age of 22, young William had found himself a wealthy heiress – Jane, the daughter of James Cooke, 'a wax chandler and citizen of London'. Luttrell wrote in his *Diary* for 15 August 1706: 'Yesterday William Grimston, Esq., gentleman of £6,000 per annum…was married to one Mistress Cooke, her fortune £20,000'.

To add to the existing problems of maintaining the Tudor fabric of the house, Gorhambury suffered badly in the extremely violent storm which took place on 26-27 November, 1703. Bristol and the country surrounding it were completely inundated; the Bishop of Bath and Wells was killed in his bed; the Eddystone Lighthouse was entirely removed from its rock; and in London the damage was estimated to amount to one million pounds. At Gorhambury itself the steward noted in his accounts the following payments:

'1704. Jan. 11. John Bradwin's bill of bricklayer's work at Gorhambury and Sopwell, most of it since the storm – £11.0.0.
Feb. 1. Joseph Kent's bill for glazing – £3.18.0.
Feb. 1. Another bill of Joseph Kent's after the storm – £0.15.6.'

One of the ways in which William sought to economise was by letting the larger part of Gorhambury to a Mr. Thomas Frederick. Initially the lease (which was drawn up on 29 September 1707) was for one year only, with an option to extend it to three years, at an annual rental of £60. The Bowling Green Close was additionally rented at 30s per annum. 'Thomas Frederick may hawk, hunt or fish on the demesne, except in the ponds. The painted window glass is to be repaired by Thomas Frederick, Esq., but the said glass is to be delivered him by William Grimston, Esq.'. From this it would appear that the treasured enamelled glass from Bacon's time had been damaged.

An inventory of the rooms at Gorhambury and their contents was made in the same year. This is of great interest, for it tells us what remained of Sir Nicholas Bacon's original buildings, and also gives a picture of a wealthy household, providing colour descriptions of the furnishings, including the tapestry hangings and rich velvet-covered furniture. It also, incidentally, confirms the story of old Sir Samuel's escape room, his 'Mount Pleasant'. The house had 55 rooms. In the Great Hall were '26 Turkey worked chairs, brass andirons, fire shovel and tongs', a table covered with a Turkey carpet, and brass sconces. The table in the 'Lower Chapel' was covered with a Persian carpet, and in addition there was 'an embroidered cloth carpet, three red plush cushions, seven Turkey worked cushions and silk curtains', whilst in the 'Upper Chapel' there were 'eight Dutch chairs with cushions and two embroidered cushions'. In the Great Dining Room there were 12 figured velvet chairs and seven pieces of tapestry, the usual fire-irons and 'two china candlesticks'. Two India cabinets on two stands, three pieces of tapestry, six figured velvet chairs and 'two copper images' graced the 'Withdrawing Room'. In the 'Passage Room' there were 'six cane and mohair chairs and mohair hangings' as well as 53 pictures.

The furnishings upstairs were equally luxurious. The bed in the 'Best Chamber' was damask-covered, and there were four matching damask window curtains, and a 'Japan table and stand with a glass'. The 'Green Damask Room' sounds beautiful, with its green damask bedcase curtains, white window curtains, two pieces of tapestry, 'a walnut tree table stand and a black glass, and 12 chairs'. In what was described as 'Sir Samuel's Summer Room' there stood 'a bed of purple cloth', a table, a looking glass, 'ten chairs...one close stool box with a pan'. Sir Samuel's 'Mount Pleasant' was sparsely furnished with three chairs, 'the fire grate, shovel, poker and tongs'. In 'His Man's Room' there was one bed, a table, a chair and 'two dogs'. The room kept especially for William's mother-in-law, Mrs. Cooke, had bed hangings of warm mohair and ten yellow damask chairs. Another room specifically assigned for a particular visitor was that kept for Lady Anne Savile, to whom William was so indebted. This room contained 'a wrought bed, four chairs and one stool, a glass, a table with a cover, tapestry hangings' and for her private use, 'in a closet', was a close stool. A 'perriwig block' stood in a room over the Great Hall. In the 'Garden Cloister' there was a marble table, and six wooden chairs; there was a room assigned to the chaplain, and also a 'Pilgrim's Room', which contained three pieces of tapestry, six red chairs and a table, the usual fire-irons and bellows and 'a closet with two cane chairs'.

The inventory also gives us a picture of the servant's quarters. The 'Footman's Room' contained a bed, six chairs, two stools, a table and a 'press'(a type of cupboard), while the Laundry boasted three tables, a 'horse for clothes' and a 'napkin press'. The 'Maid's Chamber' slept three. There were two chests and they had their own 'stool'. The Kitchen was well-equipped and listed among the many items therein are 'six pewter dishes with arms, 12 plates marked with G.' These are still at Gorhambury. The Cellars and the Pantry held 'seven double hogsheads, 19 hogsheads, two barrels, two carrying tubs, one tunnel, one trough, one tub, one sling'. Gorhambury had its own Brew House, which contained 'two coppers, 2 mashfatts, one underback, one cooler, five troughs, two pumps, two upright tubs, seven working covers, a malt mill, one brass cork, one working vat, two jets, both old'. The Brew House also included a chamber with a bed for the brewer. The Well House contained 'a large cistern of lead with three turn cocks, the tubs of the well lined with lead, two large buckets, a long new rope, two iron catches, a large wheel'. The Wash House (apparently distinct from the Laundry) contained 'a copper fixed to a leaden cistern' as well as '12 tubs, four forms, one stool, one horse for clothes, one table'. In the Stables we find along with '20 dozen of quart bottles and four bottle racks, a horse, cart and harness' there was 'the horse that works the "Wheel" that pumps up water from the Great Pump House' and a bed for the ostler. There was also a bed in the Porter's Lodge.

Although this inventory makes Gorhambury's size apparent, the part of the house left in William's occupancy was wretchedly small:

'Memo, 28th April 1708, of what rooms in the dwelling house of Gorhambury, Mr. Frederick consents Mr. Grimston shall have during his tenure ...
The side of the house next the stable
The bailiff's room
The whole side next the stables below stairs with the cellar under the servant's hall
From Sir Samuel's room to the end of the black gallery above stairs
The whole length of the garrets over the outhouses fronting the three new parlours'.

The best rooms were thus set aside for Mr. Frederick, and William and his family lived in what remained. (A very similar situation was to recur at Gorhambury 200 years later during the Second World War, but, of course, in the 18th century successor to the Tudor house William Grimston knew). On the back of this 'memo' is an endorsement which reads: 'for mending the glass windows, a bed or two spoilt and some things lost and broke, several deer killed, the house left very dirty'. There is a short account of monies due, which included 'Paid labourers for carrying out the snow from the Long Gallery and that side of the house – £0.5.0.'.

In time, the obligation to Anne Savile was paid, and William Grimston was able to enjoy his inheritance fully. Harriot again takes up the tale in her narrative written for her nieces:

' ... and then our great-grandfather walked freely about his house, boldly ordering the glazier to be sent for, the plumber to appear, and the carpenter to come ... He could likewise afford to occupy the whole of the dwelling and an increase of space became very essential to the comfort of the family, for every year added a child to their number. This was a happy part of Mr. Grimston's life, and I never heard that he envied the laurels of his neighbour, the Duke of Marlborough, and certainly would not have exchanged his Jane for the Sarah belonging to his Grace. With her, he [William] was always at enmity;

Details from the Harbottle wool carpet, showing two of the three coats of arms: VI The Royal Arms; VII the arms of the City of Ipswich, where the carpet was probably made.

VIII A 'fan' device to show the positioning of the pictures in the Great Hall in the early 19th century, possibly painted by Charlotte Grimston, the 1st Countess, or one of her daughters.

IX   The Hon. Mrs. Edward Walter, mother of Harriot,
3rd Viscountess; portrait in pastels, probably by Glain.

X   James Bucknall, 3rd Viscount Grimston; portrait
in oils, by Pompeo Batoni.

XI   Harriot, 3rd Viscountess Grimston; portrait in
pastels by Glain.

both were Whigs, yet the anxiety both felt to return two members for the Borough of St Albans was productive of interminable quarrels between them, which were left as legacies to our respective families, and were kept up with great spirit many years'.

Sarah Jennings, Duchess of Marlborough, was a strong-minded woman, and full of malice as far as William Grimston was concerned. When William was only a schoolboy, he had allowed a 'Grub Street writer' to use his name as the author of a play of the man's composition, the real author thinking he would get a better sale with a gentleman's name appended to his composition. It was a foolish play called *The Lawyer's Fortune* or *Love in a Hollow Tree*. The whole episode was forgotten until in 1705 an election was approaching in the borough of St Albans. The Duchess of Marlborough procured a copy of the play, reprinted it and distributed it amongst the electors. She added a frontispiece with the following verse, which the Duchess had commissioned from the poet Alexander Pope:

'The leaden crown descends to thee
Great author of the Hollow Tree.
Shades that to Bacon did retreat afford
Become the portion of a booby lord'.

Pope was paid £400 for this satire. Incensed with fury, William Grimston immediately bought up the whole impression of *The Lawyer's Fortune*. Not to be outdone, the Duchess sent a copy to Holland where she had it reprinted! Horace Walpole refers to the episode in *Fugitive Pieces by Noble Authors* and remarked that Sarah made ample reparation to William later by publishing her rather silly memoirs, which were not, after all 'written in her childhood'. William Grimston represented St Albans in Parliament in 1710, 1714 and 1729.

During the 1715 Jacobite rebellion, William raised a body of troops in support of George I. For this service he was created a peer of Ireland by the titles of Baron Dunboyne and Viscount Grimston, on 29 May 1719. His great-granddaughter recalled seeing in the old Armour Hall at Gorhambury a number of rusty iron pikes, said to have been captured from the Scots on this occasion. William was so delighted with his new titles that he went to Ireland to take his seat in the House of Lords, an example not followed by any of his descendants.

On 4 February 1736, he succeeded his elder brother Harbottle in the baronetcy of Luckyn which had been conferred in 1628 upon his great grandfather William Luckyn. It was in this manner that the Messing estates came to the Grimstons. In the family archives there are the court rolls of Messing manor, which are unusually complete and date from 1275.

In May 1731 John Loveday of Caversham, a student of Magdalen College, Oxford, was riding through Hertfordshire with a friend, on his way to Cambridge. On the 4th they visited St Albans Abbey and stayed the night at the *White Hart Inn* on Holywell Hill. The next day they trotted up to Gorhambury and in his diary Loveday wrote:

'Gorhambury, the Lord Grimston's, built by Sir Nicholas Bacon, is 2 short miles from St Albans. 'Tis a very large building; two round towers at the extremities of an extended front. The Hall, adorned with paintings (as indeed the house very plentifully throughout) among which are at full length Lord Bacon, Sir Thomas Methouse [? perhaps Meautys] and a Duke of Norfolk, with King George I on horseback. The Gallery here is a noble room. Pictures at length in every panel, among which is a good one of Queen Elizabeth, George Lord Carew, Earl of Totness, Duke of Buckingham, Earl of Portland, Lord Admiral &c. In the windows on one side is most curious painted glass in little panes, representing birds, beasts, &c., in lively colours. A larger painted window at one end. In one of the rooms are Sir Nicholas Bacon and his wife if I'm not mistaken: (as I'm not, for see Ballard's *Memoirs*). In a closet, a very beautiful Mary Magdalene (they said) reading. A very good piece in another room drawn by Sir Nathaniel Bacon, who was no limner [artist], but who took a fancy to the cook-maid of the house; whom he draws sitting, a fellow behind her who has brought in fowl, the several kinds of which are exactly represented. In a room above stairs is a good piece of the prophet fed by ravens. Paintings of the Grimston family in the library. A table in this house of above 100 different sorts of marble squares. There is no water nigh this pleasant seat'.

The marble-topped table is still in the family's possession today, together with most of the paintings Loveday refers to.

William and his wife Jane (now Viscount and Viscountess Grimston) sat to Michael Dahl, a Swedish artist, for their portraits. Eveything about them suggests solid comfort; he in his well-powdered wig and robes, and she, painted with a little dog wearing a red collar with bells in her lap. Jane and William had 19 children. When she first came to live at Gorhambury, she was shocked by some of the paintings there, which depicted female figures wearing very little clothing. In particular, she disapproved of Sir Nathaniel Bacon's 'The Cookmaid' and of some of the ladies of Charles II's time. At Jane's request, William hired a painter who, for half a guinea a week, painted 'handkerchiefs' across the bosoms of all the ladies wearing almost topless dresses. At that time there was at Gorhambury a glorious painting of a Venus, said to be by Titian, with her beautiful back and bottom turned towards the observer. Jane decided that her hired painter must put a petticoat on Venus. However, the result looked so ridiculous that Jane decided the only thing to do was to cut off the offending two-thirds of the painting, leaving only the beautifully painted head of auburn hair and golden shoulders. This remaining fragment was sold at Sotheby's in 1956. It could have been the same painter who added the exceptionally blue landscapes – remarkably similar to that in Jane's own portrait – to several other paintings, the sitters being clearly earlier in style than their backgrounds would suggest. The quantity of canvas this anonymous painter seems to have covered is quite astonishing. Harriot says that he liked to paint biblical scenes – one of Moses with the ten tablets, and another of Elijah fed by ravens ultimately went to Redbourn Church. He also painted an immense canvas depicting the whole Grimston family, but 'having hung on the walls of the Hall in the old house long after it had been deprived of its roof … it dropped to pieces'. There was also a portrait of Jane Cooke's brother who 'chose to have his countenance immortalised and for many years smiled on a canvas in a full bottomed wig, and a blue coat embroidered with gold, till his great-nephew William, having a fancy to see how he would look in the costume of his uncle, cut the face out of the picture, and standing behind it, placed his own head in the vacant space'.

An estimate for the cost of a new staircase at Gorhambury survives from the 1st Viscount's time. It was 'to rise out of the south side of the hall of the upper end next the chapel, to the floor of the dining room above ... all to be made of good oaken wainscot, viz. treads, risings, rails, ballisters and brackets, and also to be wainscoated rail height with oak and pilasters answerable to the columns on the rail work; ... the dining room door to be the same with architrave on both sides carved, and shutters and linings to the two windows on the stairhead, all oaken wainscoat. The ballisters, brackets, rails, and cappings of the wall work and architraves under the stairs with the columns are to be carved. The chapel door is to be sashed with 2 inch hard stuff, from the middle rail upwards; and those pairs of door that are now in the chapel to be put into the parlour partition underneath the stairs, and the steps down to be made from the hall floor down to the parlour with the old treads that are now at Gorhambury'. It was to be a neat alteration, making use of old materials as had often happened before at Gorhambury. It is not known whether it was actually built, but if so, it probably replaced an outmoded spiral staircase in a turret. The door to the Gun Room in the 18th century Gorhambury of today could have come from this period; it is of oak with beautifully carved architraves.

Estate maps tell us that the 1st Viscount, towards the end of his life, was responsible for the alteration of the grounds. The intention was the creation of a park to 18th century taste, and to that end several adjacent fields were thrown into one enclosed whole, and the approach to the house was reorientated.

The 1st Viscount was the last of the Grimstons to acquire a royal portrait to hang at Gorhambury; he purchased a fine and rare equestrian portrait of George I. This King spoke little English, had been born in Hanover, spent much of his time there even after becoming King of England, and was actually buried there. It is small wonder that the ordinary English yeoman was suspicious of him. William's great-granddaughter Harriot tells us how the 1st Viscount overcame these fears amongst those on his own estate:

> '...When George Ist arrived in England he [William Grimston] took a party of yeomen to see his Majesty that they might be convinced by ocular demonstration that neither the King, nor the Hanoverians who accompanied him, had tails, which opinion the Tories took the utmost pains to impress upon the minds of the people, and so little enlightened were the commonality in those days, that few doubted that the reigning Sovereign bore the resemblance to a monkey ... It might be in consequence of the desire of showing that the King was not a monster, that Mr. Grimston bought the portrait of George I ... His tenants after that purchase could easily satisfy themselves of the King's appearance without the trouble of a journey to London'.

If it was also William who brought to Gorhambury the exceptionally fine portrait of Colonel Tayler, also by Sir Godfrey Kneller, signed and dated 1700, then there is further cause for gratitude to him. William was not unknown in the sale room, for in 1728 he bought at 'Mr. Phillips's sale, Lot 64,

A piece of ruin, 3 guineas; Lot 65, Its companion, by Viviano, £19,19.0d'. Perhaps other such fine pieces at 'The Lady with the Fan' by van Ravestyn, the provenance of which is unknown, may also have been purchased by him.

The 1st Viscount's eldest son was another Samuel, born in December 1707. He died in 1737, predeceasing his father. Seven years earlier, on 5 November 1730, Samuel had married yet another Mary, the daughter of Henry Lovell, a member of the Fishmongers' Company of the City of London. There was one short-lived child of this marriage, who died just over a month after her birth in 1736. Samuel himself died the following year, and was buried at St Michael's. His widow continued to live with her parents-in-law until 1740, when a marriage was arranged between her and William Wildman, the 2nd Viscount Barrington. The marriage took place by special licence in the chapel at Gorhambury, and William Grimston provided the wedding ring.

From the time of Samuel's betrothal to Mary Lovell, his father kept an account of what he called 'Extraordinary Expenses on my Son Grimston's Account, in 1730'. From these accounts, which span the last 10 or 12 years of his life, we can learn more about William Grimston. An extract from the accounts is given in Appendix Four. We learn his pet names for his children, for instance: Samuel was 'Sammy' and Harbottle, delightfully, 'Botty'. It is good to know that Jane Grimston had a 'new gown and lining' for her son's wedding, which cost £24.10.0d, and that William bought himself a new wig at a cost of seven guineas. He was as generous to 'Miss Lovell's servants' as to his own. When his daughter-in-law's second wedding was being arranged, it is surprising to find that he did not only pay the new bridegroom 14s for the wedding ring, but also £2,261.4s.0d. for other jewellery. The 'Extraordinary Account's' Final Entry reads:

> 'Paid off two debts for monies borrowed to clear and discharge in full Lord Bruce's [Lady Anne Savile's husband] claim upon my estate of £30.000 pounds left his lady by Sir Samuel Grimston's will without which I could not settle my Hertfordshire estate upon my son clear at marriage but must have been subject to this sum then owing'.

His final, telling, words were 'Great fortunes know not what to demand and when bought at so great an expense not worth having'. William, 1st Viscount Grimston, died in 1756 and was buried in St Michael's.

There are two portraits of Mary Lovell at Gorhambury, one a half-length showing her with dark brown hair drawn back from a high forehead. She is wearing a loose white blouse, cut low, with a blue scarf over her head and shoulders. The portrait is in a fine Chippendale frame. The second shows her sitting at a dressing table which is covered with a deep pink cloth. In her hand she holds the quill with which she had been writing on a sheet of paper. She wears a white satin crinoline dress, the full skirt opening to reveal an underdress of pale blue quilted and brocaded satin. Her features are plain, but she has attractive ringlets. The background shows the interior of a room, with a high mantelshelf on which glass vases are arranged; tradition had it that it was painted at the *Peahen Hotel*, St Albans. In 1911 the portrait was ascribed to

William Hogarth, but more recent scholarship identifies the painter as Highmore.

On the great pedigree of Grimston, after the marriage of William Grimston and Jane Cooke the old Grimston motto of *Gratia dei Grata* [by God's grace and favour] no longer appears. It has been replaced by the motto of the Bacon family, *Mediocria firma*, which has been the Grimston motto ever since. Could the reason for this be that at that date the family really believed – as they did for many generations afterwards – that there was a blood relationship with the Bacon family? The pedigree, which was begun for Sir Harbottle Grimston, the 1st Baronet, measures 22 feet long by 27 inches wide. It was certified by William Camden, Clarenceux King-At-Arms, in 1619. The continuation of it, after the 1st Viscount's achievement of arms, was signed, but not dated, by Isaac Heard, Garter Principal King of Arms.

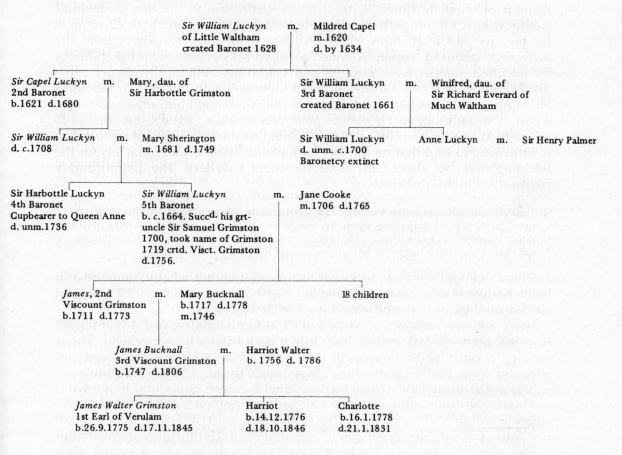

Grimston Family Tree (17th - 19th centuries)

Chapter Seven

James, 2nd Viscount Grimston

It may be recalled that the eldest son of the 1st Viscount had died in his father's lifetime. Thus it was the second son, James, who inherited in 1756. At that time James was 45, and had been married for ten years to a Hertfordshire heiress, Mary Bucknall, who was the only daughter of William Bucknall of Oxhey near Watford. The marriage had taken place at Watford on 18 June 1746. Not only did James succeed to the Grimston estates, but also, at the death of his brother Harbottle in 1766, he inherited all the Luckyn properties in Essex and Norfolk. Little remains to recall James Grimston today. It is even disputable whether the dilapidated portrait found in the attics in 1911 is really of him.

For fifty years Sarah, Duchess of Marlborough, had battled with the Grimstons for control of the Borough of St Albans in Parliament, and it was not until 1743 that she gave up the struggle. In that year James – who at that time had not yet come into his inheritance – put himself forward as a candidate at the St Albans by-election. However, he refused to offer big enough bribes, and was defeated. At the general election of 1745 he again declared himself a candidate, and was returned after coming to an agreement with the Duke of Marlborough, whereby he pledged his support for the Duke's nephew John Spencer at the next general election. No vote or speech by James in the House is recorded. He did not stand again after 1745.

James's mother lived on until 1765, nine years after her husband's death. She was buried in St Michael's. All her property was left to her brother James Cooke; only her coach and horses were left to her son.

James's granddaughter, Charlotte Grimston, wrote an account of the state in which James found Gorhambury when he inherited:

He married Mary, daughter of J. Bucknall of Oxhey [sic: actually William Bucknall] in the County of Hertford. Their union was deferred some months on account of the alarm produced by the rebellion in the year '45, which horrified the Whigs to such a degree that it was considered an act of imprudence in any man belonging to that party to form a matrimonial connection. After the defeat of the rebels the marriage took place and Mr. Grimston resided with his brother-in-law at Oxhey until the death of his father (1756) which put him in possession of Gorhambury, as the 2nd Viscount Grimston.

On coming to the property, Lord G. found the mansion considerably out of repair, and the farm houses on the estate running to decay, with very little timber left excepting the ornamental trees in the park, for the younger sons of the late Ld. Grimston, having been apprised that it was their father's intention to bequeath his monied property to them, made use of every means in their power to increase it, and as the advanced age and consequent infirmities of Ld. G. prevented his attending to the management of his estates for some years previous to his death, his younger sons took the direction upon themselves, and had by that means ample opportunities of forwarding their own interest to the great detriment of the estate.

As soon as James. G. (2nd Viscount) became possessed of Gorhambury he improved the condition of the farm houses and he turned his attention to the improvement of the mansion, one part called the Ball Room being placed in a very awkward position, and besides considered useless, was pulled down by him. It is not upon record when this room was built, it was certainly erected subsequently to the rest of the house, and being of considerable size and placed at right angles with the eastern turret was at once both ugly and inconvenient.

Ld. G.'s next object was the improvement of the appearance of the place, for in the age preceding, picturesque beauty had not been attended to, and Gorhambury was like most old houses surrounded by high walls enclosing a kitchen garden and outward courts and accessible only through an entrance through two immense iron gates kept constantly shut. It is probable that our forefathers adopted this gloomy fashion for the purpose of security against the attacks of robbers, but the improved state of the police having superseded the necessity of such precautions, the high walls have disappeared throughout the country. Those at G. were destroyed by the advice of Mr. Richmond, one of the first professional ornamental gardeners. The garden was also moved from the front of the house to the back, and a straight road made from the turnpike [road] to the house.

From Charlotte's account, we may deduce that most of James and Mary's family of eight were born at Oxhey, and only the two younger girls at Gorhambury. When the family did move in, however, the old house must have been filled to overflowing, since seven or eight brothers and sisters of the 2nd Viscount were still living at home, and his elder brother's widow was also still resident there.

A treasure from this period is the delightful conversation piece of four young people, painted in their late 'teens, who were four of James's eight children. The children's uncle, John Askell Bucknall, who was devoted to the family of his only sister, commissioned the work from Sir Joshua Reynolds. The painting shows us William, who, at his uncle's desire, took 'Bucknall' as his own surname and inherited Oxhey; it was also William who pulled the property down in 1799. On William's right there is James, the eldest son, who will be the subject of the next chapter. At the centre left is Jane, the eldest daughter, and to her left is the second eldest daughter, Mary. It is evident that Sir Joshua enjoyed his commission. An extract from the pocket book in which he noted the names of his sitters shows that he was working on the painting from 1767 to 1769. These were important years for Reynolds, in which he received his knighthood and became the first president of the Royal Academy. His pocket book entries read:

1767, May: Miss Grimston
1767, August: Mr. Grimston
1768, April: Mr. and Miss Grimston
1769, January: Mr. W. Grimston

There follows a note – 'to be finished, framed and packed up'. At this period of his career, Sir Joshua's charges were as follows: 'whole length, 7 ft. 10 ins. by 4 ft. 10 ins., 150 gns; half length, 70 gns; Kit Kat, 50 gns; 3 quarter, 35 gns; pela di testa [of head], 30 gns'.

   This superb painting which so enhances the yellow drawing room at Gorhambury today did not always hang on Gorhambury's walls, for it was painted for Oxhey. A bundle of letters reveals that after the death of her husband Thomas Estcourt in 1822, the now elderly Jane Grimston, who had been one of the sitters for the painting, wrote to her nephew Walter, the 1st Earl of Verulam, asking if he would return to her the Reynolds painting, which had been left to her by its owner, her uncle John Bucknall. The nephew's reply was predictable. He argued that if Oxhey had still existed, and if it had still been occupied by a Bucknall, then he would have surrendered the painting. With some drama he referred to the 'total neglect in which the picture was held before it came here ... how it was brought to Gorhambury in an open cart, the frame broken in pieces, with many holes in the picture itself'. Eventually Jane Estcourt sadly agreed to leave this precious picture at Gorhambury; 'how well', she said, 'she understood the distress which its removal might cause'. She suggested that it should remain at Gorhambury during Walter's lifetime, but that after that it might return to her own house of Estcourt, 'where it really belonged'. It was this Jane's son Thomas who released to Gorhambury for all time this painting which recalled his mother's girlhood. In 1848 he wrote to the Earl to say that 'he wished to present to Gorhambury now' the Reynolds picture. 'Now', he wrote, instead of 'after my own death', which had, he said, been his previous intention.

Chapter Eight

James Bucknall, 3rd Viscount Grimston

The Grand Tour and other Travels, 1768-1772

In 1768, during his summer vacation from Trinity College, Cambridge, James Bucknall Grimston, son and heir of the 2nd Viscount, made a riding tour of northern England. He kept a diary of his journeyings; as well as describing the soil and the countryside through which he rode, he was formulating a keen perception of the architecture of the country houses which he visited. Of Woburn Abbey he remarked that 'the rooms are very small'. He found Lord Northampton's Castle Ashby 'a very ancient seat without beauty or anything to recommend it'. There were, however, several houses that very much appealed to this young man of 21. He admired Kedleston, belonging to Lord Scarsdale, and described it as 'a most noble modern-built house of stone, with 26 windows in front; the entrance ... a large hall supported with 20 pillars of Derby marble, many of them one entire piece; on the right of the hall [an] eating parlour, ornamented with pictures of the best hands, pier glasses etc., beyond this is a print gallery; on the left of the hall a music room, dimensions 24 yards by 16, most elegantly adapted for the purpose; beyond this a complete library; each room filled with noble pictures, both of landscapes, seapieces and portraits. The park is as yet rude, but is intended to be laid out in the modern taste, part of which is already begun; the grandeur of the house, the beauties of which there must be in the park when it is finished, and the civility and politeness of the possessor, unite to make it the best worth seeing and the most agreeable seat in this part of England'.

Manchester he found to be 'very handsome, full of good houses, well paved, and carries on a great trade, particularly of tapes. The place is now remarkable for the Duke of Bridgewater's works, which are a great canal cut through, in many places, the solid rock, for the distance of 37 miles, for the convenience of water carriage. This work would be justly called one of the wonders of the world, exceeding in magnificence, use and grandeur every work of that kind, and proving indisputably the judgment, caution and courage in making the attempt, of the noble contriver'.

He found Chatsworth, the seat of the Duke of Devonshire, to be 'a square stone house and windows in front', which appeared, he wrote, 'magnificent'; the inside of the house, however, was 'not answerable to the grandeur of the outside'. Duncombe Park also pleased him. 'The front of this house built in the Ionic order looks on a spacious lawn; limited on each side by a sloping wood. The other front built on four Ionic columns is approached to by means of a flight of steps, and looks on some pleasure grounds laid out … into walks'. He also admired Harwood House, belonging to Mr. Lascelles. 'Mr Adam, the architect; it is built on Corinthian columns, with two wings with thirteen windows in front. The whole makes a very grand and magnificent appearance'. He ended his six week tour with a very satisfactory note to the effect that 'though each county may boast of its own particular excellencies … none can exceed the beauty, or be preferred to that regular uniformity, which is to be met with in every part of Hertfordshire'. He might still prefer his native county to any other, but it was becoming apparent that, love it though he did, the rambling asymmetrical old house at Gorhambury, which had been built 200 years before and considerably altered since by his own ancestors, was out of keeping with James's forward-looking ideas.

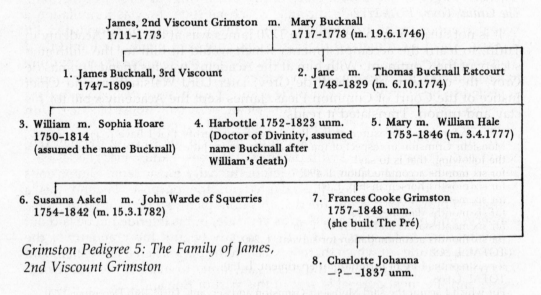

Grimston Pedigree 5: The Family of James, 2nd Viscount Grimston

The next year, 1769, James made another tour. This time he went to Wales, again on horseback. He left his mother's family home at Oxhey on 8 August, and as he journeyed westwards he visited places of interest, including Oxford and West Wycombe House, where the pictures in the saloon delighted him. He became lyrical about Stowe, and quoted Alexander Pope –

'Here order in variety you see
Where all things differ, yet where all agree'.

'If any house can claim the epithet of magnificent', he wrote, 'it must be this: if any garden that of beautiful, it must be that at Stowe'.

At each country house he visited, James's awareness of and interest in good architecture was more and more apparent, and his taste for art increased. He took care to note down pictures which he especially liked. Perhaps his first introduction to the artistic world had been two years before, when at the age of 20 he sat for Sir Joshua Reynolds with his brothers and sisters for the painting discussed in the previous chapter.

James's journey to Wales lasted 11 weeks and three days. He kept a meticulous note of his expenditure. At Blenheim he spent 4s 6d and gave a shilling to two poor people. He paid a hairdresser 5s; his servant Jacob's expenses came to 4s at Bath, and to £1 9s 6d at Dolgelly and Welshpool. He gave a Welsh harper a shilling, and left a 6d tip at Lord Grosvenor's. The 'maid at the bishop's palace at Chester' did better, receiving 1s, while at the *Lyttleton Arms* at Hagley he had a bill of 7s 5d and tipped the servants 1s 1d. His bills at Dunstable came to 19s, and his tips to 3s. These two expeditions in 1768 and 1769 had stimulated James's taste for travel, and his taste for art and architecture.

The Grand Tour, 1770-1772

It is not surprising to find that in 1770 James was at the Royal Academy in Turin, to learn the accomplishments which would fit him for the cultivated society of the Continent. With him at the Academy was his friend Thomas de Grey, the only son of William de Grey, later Lord Walsingham and Chief Justice of the Court of Common Pleas. James kept the Academy's bill for his stay and tuition. Translated it reads:

> I the undersigned Treasurer of the Royal Academy, certify that I have received from Monsieur Grimston in respect of the first apartment [sic] the sum of 818 lire made up of the following, that is to say:
> for six months accommodation, L.490
> for six months horsemanship, L.60
> for six months fencing, L.36
> for six months dancing, L.36
> for six months arms and defences, L.36
> for six months accommodation for servant, L.200
> TOTAL L.818
> for six months hire of furniture for apartment, L.150
> TOTAL L.968
> For which I acquit the said Monsieur Grimston and servant, Turin 18th December 1770.
> L.818, Guido Piero Bajano.

It may be noted that James paid only L.818, although the Academy's account came to L.969! The name of his personal servant during the 22 months of his Grand Tour was Carrell. Carrell's monthly wages were 205 'livres de Piedmont'.

It seems likely that the Academy's account was retrospective, although the date of James's departure from England for Italy is unknown. However, the presence of James and his friend Thomas in Turin was noted by one W. Lynch in a letter he wrote to Sir Horace Mann, the British plenipotentiary at Florence from 1740, on 15 December: 'There are only two English here. One Mr. de Grey, the Attorney General's son, the other a son of Lord Grimston, both in the Academy'.

The Academy's bill is not mentioned in the very full account of his tour which James kept, written in French. The book is at Gorhambury, and covers 22 months, itemised from January 1771 to the end of August 1772. It is a modest notebook, 8" by 5", hand-stitched, with paper covers decorated with coloured inks in a geometric design. From it we can glean much about the Tour, and also about James himself. We can follow his route, learn where he stayed, and how much he paid. He noted what he spent on clothes, what he won and lost at cards, how much he gave in charitable gifts, and how much he tipped servants at houses where he stayed. His bankers in Turin until April 1771 were Paul and Pierre Torras, and James notes on the credit side of his book the sums he received from them. There is also a letter from the Torras brothers to James: it seems that he had complained of the low rate of exchange they were giving him.

In the spring of 1771 we find James fitting himself out in a dashing new outfit of light velvet, with silk stockings, 'superb' black drape and lace – *'pour un velour de printemps, &c, 428 sequins romains; pour un broderie, 600 sequins romains; pour avoir attaché une broderie, 48 sequins romains; pour des bas des soie, 145 sequins romains; pour de drape noir superbe, 90 sequins romains'*. He also bought a cooking stove, and a month later in June a pair of cheap breeches to wear whilst travelling – *'au taileur à Milan pour un habit et culotte de camelot, 189 pauls'*.

He travelled via Bologna – where he bought a bearskin – to Florence, where he gave 20 pauls to 'a poor person at the house of Lord Tyburg'. He spent 233 pauls on clothes and 30 pauls on a new wig. Something else caught his eye, *'un violon de Gabrielli'* which he bought for 400 pauls. This was to be sent to England from Livorno by the captain of the ship *Hananel*, a service for which he paid 30 pauls. James then travelled on via Pisa to Siena, where in August he took lodgings with the Azzoni family, eating, however, at the *auberges*. He had a brief but passionate affair with the daughter of the family, Caterina Azzoni; she became so infatuated with him that he was forced to make a somewhat hasty departure from the city. A letter from the Countess Messarati (née Baroness Bradi) refers to this episode. She was not at all shocked, but sympathised with the 'cruel situation' which had obliged him to leave Siena. It appears that the Countess herself had not been unaffected by James's charm, for she speaks of a flower she had given him as a 'symbol of constancy'; 'the flower will be for you the image of your passing loves'. The Countess continues her letter with the sultry declaration that 'As far as I am concerned, I hate ephemeral pleasures, my heart not being made for weak feelings. I prefer the dull sadness, which is more in keeping with my heart, to the despicable pleasures which only touch the surface of the senses. He who loves by habit only enjoys himself in theory'. She ended by reminding him that he had been 'more than amorous' with her, and likened James to 'Horace de Calage, whose quick and bright humour touches the deepest springs of human nature'!

Caterina Azzoni had provided James with introductions to the Abbot Agossimo Borghesi in Rome and to the singer Senducci, 'who although possessing a good voice is not really versed in the science of music'. She wrote of her longing for him to return to Siena, or alternatively that she could join him in Rome. Thomas de Grey had not, it would appear, left Siena at the same time as his friend; in fact he remained there until March 1772. Caterina wrote to James that 'I am glad that your vivacious disposition has found so many sources of entertainment. It would certainly have been different had you been here … where we only had one *opera buffa*, a rather mediocre work, and few balls at the casino. Your English friend Mr. de Grey has found the way to enjoy himself, finding pleasure in a little ballerina, very lovely and graceful, for whom he composed a poem, which you will see printed both in the English and the Tuscan language'. James had letters of introduction to various Italian aristocrats – la Princesse Pietre Persée, la Princesse de la Rochella, and la Princesse Gerachi Grimaldi among them – but he does not seem to have made use of them. Thomas Lord Lyttelton, known as 'The Rake', was in Turin in 1771 and wrote from there to 'Madame la Comtesse Trésina à Vicenza' on 15 May, to introduce Thomas de Grey and James Grimston in glowing terms:

'Le fils de Milord Grimston anglais de grande naissance, extrêmement riche et beaucoup mon ami, m'a prié de lui addresser à quelques Dames de Vicenza ou il conte emploier une parte du temps qu'il destine pour le voiage d'l'Italie. – J'ai saisi donc cette occasion, Madame, pour vous remercier de toutes vos politesses, et vous recommender un cavalier qui est très digne de votre connaissance. – Le seigneur Anglais qui voiage avec lui et mon ami de tous les temps. – Il se nomme Monsieur de Grey. Son père est de nos plus grands sujets et le fils n'ai point dégéneré car il posside beaucoup d'esprit et des connaissances au dessus de son age … &c'.

Armed with this recommendation and others like it, James Grimston travelled on to Vicenza, the city of Andrea Palladio, the famous architect. Palladio's style, modelled on ancient Roman architecture, and based on the principles of the classical architect Vitruvius, appealed enormously to James. Palladio was to be one of the major influences on the new house James built at Gorhambury. Then James travelled on to Rome; by November, 1771, he was staying there with the Barazzi family. His letters home tell of his enthusiasm for the ancient city. On 10 November he wrote to his brother William, recommending him to study 'the best authors who have written about Rome', and saying that his own descriptions of the place were unworthy. He considered that the 'four volumes in quarto lately published by the Abate Ridolfino Venuti Cortonese' gave the most 'perfect' account. For a visual impression, he considered the 'prints of the antiquities by le Chevalier Piranese' as fine and exact as one could wish. He was so enthusiastic, in fact about the work of Giambattista Piranesi that he wanted to add some of his drawings to his collection and went on to say 'this man is exceedingly clever and was ennobled the latter end of the last Pontificate; it is immense the sum of money he has got by the statues, vases, tripods, &c. that he has found by searching amongst the ruins of the Villa [H]adriana; the greater part may still lie undiscovered and may be found to astonish a future age; it is nearly certain that the Tiber conceals in its bed what would well repay its cleaning but they are afraid to venture on such a work lest the stench rising from the mud should breed some pestilential disorder in Rome'.

10 November 1771 was a day in James's life which he would always recall, for on that morning he and some other English travellers were received in audience by Pope Clement XIV, an accomplished though not universally popular Pope, who was to suppress the Jesuit order in 1773. James wrote an account of the meeting for his brother William:

> 'I have been this morning introduced *alla sua Santita*; he was too gracious to permit us to kiss his foot and would scarcely permit us to go through the usual ceremonies of kneeling. He talked in the most familiar manner with us for half an hour and then gave us his benediction; he told us that he was glad to hear that the children of his communion were not persecuted in England and assured us that our sect should find grace in Italy. In short, his Holiness, who I fancy the London mob honour with a bonfire on the [fifth of] November is one of the most affable men and by no means such a bigot [in regard to] his religion as to imagine that there is but one path to heaven'.

There may conceivably have been another reason for James to remember this occasion; perhaps amongst the audience on that November morning there was an English family, for in that same year Mr. and Mrs. Edward Walter and their beautiful daughter Harriot were in Rome and had an audience with the Pope. It is possible therefore that James's first sight of his future wife was at the Vatican.'

James also told William that 'at Tivoli I had the pleasure of tasting of the *Fons Bandusiae*, which Horace has justly called 'Splendidior vitro dulci digne mero, &c'. The Grimston family has maintained a tradition of wine connoisseurship. In the 18th and 19th centuries a vine at Gorhambury produced grapes of superb quality which were made into a classic wine. Sadly today the grape-house and the vine itself are gone.

In another letter, addressed this time to his uncle John Bucknall at Oxhey, James reaffirmed his admiration for Rome. 'I have', he wrote 'been here three weeks and have found every day some fresh wonder; every stop offers to one's view some fragment of ancient magnificence; a temple in ruins on one side, a triumphal arch half-buried on the other, and a column which even 2000 years have not robbed of its beauty, is our usual prospect …'. He wrote of the Pantheon: 'I was in the Pantheon this morning and was struck with its grandeur, although it has been stripped of its gods: the portico, built by Agrippa, is supported by 16 columns of oriental granite of such a size that it is wonderful how they could be conveyed there, the inside now converted into an excellent church and the niches where the statues of the gods were placed into altars makes a very respectable figure on account of its ornaments as well as its form … Near this are the Baths of Agrippa, famous for their ornaments and conveniences; the old Romans made no semple[sic] of plunging up to their necks in all seasons, the mod[erns] are afraid of wetting their fingers in cold weather, and when there is a wind which they call *tramontane* nothing can persuade them to venture out of their houses till they see that the weathercock is turned round again'.

While in Rome James had his portrait painted by Pompeo Batoni (1708-1787). According to his account book he gave the artist two sittings and the result was a dignified half-length portrait, which shows James in a green velvet coat with a waistcoat edged with gold braid. His stock and tie are of lace, and his buttons are gold. His brown hair curls slightly over his ears, and his eyes are grey. Under his left arm, he carries his hat. In the right-hand corner, Batoni has signed the work, and dated it 1772. James Grimston returned home via Padua, Strasbourg, Schaffhausen and Basel. In 1773 the diarist Fanny Burney, describing a concert at her father's house at which a Signor Millico sang to his own accompaniment on the harp, noted that 'in the midst of this performance, two *beaux* entered: Mr. Grimston, eldest son of Lord Grimston, and his brother. He is just returned from making the Grand Tour ...'.

Courtship and Marriage

In 1773, shortly after James Grimston had returned from his Grand Tour, his father died. At 26 he found himself faced with many new responsibilities; however, he would not be facing them alone. Since his return from the Continent, he had become betrothed to Harriot Walter, the lovely hazel-eyed 18 year-old, whose beauty may have first attracted him when they both attended the Papal audience. The two certainly met in Italy, and he enjoyed the friendship of Harriot's parents as well as her own. The Walters were art-lovers and collectors, and with James's love of antiquities and architecture, they had much in common. The Walters had taken Harriot with them for an extensive tour of Italy and France, although at that time it was unusual for a girl to undertake the Grand Tour. Mr. Walter had many influential acquaintances to smooth his path on his journey, amongst them no less an authority in artistic matters than Sir William Hamilton, who arranged accommodation for them in Naples. Another letter from Hamilton recommended a portraitist called Glain, a Frenchman who had been much patronised by Englishmen visiting Naples. 'He really has merit in chalks and crayons very like and in good taste for a trifle' Hamilton wrote. Glain was engaged to make a pastel portrait of Harriot. It is an enchanting work. Harriot's hair is powdered, and ornamented with a pink and white rose. She wears a pale blue velvet dress with lace and pearls at the neck and frills at the elbows. It is signed by Glain, and dated 1769.

By 1771 the Walters were in Rome. At Gorhambury there is a small painting on copper, possibly the work of A. Elsheimer. On the back of it James wrote that the picture was given to Harriot by the Pope Ganganelli (Clement XIV) when she was in Rome in 1771. Love for Harriot's person was probably not the only consideration which induced James Grimston to ask for her hand in marriage, for she was a wealthy heiress. The Walters were happy to see their only child marry the heir to a viscountcy. Despite these monetary considerations, however, there is no doubt of the considerable personal affection in which they all held each other. In June 1774 James wrote his first love letter to

Harriot. He was in Colchester, where he was meeting his Essex tenants for the first time since his father's death:

My dear Harriot:

If it is true that 'Heaven first taught letters for some lovers' aid' I may justly add that they never were made use of with more propriety than at present; they are however a poor substitute to conversation, and I feel very sensibly that that something much beyond regard and esteem, which I flatter myself you are already convinced I have for you, cannot be done justice to, nor expressed with half the warmth upon paper, that even silence itself might do in your company; you are now present in my idea, but the reality is wanted to give that *fuoco* to my language which it ought to have when you are the subject of it; in short I may endeavour to describe to you my sentiments, but I shall fall so far short of what I wish to say, that I would rather depend upon you to paint them to yourself in their proper colours, than hazard the attempt myself. If I write nonsense my plea shall be that you are the cause of it, and as it is to you alone that I am to apologise, I hope that that will be considered a good one; If you think the style too free, I only beg that you will be so kind as to send me a model directed to me at Gorhambury near St Albans, and I shall be happy in being the humble imitator of it.

Nothing but necessity shall prevent me drinking your health to you on Friday next, and I look forward to that day with the same degree of joy, as I did of sorrow to the Monday morning that hurried me away from London; I must fill up the intervening space with thinking of you, and I fear much my tenants will find their landlord by no means a man of business: those I have already seen have wished me joy, and very heartily drunk a health to *la futura*. If you have half as much pleasure in reading this letter, as I have in writing it, I need not beg pardon for the length of it, the idea alone that you had not would so immediately [stop] my pen, that I should be incapable of doing it. *Adio cara mera del anima mea, v'abbracio con tutto il mio cuore* [Farewell sweet darling of my soul, whom I embrace with all my heart]. I assure you that I never said anything more sincerely than that I am most entirely and most affectionately yours Grimston'.

Harriot, probably unsure what to call her admirer, goes straight into what she wishes to say in her reply:

June 15 1774.

I would have answered your kind letter last night had I not been on the point of setting out for this place when I received it, and we did not arrive here [her family home of Berry Hill] till almost eleven o' clock; I hope I need make no longer apology to you and that you will think I would not have deferred writing, had I not been unavoidably prevented.

We are in hope of having the pleasure of your company Friday, but at the same time it will be no surprise if you should not come, as we think it impossible for you to finish your business in the time: however I hope it will not be long before I shall have the pleasure of seeing you ... My father went yesterday to Mr. Bucknall's [James's uncle], and returned in rapture with the beauties of his place, but has not yet had the pleasure of seeing its owner who had gone with three of the young ladies to Gorhambury: Lady Grimston did the honours and showed my father enough to make him abuse poor Berry Hill ... I therefore expect to see something very fine and begin to grow impatient to make a visit.

You are in *disgrace* with my mother who bid me abuse you for having forgot to mention *her* in your letter. My father is in charity with you and bid me say you was sure of always meeting with a true and sincere friend in him, and sends you his most affectionate compliments, my mother also, being of a forgiving temper, joins in all good wishes to you.

Now I have said so much for them, I am a little puzzled to know what to say for myself, imagine therefore what you please, and I will subscribe to it. Harriot Walter.

Berry Hill, which was built in 1753, was burnt down in 1950. By Harriot's marriage it came into the hands of the Grimstons, who sold it to the Barclay family in 1812. There is a description of the house written in 1841: 'Bury Hill, on the south side of the Guildford Road, about three-quarters of a mile from Dorking, is a considerable eminence which gives its name to the pleasant seat of Charles Barclay, Esq., a lineal descendant of Robert Barclay, the celebrated apologist for the Quakers. It was formerly considered as part of the waste of the manor of Milton but inclosed and planted (chiefly with Scotch firs) between 70 and 80 years ago by Edward Walter Esq., who was M.P. for Milbourne Port in the county of Somerset during several Parliaments. His first purchase here was a small farm called Chadhurst, but he afterwards greatly enlarged the estate, improved the grounds and erected the present mansion. Whilst residing at the farm he married Harriot, the youngest daughter and co-heiress of George, Lord Forrester; by whom he had several sons who all died in infancy, and one daughter ... The house is finely situated on a shelving eminence skirted by plantations and in front is an expansive stretch of water. It is a uniform and handsome building, stuccoed ...'

There are other letters immediately prior to James and Harriot's marriage. All are, to our eyes, somewhat stilted in style, and may be regarded as perfect specimens of their period. On 2 July, 1774, for instance, James wrote to his 'dear Harriot' from Harley Street, already a centre of the medical profession, where he was consulting an eye specialist.

> Although I left Berry Hill but yesterday, I yet pant for the pleasure of seeing you again, I shall however sacrifice that I most wish to the convenience of my friends and defer my visit till you send me word that my company will not be disagreeable. Mr. and Mrs. Walter were so obliging as to give me an invitation for next Tuesday, and I would be happy in accepting it, if I did not fear that it proceeded from their affability without considering the number of persons they expected with them: I shall depend upon you to clear up this point to me, and you may be assured that I shall be anxious to acknowledge the *favor con viva voce* ... I am going down to Gorhambury this evening and shall carry you with me in idea, you will see from thence that this is but a partial separation from you, but, as such, is sufficient to oblige me to exert all my philosophy; it is some consolation however that you have given me leave to assure you in this way of what I flatter myself you are already well convinced of, which is that I am so much as I can be most sincerely and most affectionately, yours Grimston. I shall beg of you to pay my proper compliments to Mr. and Mrs. Walter, and to tell them that I love them for your sake, and that I respect them for their own. My direction is at Lady Grimston's, Upper Grosvenor Street.

Seven months after succeeding to the title, James Grimston married Harriot Walter at St George's, Hanover Square, London, on 28 July 1774. Arrangements and negotiations for the marriage must have been going on before James's father's death, for otherwise the complex exchanges between the contracting parties could not have been completed by that date. There is no account of the marriage preserved at Gorhambury. It would have been very much a family occasion. As well as the Dowager Lady Grimston, there would have been James's five sisters. One imagines his lively brother William as James's best man, and his other brother Harbottle, taking time off from his study of divinity, would also have been there. Perhaps Sophia Hoare, daughter of Samuel Hoare the banker, would also have been there too; she was to marry William Grimston. Certainly all the Bucknalls from Oxhey would have been there in full force, with Uncle John Bucknall enjoying every moment of the festivities. On the bride's side of the church there would have been many old friends of the Walter family like Lady Forrester and Miss Cockburn, up from Bedgebury in Kent, and Dr. Mervin Nooth and his family. Harriot's closest friend Jenny Spence would certainly have come with her sisters and parents, and surely Harriot's maids, Bessy and Philis, would have come to see their mistress married.

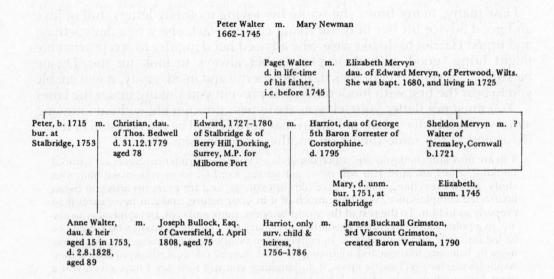

Walter Pedigree

Married Life

Until Harriot married, she and her mother had never been apart, even for a day. Poor Mrs. Walter felt quite desolate without her daughter. We should pity Harriot too, the only child of doting parents, now launched into a large family with five unmarried sisters-in-law, two brothers-in-law and her mother-in-law all living with her under the same roof! Mrs. Walter, unable to bring herself to write a long letter –'my eyes are so very weak' – ends a sad letter to her daughter with the telling words 'This is the first letter I ever wrote you'. On 12 August 1774 Mrs. Walter wrote from Berry Hill:

My dearest love,
I found some little consolation yesterday in thinking it was still in my power to be some small use to you, and set out after breakfast to the several shops to get the things you wanted ... I could not carry Lady Cranborne's [?choice of pattern] well enough in my eye to be sure of getting her stripe so ordered him to send you patterns ... He is to write to you for another measure for the window curtains, he desires the length from the cornice to the floor ... I have some hopes I shall see your handwriting tomorrow. I have been from you 50 hours, but I must grow accustomed to living without you. Adieu my love, be good and happy, and satisfy yourself that while I have reason to believe you so, though I may be afflicted at your absence I cannot be wretched. Your Father joins with me in kind love to Lord Grimston and all with you and both of us put up our prayers for you. I could say a thousand tender things but dare not trust myself till my mind grows stronger to tell you how dear, how very dear you are to the heart of your affectionate mother, H. Walter. Poor Bessy begs her duty.

How many, many times she wrote her loving motherly letters, full of love and good advice for her only surviving child; in fact, she wrote daily letters, and urged Harriot to do likewise. She advised her daughter to accept what life might bring, good or bad, imploring her always to look for the 'Divine blessing ... never forget to seek it, in prosperity and in adversity, it will enable you to bear the first with moderation and prevent you sinking under the latter ... You must not flatter yourself you are to pass through life without knowing sorrow, nobody does, I do not mean that Lord G. will be the occasion of it ...'. Returning to the same theme on another occasion, she wrote:

You are now launched into life, much depends on your own prudence. Never act without thinking, and I am sure you will never act wrong. Lord G. loves you, make him your study, avoid everything that can give him uneasiness, and try to fix his affection by an unaffected complaisance, you have much of it in your nature, and can never exert it so properly as to him. To the rest of the world be open, frank and civil, but remember to say 'no' in a polite manner is often absolutely necessary for a young woman, who would not be led into folly and imprudence. In conversation be attentive to others, you will please more by listening to them and following the lead than by taking it, those who do if they acquit themselves will excite envy, if ill, laughter; you will now say I have given you a great deal of wholesome advice. It has been the business and pleasure of my life these 18 years to make you what you ought to be, heaven prospered my labours by giving me a docile nature to work upon, and my endeavours must not cease now when in the height of youth, happiness and spirits, you may be in danger of wanting a tender friend to call you to serious reflection. I believe indeed I have no cause for a fear of this sort, but a mother's tenderness is apt to run before danger, and I know I shall not displease you by sometimes writing in a grave style ...'

At this time Lord Grimston was standing as a Tory candidate for one of the two Hertfordshire parliamentary seats. The election came very soon after his wedding, and canvassing occupied a good deal of his time, which meant that Harriot was left much alone. Letters tell of James coming home exhausted each day, of the 'fatigue' of his eyes. His father-in-law, himself a former M.P., understood the demands of campaigning, although he did not entirely approve as a father of this neglect of his daughter. On 24 August he wrote to Harriot about the situation:

My dearest child,

We begin to think 'tis a long time since we saw you and want the day when we hope to give Lord Grimston and yourself and the lively William a welcome here, I think we need not express our wishes that it may be the earliest hour that could set you down after the 12th. I know you will not disappoint our hopes, and we shall expect to see you then. I have been with the knaves of M[ilborne] P[ort] and held pretty much the language there that I held at Gorhambury. Was your Lord my dear as indifferent about a seat in parliament as I am and he appears to be, perhaps he may and doubtless would treat the County of Herts with more politeness, but with an indifference suitable and agreeing with that of mine at M[ilborne] P[ort]. I say not this my dear child to divert his Lordship from his present pursuits, nor to put you on persuading him from it, his pursuits would be laudable in better times, but as Parliament now is, and the next promises to be, I am sure 'twill be more for his honour and the quiet of his family to rejoice in his Gorhambury than mix with the most profligate and abandoned wretches alive. I cannot, will not, think it possible that his honest mind will receive taint from so pestiferous an air as that of a House of Commons, but why should he mix with a set of knaves that in any other place he would be ashamed of and avoid, believe me there is no real honour in a seat there, and why risk a quiet that one unlucky step at setting out may hazard. I believe I have said this is too tender a subject for you to touch upon to him, you'll keep it to yourself nor let drop an intimation of your disapprobation or my thoughts. I shall rest assured he means everything for the best, 'tis your duty my dear child to receive him with cheerfulness, which I am confident he will make up in kindness to you, that it may last to your latest time is, my dearest love, the constant prayer of dear dear child, your most affectionate Father, friend and sincere humble servant, Edward Walter. Make my compliments of love and affection to L.G. and best respects to L.F., the girls and the family of Oxhey.

In the same month Mr. Walter also wrote to his son-in-law. It gives no hint of disapproval of a seeming neglect of his daughter.

I should be truly miserable, my dear Lord, to be thought unworthy of your esteem and friendship, and you could not have made me more happy than by your expressions of kindness to me and tenderness to Lady Grimston, it is a happy presage my dear Lord and I trust in God for its continuance. We shall leave this place [Berry Hill] tomorrow and I purpose being at Stalbridge Sunday to dinner, we shall there expect letters from Lady G. as we have none today, that we may hear everything goes on happily at Gorhambury, and in the canvass, is very much the wishes of my dear Lord your Lordship's very affectionate Edward Walter.

Mr. Walter added a postscript: 'Short letters my good Ld. like short answers may and I hope will make long friends'.

Lord Grimston did not get a seat in Parliament; he had failed to secure the support of Lord Salisbury, a prerequisite for any Tory candidate in the neighbourhood. James's election expenses from October 1774 to September 1775 amounted to a staggering £2,750. Mr. Walter, who had predicted that Lord Grimston's 'election matters are not likely to pay for the pains he has been at, and [I] cannot help wishing that he had nothing to do with the confounded election', was proved right. James's mother, however, was so disappointed with the result that Harriot did not know what to do to alleviate her mother-in-law's distress. Her own mother wrote:

Lady Grimston is so very tender of her son she is hurt even with the appearance of his being abused to you. I think you might have set the good lady's heart at rest, by telling her these things gave you pleasure, as they were so many proofs that his enemies have nothing to say against him. This you might have said without compliments. I do assure you, it gives me great satisfaction to find his worst fault is being an Irish lord, which I can forgive him, though I confess I wish, for his own sake, he was an English one, as he would stand in no need of Hertfordshire freeholders in that case.

When James was away from Gorhambury, Harriot was unhappy, and longed for her parents and Berry Hill. Her mother understood this reaction, and 'was not surprised you felt a little when your three nearest and dearest friends were all from you'. She hoped that 'my Lord is now returned ... and your usual good spirits with him. In a married life little separations are unavoidable, happy the woman who has reason to regret them when they happen. In such a case the pleasure of meeting pays for the pain of a short absence. I hope by this time you know all this by experience, and that you have found out you was sorry not nervous. This last I hope you will never be, as I never had reason to think it in your constitution'. Harriot, her mother went on, should not 'make imaginary sorrows, as many people do, by which means they lose the enjoyment of a thousand blessings, and pine away their lives in misery surrounded by every comfort; to make a proper use of God's blessings, not to abuse but to enjoy and be thankful for them has always appeared to me as one of our great duties'.

Harriot's marriage settlement gave Lord Grimston a further £2,000 a year. Three months after the wedding Mr. Walter sent the amount for the first quarter's payment. James acknowledged it with great charm:

> 28th Oct. 1774. Received of Edward Walter Esq., the sum of Five Hundred Pounds being one quarter's payment due to me from him for having made me completely happy. Grimston. £500.0.0.

This little scrap of paper was found in one of James's pocket books. Folded with it was a silhouette of Harriot by Torond of 18 Wells Street, London.

5. Silhouette of Harriot, 3rd Viscountess Grimston by 'Torond of No. 18 Wells Street London'.

Mrs. Walter was busying herself preparing Stalbridge House, an estate which lay between Sherborne and Shaftesbury in Dorset which had been the Walter family's ancestral home, for visits from James and Harriot. Stalbridge had been acquired in 1700 by Harriot's great-grandfather, Peter Walter (1662-1745). He had been attorney and land steward to Thomas Pelham-Holles, the impoverished Duke of Newcastle. Peter Walter was something of a financial wizard, for as well as putting the Duke's finances on a secure footing, he had at the same time feathered his own nest. He seems to have been a somewhat unattractive and devious man. Walter accumulated a huge fortune, leaving the sum of £300,000 at his death. Stalbridge was bequeathed to Harriot's father 'in tail male' which meant that in the absence of a surviving male heir, it would pass to Henry Bayly. As we know, none of Harriot's brothers survived to inherit, and thus this estate was in the event to pass to Bayly (afterwards the Earl of Uxbridge). Stalbridge House no longer stands.

Mrs Walter wrote to her daughter that she was making 'the old mansion look cheerful'. She prepared a room especially for James's brother William and 'even if Mr. Harbottle comes we can provide for him in the upper regions'. She longed to hear the old house ring with Harriot's laughter at William's lively chatter. She began to brush up her Italian and read books in the language to recall the family's time on the Continent. Mrs. Walter's life was always centred around her daughter – memories of the past, thoughts of her in the present, and hopes for her future.

Surviving letters contain many details of life at Stalbridge. There was the day when morning visitors began to arrive 'at half an hour after 7':

> Mr. Walton went down and in a few minutes returned and said some of the ladies from Horsington were coming. Accordingly I heard the sound of coaches and when I got into the breakfast parlour I found the Baron, Lady Busland, Mr. and Mrs. Freke and their little girl, Mrs. Spencer and two daughters, Walter Spencer and a young man whose name is Lutterel, in all ten, and four of us made fourteen, a pretty number to make breakfast for. You may believe noise was not wanting, the Baron is in health and spirits ...Mrs. Spencer shed some tears when she saw me, but seemed cheerful afterwards. Miss Jenny [Harriot's close friend] is gone to Weymouth, they say she is not well and has lost much of her flesh ... At twelve we got clear of this possé and Mrs. Webb and I took a turn in the park to refresh ourselves for dinner ... This morning Mr. Place breakfasted here, I expected to see him in low spirits, as his eldest daughter died in childbed a few days ago, but he seemed just as usual, it certainly is as your Father observes that people at a certain time of life lose their feelings, yet I think I must be dead before I can lose mine of you.

* * * * *

There was a good relationship between the Walters and their servants, perhaps more than was usual in that period. We have already seen Mrs. Walter telling Harriot that 'poor Bessy begs her duty'. When one of Harriot's personal maids was ill, Mrs. Walter referred her to their own kinsman and doctor, J. Mervin Nooth. For the ailment, whatever it was, Dr. Nooth advised rest and sea bathing, and gave the patient a prescription for medicine. 'In the meantime ... my scheme is,' Mrs. Walter wrote, 'that you should bring her down with you from hence and we may send her to Weymouth, as you have no servant that I know fit to wait on you while she is absent, Philis who can do your hair shall ... I have some thoughts of sending Bessy with her'. She also offered practical help with the servant problem. 'If your cook and housekeeper persist in disagreeing so, you must part with that you like least, or you will never have a quiet house, which is the everlasting plague to the mistress of a family ...' Mrs. Walter returned to Harriot's problems with her servants in a later letter:

> When first a set of travellers get into a stage coach they sit uneasy, but after hunching and shoving each other for the first half hour, all goes right. I hope you will find this the case with your family. You must act the part of coachman, and if anybody insists on two places instead of one you must out with them. I think this seems to be the case with the cook and housekeeper, both wish for power, and perhaps both make an ill use of it; his disagreeing so much with the maids under him, looks as if he was ill-tempered; as to the article of extravagance, your bills will inform you whether that is founded or not. I think you should have an account kept of the corn your fowls eat, and the numbers that are killed. These should be charged at the market price on one side of the page, the corn in the same manner on the other, by which you will see whether you save or lose by keeping them; you should afterwards charge them to your house book, otherwise you cannot judge the expense of your house and consequently not know whether your servants use you well or ill. I will try to get you a dairy maid but I fear it will be impossible to get one to take care of so many cows, and to bake for so large a family. I spoke to Sidney James this morning and told him you had 16 cows, he said he supposed you had somebody to help your dairy woman. I imagine you have not that number in milk at once, but you must let me know how many you have, and what to expect. I had not time to inquire into these matters when at Gorhambury, so am not qualified to talk to a servant for you ... Stalbridge goes on as usual. It is brim full at this moment. Yesterday we had six parsons, and the Lord knows who besides ... I am vexed I did not bring the music you left at Berry Hill with me, don't forget what you have at Gorhambury. I often sigh that the organ is so silent. *Anima mia adio*, be assured I will pray for your dear Lord as often as for my dearest love'.

She adds a postscript: 'I am sorry the toad Wedgwood has behaved so, you must make him change his ware'. Some early Wedgwood porcelain is still at Gorhambury.

Mrs. Walter returned to the question of the new dairymaid in a later letter. Mr. Stephen James, the Walters' farmer, thought he had found a suitable girl at Stalbridge Fair - 'at least, he thinks she will do, if she will go so far from home ... She is a stout good-humoured looking wench, says she understands a dairy and baking very well, and does not fear work, or scruple going so far from home, but as it is so far off, hopes you will give her seven pounds a year, this I would not promise, but I think [if] she is a good servant it will not be worthwhile to stand out for 20s a year'. In the same letter she enclosed a recipe for compost! 'Two measures of grey sand, two measures of rotten cow dung, one measure of rotten leaves, one measure of rotten tan. These laid in a heap only three feet high, and turned bottom upward every month, exposed to a full south sun without any drip of trees near it. It must lie a year. It will not do for hyacinth two years following, but may for less curious flowers, and when tan cannot be got a measure of fine mould may be used'.

In September Mrs. Walter was able to tell Harriot that 'your dairy maid set out on Friday. I have told her that you will raise her wages to seven pounds if she behaves well; she promises fair. Stephen James says she is a "brave broad backed one, and very able". I could not help laughing to see him examine her as he would have done an ox. "Thou has been long biting o'thee bridle", says he "without are a place: buy thee mantle and some smocks with the money thy Lady has gid thee, and be a good wench, and behave thyself that thou mayest keep the good service thou hast gotten"'.

'Did you see Grosvenor Square house when you was in London?' Mrs Walter asked her daughter. 'How goes it on?' The Grimstons had a house in Upper Grosvenor Street, but the Walter's London residence was at 42, Grosvenor Square. It was being renovated by Mr. Walter for the use of James and Harriot. This house is still remembered at Gorhambury today, for there is a small square landing in the bathroom area of the Lea Wing at the top of the 'family stairs' by the lift, between the north wing and the main block, which is affectionately known as 'Grosvenor Square'. In 1780 Lord Grimston decided to let the house in Upper Grosvenor Street, and wrote to a Mr. Claridge on the subject on 24 December:

The house to be let or sold, which you enquire after, was the residence of my father [and] is situated on the left in Upper Grosvenor Street, going towards the park, next door to the Duke of Montrose's ... It consists of three rooms on a floor, exclusive of the hall, in which the staircase stands, one of which rooms makes a good bedchamber; over there are four good bedrooms, and the garrets are perfectly convenient, and sufficiently large for the servants of any family that such a house would suit. The kitchen and its contingencies are out of the house, connected, however, with it by the advantage of a covered way. There is stabling for seven horses, coach house contiguous, and I think every office that can be desired in good order ... I shall confine myself to the rent *per annum*, which will be £200, clear of all deductions. I have to say that the taxes are not exorbitant, the ground rent being only £13 paid to Lord Grosvenor. There is some damask furniture ...'

Long before the date of this letter, James had become a father. The first hint of the news comes in a letter from Mrs. Walter written on 5 September 1774, who thanked Harriot for 'two letters full of information of a kind indeed that would not be pleasing to anybody who loved you less than I do, but there are things I like to be informed of ... and know that a regular family is a very necessary thing, and contributes more to one's happiness than people may think'. James and Harriot moved to 42 Grosvenor Square for the birth of their first child, James Walter, who was born on 26 September 1775. Harriot then went to Berry Hill to recuperate, where James wrote to her on 3 November:

A separation from you teaches me how well I love you and my feelings since I left Berry

Hill convince me that to be absent from you and to be happy at the same time is impossible; the idea I have of the pleasure I shall receive at our next meeting is my present consolation, and though that will not make the hours that separate us pass away more quickly, yet it assures me that I have the best of wives, and that I fundamentally am the happiest of men ... I am going this evening to the much celebrated St Albans Ball where I suppose I shall exhibit as Master of Ceremonies, and probably sport a minuet for the benefit of Mr. Sherman and some despairing Miss who dies to make a figure. I really think husbands might be excused the formal part of these assemblies, especially those who would so willingly give up the whole for an hour of his wife's company, as I would do ... You must present my love to Mr. and Mrs. Walter, kiss a blessing into the dear pledge of our mutual loves, and believe me to be most sincerely and affectionately yours Grimston'.

The couple were to have two further children, both daughters: Harriot, who was born on 14 December 1776, and Charlotte, born on 16 January 1778. A note in the family Bible tells us that 'all had the smallpox April 1779, the whooping cough 1791, the measles 1793'.

In their early childhood, Harriot often took her offspring to spend long periods at Berry Hill. It was far more comfortable there than at old Gorhambury, with its leaking roof and damp and crumbling walls. In 1778 a letter from James to his wife makes the first mention of the 'Great Work'– the construction of a new Gorhambury which was just beginning. This topic will be discussed more fully below. His letters were full of affectionate messages to the 'bambini', a term which recalled his romantic Italian courtship of the children's mother. He told Harriot 'I never can call any place where thou art not, my home, otherwise I ought to think my journey finished at Gorhambury'. In the same letter, James gave his wife news of the family and related that his sister Mary, now married to William Hale, was staying at damp old Gorhambury and 'she feels aches and pains every day ... Hale is wonderfully attentive to her and if I did not assure myself that I should act in the same manner as he does in the same situation, I should call him the very best husband in the world; I pray God I may never have an opportunity of showing my sincerity'. Little did he know what was soon to happen.

Living at Brooks's Club, with Harriot still at Berry Hill, in the summer following James passed his time playing whist and visiting the opera. His subscription cost him £21. 'The *amatori* declares against the opera, although the performers are good; the opera house is quite neglected, and in short the only well frequented public place is St James's'. How he resented those 'seven and twenty miles between us'; how 'heartily tired' he was 'of this limited manner of assuring you that I am your affectionate Grimston'.

From 1778 onwards James began to keep a series of vellum-bound letter books, in which he put letters received and also copies of the letters he wrote, or at least a précis of them. Six such books have survived which together cover 1778-1808, the last 30 years of his life. They show him as a country gentleman occupied with family affairs and the management of his estates, which were spread across seven counties – Hertfordshire, Norfolk, Surrey, Essex, Dorset, Somerset and Wiltshire. He was also involved in parliamentary affairs, served on the Bench, was a Deputy Lieutenant, and was responsible for appointing clergymen to the various livings in his gift. Occasionally he writes a letter and then notes that after all, he did not send it. We learn what he would have liked to have said, and what in fact he did say. These alterations reveal his sensitivity and his respect for the feelings of others. Whoever his correspondent, whether Pitt, the First Minister of England, or one of his own estate workers, there is in each letter the same dignity, the same courtesy, the same endeavour to be of service. It is clear that in all he undertook, he showed the same sincere concern to carry out the duties of his position.

By 1780, work on the new house at Gorhambury – more fully described below – was coming along very well. James reported on its progress to Harriot at Berry Hill:

> I found everything at Gorhambury in order; the rooms were warm, the house has got up to the point I expected, and the dairy maid to save her credit was legally married. I am told that in her serving capacity she has long been no better than she should be, so that we may easily console ourselves for her loss, and I fancy shall have small difficulty in supplying her place, for though fit and able men for church and state may be wanting, I hear there is no scarcity of dairy maids. The raven croaks upon the same old tree in the Long Walk, and I have retained the Keeper in its favour; I sauntered under the shade this morning with such a pleasure that few things could have lightened, and one of these would have been the having you with me: If I had made this declaration before marriage you would have placed it under the article of gallantry but now I think near five years of honest cohabitation will stand between me and such an idea, and you may fairly put it under the chapter of truth and fidelity. I thought of our children before I wrote the last sentence, it is just now to make my best wishes for them; I shall be very anxious to hear how our care in the nursery goes on; I take it for granted that the boy is getting better every hour, and it is probable that the little girl is beginning to sicken; a short time I hope will get us clear of this terrible disorder. The workmen here all made holiday today being Easter Monday, and most of them have passed it very agreeably in going to sleep in the barn; they prefer negative to active pleasures and perhaps with good reason ... Love to the *Bambini*.

* * * * *

During the following year Harriot kept a little pocket notebook, a strangely poignant relic today. It is bound in red morocco leather, is lined with pigskin with marbled end papers, and measures 2 inches by 4 inches. In pencil, using minute handwriting, we see her motherly note about the behaviour of little Walter, now aged five:

> April the 22nd – Walter was very good
> April the 23rd – Walter deserved but one pin though he was very good in every other respect but reading
> April the 24th – Walter deserves two pins and has been very good all day
> April the 25th – Very good

The little book has a gusset pocket, and inside it, folded neatly to fit, are two newspaper cuttings of songs. One of them shows that Harriot saw a funny side to marriage:

SONG – MR. DARLY
As you mean to set sail for the land of delight,
And in wedlock's soft hammocks to swing every night,
If you hope that your voyage successful should prove,
Fill your sails with affection, your cabin with love.

Let your heart, like the main-mast, be ever upright,
And the union you boast, like our tackle be tight;
Of the shoals of indifference be sure to keep clear,
And the quicksands of jealousy never come near.

If husbands e'er hope to live peaceable lives,
They must reckon themselves, give the helm to their wives,
For the evener we go, boys, the better we sail,
And on ship-board the helm is still ruled by the tail.

Then list to your pilot, my boy, and be wise;
If my precepts you scorn, and my maxims despise,
A brace of proud antlers your brows may adorn,
And a hundred to one but you double Cape Horn.

In the inner pocket of Harriot's account book for the same year, in which she noted what she had paid for her bonnets, ribbons, cottons, and stays, and toys for the children, there is a list of clothing 'for 12 girls'. Twelve girls! Was it Harriot, then, who as early as 1781 started the school in St Michael's which was to be fostered by her future daughter-in-law? The list of clothing also mentions a school mistress, and seems to correspond to the clothing provided for the school 40 years later.

For twelve girls			
School mistress	21	0	0
House	3	0	0
1 gown each	2	8	0
4 shifts each at 2s.6d. Russia	6	0	0
2 petticoats each at 2s. Wolsey	1	4	0
1 upper petticoat each at 3s.3d.	1	16	0
2 tippets each		6	0
2 caps each		6	0
Hanover lace for ditto		4	0
2 aprons each	1	7	0
2 pairs stockings each	1	16	0

I hat each
1 red winter cloak
2 pairs of shoes each as 3s.6d. per pair

Harriot also noted local people from Redbourn and St Albans who were 'cured of the ague in 1781'. We do not know if she herself was responsible for these cures, making use of the recipe provided by her mother:

Two ounces of bark infused in a glass of brandy with a little snake root, taken night and morning, will cure the ague. A quotidian ague returns every day. As to the cure in tender constitutions, 10 grains of ipecacuanha may be given alone; but to more robust, a grain or two of emetic tartar may be added. If it is necessary to purge, take half an ounce of Epsom salts, and two or three grains of emetic tartar. Mix them and make them into a powder; to be dissolved in a pound of lukewarm water and taken two hours after the fit. Then take the following electuary: rob of elder, one ounce; five drams of Peruvian bark, two drams of camomile flower in powder, extract of the lesser centuary, and powder of gillyflowers, of each half a dram; add as much syrup of lemon as will make an electuary. Half a dram to be taken every two hours.

There are other odd little notes: 'Plunket behind Curzon Street Chapel, cures cancers'. 'Mrs. Smith of No. 77 Dean Street, Soho, is a Rat Killer'. 'Lord G.'s annual income at £7324'.

In 1784 the main block of the new house was almost completed; this year seemed in many ways a happy one for the family. On 20 October James Grimston noted 'Took possession of our new house at Gorhambury on this day, after having been employed on building it seven years the second of last month – '. Everything seemed to be going well. James was playing a prominent part in county and parliamentary affairs. He had been elected a Fellow of the Society of Antiquaries, and also of the Royal Society. Harriot was busy choosing furnishings for the new house, with new porcelain and curtains as well. They chose the preparatory school at Cheam for their little son, where 'for the sum of about £20 a year Mr. Gilpin undertook to prepare our little boy for public school' as James noted in his account book for the year.

In February 1785 Harriot found she had something wrong with one of her arms. A Mr. Kent was paid a guinea to examine it. It was still troubling her in May, and a Mr. Gains was consulted. He recommended a 'collar', and James paid £3.0s.6d. for 'a collar for Harriot'. What was wrong? At the same time little Walter had some stomach infection; Harriot and the children were sent to Eastbourne in the hope that salt water bathing might benefit them. A year later Harriot wrote to her girlhood friend Jenny Spencer, now resident at East Wenford, Exeter:

> My dear J.S.,
> I have much too good an apology to make for my long silence, that of illness, first in myself, and then in our little boy, who has been in great danger from an inflammation of his bowels, which he is but recovering the effects of: I hope to be able to give you a better account of my family some time hence, that my child will be re-established in his health, and that a journey we are to take, when the season permits, will set me up again. It is to Buxton we are to go, I do not like the thoughts of it, but health is to be purchased at any rate, and I feel myself bound to take care of mine for the sake of my children. I am sorry my dear J.S. feels any afflictions, but in this world it is the fate of all to suffer and those who have not real miseries, make them – but I will not sermonize, my friend, nor can I make my pen speak mirth – The days which were decked with flowers that we passed in youth together are gone, the *allegro* has given place to the *penseroso*. They both have their charms, but the latter are the most solid; my own ill health, and my child's illness have thrown a melancholy over me, which not the tenderness of my husband and mother can prevent my feeling, though before them I put on a cheerfulness I do not feel, but which I hope will return – Adieu my dear J.S. This detail of myself I thought I owed to our friendship, believe me with best compliments to your family, yours affectionately, H.G.

Harriot's health did not improve, and the proposed visit to Buxton was made in July. The doctors began to take a grave view of her illness. On their return James Grimston made this note in his account book – '1786, Aug. 26. Journey to Buxton and return to Gorhambury on the 19th inst. having been absent seven weeks: a miserable journey and the consequences even more so – £135'. They then tried the waters at Tunbridge Wells. From there, on 16 September 1786, Harriot wrote once more to Jenny Spencer:

> My dear J.S.,
> Though I have not one thing to say, nor a single idea in my miserable brain to furnish matter for a letter, yet I must write to you, to return my thanks for your goodness in forgiving me my long silence, and my impudence in scolding, when all the blame lay with *me*; but you are a particular creature, and have so natural a turn to forgive, that if ever you live much in the world, every body will be trampling upon you. This is my manner of returning thanks for favours! I have got our little boy with me who has now become a very entertaining companion, which is a thing I stand a little in need of in this dull place, where Heaven knows, nothing should have made me come, but the want of the most valuable of all the blessings its bounteous hand pours on us! but my dear we can't have everything, and as I am happy in all other circumstances I must not expect health.

The neat handwriting flows on, playfully recalling their days together at Stalbridge and their old friends, and then Harriot ends by teasing her dear J.S.:

> Well, I suppose you are almost asleep, but open thy eyes Jenny and read the conclusion of this epistle, which consists of all good wishes to you, such as that you may have a husband that will beat you twice a day at least, and hate you as much as your sincere friend, H. Grimston.

The two letters were sent back to Gorhambury by a descendant of Jenny's in 1817, to Harriot's son, who was by then the 1st Earl of Verulam. This was the last letter Harriot ever wrote. Less than a month later, on 7 November 1786, she died in the new house at Gorhambury. She was just 30 years old. James's diary noted a payment:

> 1786, Nov. 10. To Dr. Hunter fee for visiting Ly. G. at Gorham. £21.0s.0d. My dear wife died.

During that last summer of her life, workmen were still busy putting finishing touches to the inside of the house. The tragedy that seemed likely to strike was apparent even to them. In 1958, over 170 years after Harriot's death, a fire occurred at Gorhambury below the State Dining Room. In 1786, this room had been intended as James Grimston's business room, and that summer the oak flooring was being laid. When some of the flooring had to be removed in 1958, on the underside of one board was a message written in chalk. The joiner had written 'Pray God prosper the noble family that walks on this floor, and pray God spare the life of the Viscountess Grimston'. He had signed his name – Matthew Kirk – and dated his inscription 14 June 1786.

Another touching memento of Harriot was found in her 1782 account book. At first sight it seemed no more than a tiny folded piece of faded tissue paper, but inside it lay a tiny piece of lace, and its design is centred around the initials 'J.S.' Did Harriot make it as a gift for her friend?

Three years earlier, Harriot had written instructions to accompany the will which she had made at the time of her father's death, which took place in 1780.

> Whereas I have a great dislike to all pomp in a funeral ceremony, I desire mine to be conducted in the following manner. That my body should not be embalmed, or opened (unless I should die of some disorder that may make the opening of it useful to mankind), that it may be wrapped in a plain woollen shroud, and if I should die at Gorhambury, that eight of the labourers, who have the largest families, and the best characters, should carry me to the grave, for which trouble I order to each man one guinea, and a good brown suit of clothes, hat, stockings, shoes and a crepe hat band, and it is my desire to be followed by only two maids and two men servants. If I die at a distance from St Albans, it is my desire my body may be conveyed thither in a plain hearse, attended by one mourning coach, and that the aforesaid labourers may take my body from the carriage into the church to be deposited in my dear husband's family vault in the church of St Michael's near the town of St Albans, for which I desire they may have the aforesaid legacy, and that all superfluous ornaments of ciphers, escutcheons, and black hangings in the church may be omitted; and I desire that the money which used to be expended on bread and beer at funerals in my dear husband's family, may be laid out in meat the Christmas after my decease, to be distributed to the poor in the neighbourhood of Gorhambury, that they may rejoice at the season in which our blessed Redeemer came to the world'.

She wrote a second letter of instructions, almost identical, but differing at the end, where it reads:

> It is my desire to be attended to the grave by only my housekeeper, my own maid, the house steward, and one other manservant out of livery, and that all the superfluous ornaments of ciphers and escutcheons, and black hangings in the church may be omitted; and that no bread and beer may be given away to make a day that should be one of sorrow, a scene of riot and debauchery'.

James honoured his wife's wishes. In the January following her death he noted in his account book: '1787, Jan. The funeral expense of my dear wife the Viscountess Grimston, conducted in pursuance of her own directions, which were strictly followed ... £190.14s.7d. Bread and meat to the poor of St Albans ... £70, £20 of which was given at my dear wife's funeral ... £50'

In her will, Harriot left a little tortoiseshell box with a miniature of her mother as a child in it to her cousin, Lady Forrester. This was to return to Gorhambury, at Lady Forrester's own death. Harriot left Berry Hill in trust for her children, with the clause that the 'household furniture &c. belonging to Berry Hill shall not be removed from the House but shall be used and enjoyed therewith'. She also left £50 to 'my father's faithful servants, John Dober, and David Browne. The will can be seen in full in Appendix Seven.

6. *Tiny fragment of bobbin-lace with the initials 'J.S.'; a present made by Harriot Grimston (née Walter) and intended for her childhood friend, Jenny Spencer?*

Chapter Nine

The Building of the Eighteenth Century Gorhambury

From the time of their marriage, James and Harriot had been giving consideration as to how to improve old Gorhambury, that once pleasant Tudor house built by Sir Nicholas Bacon. The fabric of the place was deteriorating rapidly. Many structural weaknesses were revealed when architects were consulted. The walls, which were built of rubble and chess-work, were so unsafe that there seemed to be no way to make them proof against cold and damp. It was plain that this was no place to bring up a young family, nor to house the many valuable family possessions, in particular the fine portrait collection. As early as 1775 there is an estimate from an architect called Joseph Saunders:

> To making working drawings for a summer house at Gorhambury, going down there and setting out ditto ... £10.10.0d
>
> To surveying the house, giving instructions for shoring it, taking the plans of it, &c ... £15.15.0d
>
> To making designs for a new house at Gorhambury, making fair drawings of ditto, &c ... £52.10.0d

The amount so astonished James that he wrote to query it! Nothing, apparently, resulted from this estimate.

There is little doubt that it was Mr. Edward Walter, Harriot's father, with his practical experience of designing his own new house at Berry Hill, who persuaded James and Harriot to build a new Gorhambury. Tradition relates that Edward Walter chose the new site by planting his cane where the portico of today's mansion now stands. It was a free and open site, 400 yards east of the Tudor house, with glorious views over the parkland. We are left to guess the names of the 'best architects of the day' who were consulted. Doubtless Robert Adam was one. On his northern tour, years earlier, James had greatly admired Lord Scarsdale's house at Kedleston, which was designed by Adam. However, James's eventual choice was Robert Taylor (later Sir Robert), who was 63 at the time. Gorhambury and Heveningham Hall in Suffolk were to be his last important works. Having studied in Italy, Taylor was an excellent choice to build a house which would remind the Grimstons of those days of their courtship in Italy; for he submitted a design based on the ideas of Palladio.

Taylor's father had apprenticed him at the age of 18 to Henry Cheere, a sculptor, for the considerable fee of £105. In 1741 Mr. Taylor senior had further managed to provide his son with enough money to 'travel on a plan of frugal study to Rome'. Despite his rapid success as a sculptor, Taylor began to devote time to architectural studies as well. From 1750 his career in this sphere is well documented: he carried out decoration and alterations at Braxted Lodge, Essex, and at Longford Castle in Wiltshire from that date. He built up a large clientele mainly amongst City merchants, for whom he designed both London properties and country villas. In 1765 he was appointed to the surveyorship of the Bank of England, and carried out extensive alterations there; in 1769 he became Architect of the King's Works, the first of a series of posts he was to hold at the Office of Works. A feature of his work is his use of domes, usually suspended over the main staircase, as at Gorhambury. Staircases were, in fact, always focal points in his designs. Most are circular or oval and wind in a continuous floating spiral because they are cantilevered, the weight of each step resting entirely on the one below. Again, this feature can be found at Gorhambury.

Taylor's first plan showed a starkly classical main block, with two curved extensions to the north and south, sweeping from the rear of the house. This project featured an elegant staircase, an oval scalloped hall, and two wings separated by wide arcs from the main block, in a manner derived from Palladio and reminiscent of the design of Kedleston. This plan for the hall was rejected, on the grounds that the curved walls would not afford suitable hanging surfaces for the family's collection of paintings. However, niches were incorporated on either side of the door leading to the library from the Great Hall (see colour illustration no. 9), a feature which had been used at Kedleston. These niches were later blocked in, presumably to provide more hanging space for pictures. Another link with Kedleston was the decision to employ the same plasterer – Joseph Rose – who had worked there. He was the most famous man of his craft in his day, and was responsible for all the lovely restrained plaster work on the ceilings and friezes at Gorhambury. Rose was paid £985.15s.8d. for his work, according to James Grimston's accounts.

The curved wings of the original design were altered to become detached wings, connected to the main house by straight covered passages. The south wing was to house the kitchens and the bakery; the north wing included the laundry, the brewhouse and the dairy. These two wings were not, however, built until 1788-90, and their workmanship is somewhat inferior to that of the main house. All rooms below ground level and the passages in the higher parts of the house are vaulted in brick and plastered. Some of the upper bedrooms have fine curved walls: the corridors here are top-lit above small elegantly-friezed domes at intervals along their length.

The main work of building began in 1777, although the foundations were started somewhat earlier. Most of the external facing was of Totternhoe clunch, from nearby Bedfordshire. The plinths, the bases for the columns, the sill courses, the steps and the balustrading were all of Portland stone. The material to in-fill behind the clunch was looted from the Tudor Gorhambury. The capitals of the impressive Corinthian columns that support the vast

. Edward Grimston, Comptroller of Calais, in middle life; oil painting on panel by an unknown artist.

2. A contemporary painted terracotta bust of 1568, representing Sir Nicholas Bacon, Lord Keeper and builder of the Tudor Gorhambury.

3. A contemporary painted terracotta bust of 1568, representing Sir Nicholas Bacon's wife Anne Cooke.

A contemporary painted terracotta bust of
1568, representing one of Sir Nicholas Bacon's
two sons by Anne Cooke, either Anthony or
Francis, as a child.

The Tudor Gorhambury: an 18th-century watercolour drawing.

6. Anne Bacon, daughter of Sir Nathaniel Bacon of Culford, and wife firstly of Sir Thomas Meautys and secondly of Sir Harbottle Grimston: portrait in oils attributed to Jan de Baen.

7. Sir Thomas Meautys, showing him in his 'newly-acquired park of Gorhambury': an oil painting by Paul van Somer.

8. Sir Harbottle Grimston, 2nd Baronet, who began his family's long association with Gorhambury: portrait in oils by an unknown artist.

9. Mary Grimston, daughter of Sir Harbottle Grimston. She is the link between the early and the later Grimstons: portrait in oils attributed to Theodore Russel.

10. Sir Capel Luckyn, who married Mary Grimston, and whose descendants live at Gorhambury today; a painting in oils attributed to Van Diest.

11. Mary Grimston, granddaughter of Sir Harbottle Grimston, with her negro page; oil painting by William Wissing (reproduced by permission of the Paul Mellon Centre for Studies in British Art).

12. William Luckyn/Grimston, 1st Viscount Grimston, aged 17; a portrait in oils by Sir Godfrey Kneller.

pediment are of Coade stone, a cream-coloured fabricated stone of great durability, made by a Mr. Coade from a secret recipe. At his death he passed his secret on to his wife, but at her death it was lost for ever. Lord Grimston paid Mrs. Coade £342 for these capitals. The fenestration conforms to the fashion of the time: the main rooms have tall double-hung sash windows, surrounded by moulded stone architraves, flat friezes and delicate cornices. The basement and bedroom windows are simple square openings. The house's main feature, the enormous east portico, which is very reminiscent of the Pantheon in Rome, was the last section of the main block to be built. Until it was completed, the great area of the main roof was thatched to keep out the weather.

In 1771 James Grimston had written home from Rome, extolling the work of 'le Chevalier Giambattista Piranesi'. Whilst James merely bought some engravings, his father-in-law acquired some original pen-and-ink sketches by the artist. These drawings were eventually to come to Gorhambury, and are discussed at some length by Jonathan Scott in his definitive study of Piranesi. He suggests that they may even have been a gift from Piranesi to Edward Walter. There are two marble chimneypieces at Gorhambury, which present something of a problem. Past generations of Grimstons claimed that they were the work of Piranesi and had been made especially for Gorhambury; this would have made them unique examples of his talent in this kind of work in England. While there is documentary evidence proving that Piranesi was responsible for many examples of his work at Gorhambury – their purchase is noted, and in many cases the item itself is signed by the artist – there is no record of chimneypieces. However, at Lord Aylesford's house at Packington in Warwickshire, Marcus Binney found drawings by the artist Joseph Bonomi of chimneypieces exactly like those at Gorhambury. Bonomi was in London in 1767 to decorate buildings for the Adam brothers. The fact that one drawing shows an overmantel which is not featured in the actual objects themselves would seem to suggest that these drawings are designs for, not copies of, the Gorhambury chimneypieces.

Who sculpted Bonomi's designs? In the accounts for 1784, we find the payment of an unspecified amount 'to Mr. Westmacott for a chimneypiece for the library'. Richard Westmacott was a sculptor resident in Grosvenor Square in London. In 1777 he published a series of 20 engraved designs for chimneypieces. Could Richard Westmacott have sculpted the chimneypieces from Bonomi's designs? Their design does incorporate so-called 'Roman antiques', but these are quite possibly copies.

Even if Piranesi was not responsible for these particular pieces of sculpture, his acquaintance with the Walter family was more than a slight one; he dedicated one of his beautiful vases *'all Ill'ma Signora Harriot Walter in atto d'Ossequio il Cavaliero Gio. Batta. Piranesi'*, and with two other vases, it can be seen at Gorhambury today.

After Harriot's death, there was a lull in building activities for two years. James did not build on the two wings until 1788-90. By that time Sir Robert

Taylor was dead, and the work was completed by his son Michael Angelo
Taylor. The family, as we have seen above, had moved into the new mansion
in October 1784. The basement rooms and passages with their stone-flagged
floors must have served for domestic rooms for the first five years of their
occupation. It is strange to find in this obscure area of the house some
interesting fragments of stone carving from the Tudor mansion: there is a
mask-face of Pan and a stone block bearing Nicholas Bacon's initials.

Externally, the house – with its parkland meeting its classical portico in an
uninterrupted sweep – surveys its woods and meadows to the east. To the
west, it looks across the ruins of the Tudor house, to a mock temple beyond
the straight lines of its terraced gardens, which are enhanced by enormous
classical urns. Inside the house, the elegantly-proportioned rooms with their
restrained classical ornamentation provide an appropriate setting for the fine
furniture, the paintings, bronzes, porcelain and all the other items which
recall James Grimston's Continental tour and his influence on the 'new
Gorhambury'.

7.   *Pen and ink colour-wash drawing of Sir Robert Taylor's original design for the 18th-century Gorhambury,*
built 1777-1784 for the 3rd Viscount Grimston.

A widower at 39, James now faced the bleak prospect of life without Harriot in that unfinished mansion, every detail of which would recall her. For a long time they would have known what was to happen, and no doubt discussed the future. Lord Grimston went on to complete the house, and continued with his public duties. In these actions he was carrying out his wife's wishes. The 22 years of life that were left to him were to be important ones. He devoted himself to Parliamentary and public affairs. Nearer home, he became Major Commandant of the St Albans Corps. He had been granted the freedom of the Borough of St Albans and became its mayor in 1807. His unsuccessful candidature at the 1774 election did not deter him from further involvement in Parliamentary affairs. Harriot's cousin, Lady Forrester, urged James to stand again. 'Unite with Lord Salisbury and nothing can shake your interest' she stated. In 1783, on the death of his family's nominees John Radcliffe, James stood again for St Albans and this time he won. In this Parliament he voted with Pitt, and presented the address from St Albans thanking the King for having dismissed the Coalition government.

In the General Election of 1784 Lord Grimston canvassed St Albans, but withdrew at the very last minute, on the morning of the election, in favour of his brother William, who was successfully returned with Lord Salisbury's support. James himself obtained a seat as a member for Hertfordshire.

In Parliament James was an independent who supported Pitt's government. He gave the First Minister his support during the Regency crisis, explaining to one of his constituents that 'you are not unacquainted that I am a wellwisher of Mr. Pitt and his administration, and I hope you are equally convinced that I would not upon any terms give any support to a grand constitutional question which I thought subversive of our common rights in compliance with any party whatever'. At the request of the Marquess of Salisbury, Lord Grimston was made a peer of Great Britain in June 1790 for his support of Pitt's government. He became Baron Verulam, with a seat in the House of Lords. How pleased Mrs. Walter must have been: she had lived to see her wish of 1774, that her son-in-law should have an English peerage, become a reality. Gorhambury today possesses a very fine portrait of William Pitt, painted by John Hoppner in 1805. It is a three-quarter length view of the Prime Minister, facing the spectator, and turning slightly left. His right hand rests on the back of a chair, over which lie his robes of office. His left hand is on his hip. He is dressed in black and his tightly buttoned coat is open at the neck, revealing a high white stock. A black satin waistcoat is visible below the short front of his coat.

James did not forget his dead Harriot in his time of triumph. In the summer of 1790 he wrote some poignant lines recalling her:

If purest virtue, sense refined in youth:
Religious wisdom, and a love of truth;
A mind that knew no thought ignobly mean;
A temper sweetly cheerful yet serene;
A breast that glowed with those immortal fires;

Which godlike Charity alone inspires;
If these could length Fate's tremendous doom,
And snatch one moment from the gaping tomb:
Death had, relenting, thrown his dart aside,
And Harriot, Oh! my Harriot, had not died.

After Harriot's death, there are few insights into Lord Grimston's private life: as intruders we merely peep. Items randomly selected from his account books show that he was a loving father, a considerate friend, and also a man intolerant of other's failings:

1787. May 7. A bat and ball for Walter – £0.4.0d.

May 11. To a man for thrashing a fellow for ill-using his jackass – £0.2s.6d.

1788. January 10. Mr. Gold for flax, etc., for the use of the poor – £12.14s.9d.

1789. February 15. Fee to Dr. Nooth. N.B. the first I ever gave to a physician on my own account – £1.0s.0d.

March 13. To Dr. Warren to consult with Dr. Nooth on my case; at which it was perfectly apparent that Dr. Nooth knew nothing about it, after having had me in his hands one entire month – £2.2s.0d.

June 12. To Mrs. Walter for the children – £205.9s.7d.

1791. March 17. Fee to the clerk at House of Lords on certifying my pedigree – £2.2s.0d.

1792. February 1. To Mr. Stone for my robes – £27.0s.0d.

1797. May 20. Tax for hair powder – £8.8s.0d.

May 24. To Mrs. Faith. Court dresses for the girls – £60.7s.0d.

1799. May 12. Certificates for hair powder, self and five servants – £6.6s.0d.

October 30. To Mr. Josh Gape, subscription to the Blue Coat School at St Albans – £2.2s.0d.

November 2. Subscription to the widows and children of soldiers employed in Holland – £10.10s.0d.

1800. November 9. To Mr. Thomas Rose, grocer in Davies Street, for 7 cwt and 17 lbs of rice for the use of the poor – £13.8s.0d.

December 24. Gift to the prisoners, being seven of them – £0.15s.0d.

1801. April 30. Gift to the soup shop, St George's parish, for the better supply of the poor – £10.10s.0d.

1802. June 21. Gift to the groom boy when he quitted for being drunk – £1.1s.0d.

1803.June 18. Three tickets for breakfast at Cumberland Gardens, £1.11s.6d. To hire of boat, &c. £3.18s.6d.

1804. December 10. Fees on account of Charlotte's illness, the scarlet fever – £164.1s.0d.

December 25. Dinners to the prisoners in gaols – £2.0s.0d.

1806. April. To Mr. Thomas for a billiard table, &c., complete, purchased at Lord Lansdowne's sale – £91.12s.0d.

Chapter Ten

The 3rd Viscount's Daughters: Harriot and Charlotte

Grandmama Walter, with her wise husband and the daughter she idolised both dead, did not falter. She wiped away her tears, and took charge of the motherless family Harriot Grimston had left behind her. Eleven-year-old Walter was sent to Cheam School, as arranged; ten-year-old Harriot and little Charlotte, who was only eight, were taken under her own wing. All the devotion Mrs. Walter had bestowed upon her daughter was transferred to her little granddaughters. Fortunately, she was still young enough to guide them through childhood, and to see them grow up into young women. She saw to it that their penmanship was neat and clear, and that they were good needlewomen. Both girls showed talent as artists in water colours and in miniature painting; they were to contribute much to Gorhambury. Their father paid Mrs. Walter £205.9s.7d for their keep every half year.

After Cheam, Walter went on to Harrow School, and then to Christ Church, Oxford, where he took his M.A. degree in 1796. His father's letter book records that he wrote to Walter on this subject: he recommended that he should take it in the usual manner if he felt himself sufficiently able to go through the examination. He advised him to study 'the common law of England, not only at present, but as a future employment'.

During their childhood and adolescence Harriot and Charlotte were never short of relatives to entertain them. They were often on the farm at Estcourt in Gloucestershire with Aunt Jane and Uncle Thomas; they stayed with Aunt Mary at the Hale home at Kings Walden. By now their Uncle William, who had inherited Oxhey and taken the name of Bucknall, was married to his elegant golden-haired Sophia Hoare. Their favourite aunt was Aunt Susanna, who had been a close friend of their mother's. When Susanna had become slightly uneasy about her betrothal to John Warde of Squerries Court, she had asked for Harriot's opinion of him. Harriot replied that 'I know but little of him, except that he bears the character of a worthy, goodhumoured man, that he is polite, and my own eyes have informed me that he is handsome: if with these qualifications you can love him, I think you have the prospect of happiness with him'. Susanna did marry John Warde and kept her considerable sense of humour. In a letter to Harriot's daughter of the same name, written in 1795, she gives a lively account of a burglary at Squerries:

I am sorry to send you such a scrawl but the carriage waits ... added to which we have
lost our silver inkstand and the rogues have left me such a blackguard pen and worse ink
that I can scarce write legibly. Charlotte, who is with me, is mad that I can give her no
good tea, the best Hyson is likewise gone in the silver tea-chest and pray excuse a wafer
[i.e. the small disc of dried paste used to fasten letters] as they took a fancy to some of our
seals and don't trust me with any secrets as the padlock is taken away from my pocket
book. But it is fair to tell you after this we were not alarmed at the housebreakers on
Thursday night last.

In time, Harriot and Charlotte were launched into society, and Mrs. Faith
made them court dresses for which their father paid her £60.7s.0d. During
1802, 1803 and 1804 he gave three balls for them at 42 Grosvenor Square. By
now the girls were no longer dependent on their grandmother and lived at
Gorhambury, enjoying the new house to which finishing touches were still
being added. They made catalogues of the pictures and the books in their
beautiful handwriting. Their particular hobby was that of making copies of
miniature paintings of scholars and divines, such as Donne, Erasmus, and
Cardinal Richelieu.

In 1794 poor Mrs. Walter was in deteriorating health. Charlotte and Harriot
assisted in nursing her where they could, but Charlotte in particular found it a
gruelling task and could not bear to watch her grandmother suffer. Mrs.
Walter's unmarried niece Anna Maria Cockburn (who was the 9th Baroness
Forrester in her own right) came up to London from Bedgebury in Kent to
visit her sick aunt. She was shocked to find her desperately ill and attended
only by two servants, both of whom were worn out by the work involved.
Lady Forrester summoned Lord Grimston and there 'insinuated' to him that
he and his girls should be 'more attentive to' Mrs. Walter. These remarks
greatly hurt Lord Grimston, who found these 'unkind observations extremely
grating'. The Baroness, for her part, stated that she was 'anxious that Harriot
and Charlotte should lose not themselves in the opinion of the world by
appearing so inattentive to their grandmother'; she thought it 'not quite right
that the young people should be running to balls in the present state of Mrs.
Walter's health'. However, she assured Lord Grimston that 'any coolness
between you and I will I am sure make her unhappy, so on that account as
well as our own let us be good friends and live in peace and harmony in future
which will give pleasure to, dear Ld. G., your warm and sincere friend,
Forrester'. Eventually the Baroness ánd Viscount Grimston mended their
difference: the doctors, the servants and the two girls continued to immerse
poor Mrs. Walter's ailing body into hot baths, applied leeches to her and
dosed her with laudanum.

She lingered on until March 1795. On 5 March Lord Grimston wrote to tell
Baroness Forrester that 'the event, which we have long expected in Mrs.
Walter has taken place' and that he had opened her will 'for the purpose of
pursuing any directions she might have given for her funeral'. She had
appointed him her executor and 'among other legacies, she has given you one
specific one of £200. She has directed that she should be buried at Dorking in

the vault built for Mr. Walter without any funeral pomp'. If Mrs. Walter's funeral lacked pomp, it was certainly impressive and gloomy, with its hearse drawn by six horses, and a following coach drawn by another six horses, decorated with feathers and velvet. The clergymen and 'gentlemen attendants' had 'three very rich three-quarter inch wide Armozeen hoods and scarves'. There were also attendant porters and six men on horseback who also served as bearers; these were presumably wearing the 'black cloaks and scarves' mentioned. There was a special individual called a 'featherman' who carried the 'feather lid in town and at the place of interment'. There were ten men in mourning dress, and two men as 'coach pages', carrying 'truncheons and wands' and '20 black silk headbands' were provided for the 'attendants, the clerk, sexton, servants in town and coachmen'. Beside this, there were the 'expenses in refreshments for company and attendants in Dorking and back out, 2 days, and for attendants in town' and the cost of the 'achievement in arms, painted and strained on a gilt-edged frame and an outside frame strained with black cloth'.

Rather than leave the charming Mrs. Walter on this gloomy note, we can turn to the two fine portraits of her which hang at Gorhambury today. In January 1757 she was painted by Sir Joshua Reynolds, romantically depicted dabbling her left hand in a small fountain with a slender silver birch tree behind her. Her dress is of brown satin, its bodice is elegantly tight-fitting with full-flowing white sleeves, and she wears a full, dark skirt. A black scarf, edged with gold, is draped around her and a close-fitting lace collar surrounds her slender neck. The other portrait is in pastel, and may like the one of her daughter mentioned above (p.65) be by Glain, the artist the family met in Italy. It shows her with her dark hair drawn back and with a small white feather and pink flowers adorning it. She wears a rich red gown with a square neck-line and a lovely lace fichu, with a rose at her breast. Her sleeves are faced with pink and white brocade. It is easy to see in this enchanting portrait the author of the lively letters which do so much to bring to life the 18th century Grimstons and their daily round at Gorhambury.

Private griefs, like that occasioned by the death of a beloved grandmother, were inevitably overshadowed in these years by the long years of struggle with France. In the early 1800s Britain feared an invasion: after all, had not the French assembled a mighty fleet of ships and an army at Boulogne in preparation for the assault on England? In August 1803, Walter Grimston wrote to tell the Marquess of Salisbury that he had been 'commissioned by the several parishes of the Abbey in St Albans, St Peter's, St Michael's, Redbourn, Sandridge, to inform your Lordship, that it is the desire of the inhabitants of the above parishes to volunteer their service within Great Britain in case of invasion or rebellion ... I shall take the liberty of offering my personal service as Lieutenant Colonel or Major of the above Corps when formed'. With Lord Salisbury's concurrence, Walter became Major Commandant of the St Albans Volunteer Corps of Infantry later the same year. The Corps consisted of three companies of 80 men (a total of 240), together with 14 sergeants, including a

Sergeant Major and a Quartermaster Sergeant, 12 corporals and three drummers.

In August 1803 Lord Grimston purchased a pair of colours for the Corps. The Misses Grimston were invited to present the colours at a special ceremony held at Gorhambury in September 1804, and the two girls wrote a special prayer for the consecration of the colours. Their father, brother and most of the Grimston clan were there: one who was unable to attend was Aunt Susanna Warde, however, and Charlotte wrote her a long account of the exciting event:

> The great event being most happily concluded, I lose no time, not having one moment to spare, to communicate the particulars to you, and I believe everything has been conducted with the greatest military decorum, as the Duke of York's aide-de-camp gave his sanction to it, and suggested, most good-humouredly, many little particulars which would otherwise not have been thought of.
>
> At 12 o'clock the Volunteers, with their officers, marched on the ground, which was at the back of the house, and they were drawn in a line facing it; the colours were then conveyed and laid across two drums; one is the King's colour, the other is the arms of Herts., round it the motto, St Albans Corps of Volunteers, and laurels, etc., round the whole, painted most brilliant, and a great deal of gilding, upon buff silk.
>
> We, the company, then with the chaplain followed Harriot, who leant on Mr. Paget's arm, and stood facing the soldiers, very near the colours; then the music struck up 'God Save the King'. The chaplain then stepped forward and read his prayer remarkably well; my brother stood on the other side of the colours. Then Harriot made her speech extremely well, most audibly; my brother made her a reply and a very long address to the Volunteers. I ought to have told you there was a manoeuvre to bring the ensigns, with a sergeant, forward between the benediction and Harriot's spech. My brother then took the King's colour and gave it to one ensign, who received it on one knee, and then the other colour to the other ensign, who received it also on his knee. After this, they – the Volunteers – gave a general huzza.
>
> Then my brother went to them, gave the word of command for a great deal of manoeurvring and firing towards the woods; the company stood for all this; then he marched them with the music to the front of the house where four tables were spread, making an exact square, with a small one in the middle for the music; being a fine day you cannot imagine what a beautiful effect it had. They gave the usual loyal toasts, Mr. Grimston's health and prosperity; Lord Grimston, the founder of the feast, when he had left them, with a great many cheers to each toast, and then the officers marched them off and hurried them away sooner than they would otherwise have done to give themselves time to return for their dinner with us at 6 o'clock.
>
> ... There was a good deal of the world; not many of the fine people of the country. The ground was kept by the cavalry volunteers, some of Mr. Lamb's and some of Mr. Villiers' troops, I think about eight. Harriot was immensely frightened before the thing began; her terror fortunately subsided and she went through her speech without faltering ... Harriot was very well dressed; a muslin hat, with a lace crown, her garnet ornaments at the turning up of the hat, with a bow over it, and feathers, garnet earrings, brooches and cross, her beautiful cloak, coloured gloves ... On the subject of dress, I had the misfortune to tear my fine lace cloak ...'

One reason for Harriot's extreme nervousness on this occasion was the presence at the ceremony of a captain of the Volunteers whose name was Thomas Baskerfield. Thomas had fallen in love with her: we do not know how she felt about him, but his request to court her was quickly rebuffed by her father who wrote rather pompously to the unfortunate suitor:

> I think it incumbent upon me to give you as early an answer as possible to your request for leave to pay your addresses to my daughter, Miss Grimston, and for that purpose I have communicated to her your prepossessions in her favour. She desires me to inform you that taking into consideration the disparity in years and other circumstances between you she cannot flatter herself that such an union could be attended with happiness to both parties which ought to be the object of so serious an engagement and therefore begs that this subject may be no further pursued. For my part I perfectly coincide with her in opinion.

In the event, neither Harriot nor her sister married. They lived together, either in London at 34, Hertford Street, or in the country at a place in Hertfordshire they always referred to as 'Berkhamsted Castle'. In Queen Elizabeth's reign, a mansion built by Sir Edward Cary stood on Castle Hill, a mile north-west of the ruined medieval castle. Two-thirds of Sir Edward's house were destroyed by fire in 1662, but a fair-sized building remained until it was completely demolished in 1967. This house was known variously as 'Berkhamsted House' or 'Berkhamsted Place', but a 17th century historian, J.E. Cussans, mentions that in his day it was sometimes known as 'the Castle'.

At a time when ladies of quality were expected to occupy themselves within the home, these two sisters pursued a somewhat unusual enterprise. Their talents lay particularly in the field of writing and painting, and they decided to illuminate Francis Bacon's *History of King Henry VII* with miniature water-colour portraits of almost every person mentioned in the text. In search of sources for their illustrations they visited libraries, museums, and country-houses. Charlotte's diary records these journeyings.

> 1813, May 5. To Lambeth to copy Archdeacon Warham.
> Oct. 15. We went to Hatfield. I painted Margaret Countess of Richmond.
> 1814, Mar. 16. Lord Clarendon came and lent us a picture of Henry VIII. He looked at our illustrations of Henry VII, approved, and promised us his assistance.
> 1815, Aug. 28. We went to Oxford and I had time to begin taking a sketch of Philip the Handsome in the Chapter House.

Their quest for source material did not end in the British Isles. In 1818 Charlotte went to France, and at the Louvre 'found a picture of Charles VIII, which I obtained permission to copy', and at the Bibliotheque du Roi she 'found an interesting portrait of Louis XII'.

Their self-imposed task took them the best part of 20 years. With enormous care and patience they inserted the printed text of the book into the centre of larger sheets of paper; it is almost impossible to detect that this has been done, so neat is the application. Interspersed between these pages and mounted in the same way are their miniature illustrations. The pages are each bordered with elaborate designs in the style of the Tudor period. The professionalism of the whole enterprise is extremely impressive. The massive volume (each page measures 20 inches by 14 inches) has been bound in the finest red morocco leather; on opening the box which contains it, one is struck by the bright blue velvet lining it, and again by the bright blue silk lining of the book itself – a startling choice against the dark red binding. With the volume is a small notebook, also bound in red morocco. This is headed in Harriot's writing as being 'An account of the pictures and margins of the pages of the History of Henry VII written by Lord Bacon Illustrated by Harriot and Charlotte Grimston. Begun 7th April 1812. Finished -'. The date of completion was their only omission, but we can supply it from a letter written by their brother in February 1825, in which he wrote: 'My sisters showed me the title page of the most beautiful book they have illustrated for me. It will be one of the most valuable productions of female industry and talent, that has made its appearance for ages, and I hope fully to appreciate its merits and its beauty'.

Charlotte was also responsible for another project, which was to be of the greatest interest to all interested in her family's history. This was her *History of Gorhambury*, which was handwritten in copperplate writing, and reproduced by a lithographic process. On 20 November 1822 she noted that 'on this day I received from the Admiralty the concluding pages of my *History of Gorhambury*'. Did the Admiralty play some part in arranging its reproduction? This work was illustrated with miniature copies of paintings from the Gorhambury collection.

These two ladies were wealthy enough to be able to indulge their love of fine books and indeed all their artistic tastes, for in 1822 they had the good fortune to inherit £40,000 from Mr. Richard Glover. He was a younger brother of the wife of George Grimston, who was one of the many sons of William, 1st Viscount Grimston. From this bequest not only Charlotte and Harriot, but many subsequent Grimstons, benefited; it is sad to think that so far it has not proved possible to discover the Christian name of the Miss Glover whose marriage brought about the legacy.

It seems that Charlotte inherited the same strange shaking palsy which had killed her mother, and she became progressively more unwell after Christmas 1825. During the course of the following year she lost the use of an arm and a leg 'in consequence of a nervous affliction'. She diverted her mind from her suffering by compiling, with Harriot's help, a collection of morning and evening prayers, which, she said, she had found 'during a long illness ... her constant solace'. Her object in compiling these prayers was 'to keep the mind in a habitual state of preparation for that time when worldly cares and diversions pass away like empty shadows'. The volume was later dedicated to Queen Victoria. Charlotte died, or, as she would have put it herself, 'finished her course of suffering' in 1831, aged 53. Harriot died in 1846, having reached her three score years and ten.

Chapter Eleven

The Public and Private Life of the 1st Earl of Verulam

Introductory

The character of James Walter, 4th Viscount Grimston, who was created 1st Earl of Verulam in 1815, was entirely different from that of his father. Certain weaknesses in it became apparent which are hard to account for. It is possible that the death of his mother when he was only 11 may have had some unfortunate effect; for the two years preceding her death, she had cared for him herself at home, as Walter's own illness had made it impossible for him to be away at school. He had thus witnessed Harriot's suffering and her death from close quarters. After she was gone, it is possible that the grief-stricken father allowed his only son too much licence. Walter seems to have acquitted himself reasonably enough academically; as his father had hoped, he took his degree at Christ Church successfully. However, when he was 25 we find the first signs of trouble in a letter James felt obliged to write to his son warning him about his extravagant spending on his favourite sport of racing, and about the excessive number of servants he employed.

At the age of 32, Walter married the beautiful 24-year-old Lady Charlotte Jenkinson, the only daughter of the 1st Earl of Liverpool by his second wife, who was a daughter of Sir Cecil Bishopp. The marriage was by special licence, and took place at the Liverpool family home, Addiscombe Park, near Croydon. (As a wedding present, James Grimston gave Charlotte a pair of diamond earrings and a diamond necklace, which were later stolen from the 4th Countess of Verulam at St Pancras station in 1920). The women of the Bishopp family were famous for their good looks, and Charlotte was no exception. Soon after her marriage she sat to John Hoppner for her portrait. She wore her dark hair piled in curls on top of her head, and a high-waisted black velvet gown with short sleeves that reveal her plump arms. In her right hand she held an eyeglass attached to a long chain about her neck; her short-sighted eyes looked wistful and sad. Charlotte was a tall woman – indeed considerably taller than Walter. One of the couple's great-granddaughters stated that it was from Charlotte that later Grimston men inherited their great height. Before this time, the Grimstons were not a notably tall family – Walter himself was about five foot eight inches. He had a large nose, full sensuous lips, and very plump fingers.

In 1808, the year following the marriage, Baroness Forrester of Corstorphine, whom we have already met as Mrs. Walter's devoted niece, died at her

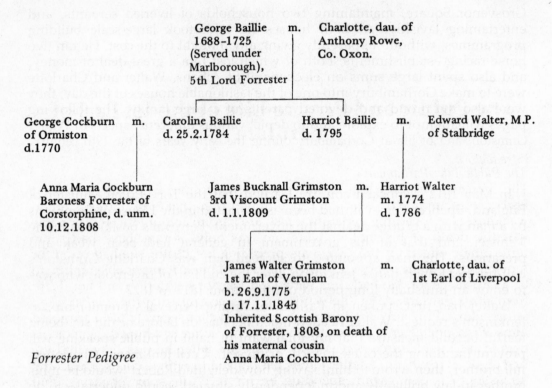

George Baillie   m.   Charlotte, dau. of
1688–1725   Anthony Rowe,
(Served under   Co. Oxon.
Marlborough),
5th Lord Forrester

George Cockburn   m.   Caroline Baillie   Harriot Baillie   m.   Edward Walter, M.P.
of Ormiston   d. 25.2.1784   d. 1795   of Stalbridge
d.1770

Anna Maria Cockburn   James Bucknall Grimston   m.   Harriot Walter
Baroness Forrester of   3rd Viscount Grimston   m. 1774
Corstorphine, d. unm.   d. 1.1.1809   d. 1786
10.12.1808

                              James Walter Grimston   m.   Charlotte, dau. of
                              1st Earl of Verulam   1st Earl of Liverpool
                              b. 26.9.1775
                              d. 17.11.1845
                              Inherited Scottish Barony
                              of Forrester, 1808, on death of
Forrester Pedigree   his maternal cousin
                              Anna Maria Cockburn

home at Bedgebury in Kent. This meant that the Barony of Forrester descended to her great-nephew by marriage, as she left no direct heir – and this was Walter's father, the 3rd Viscount. The Grimstons were all highly delighted about this new title for the head of the family, especially Walter and Charlotte. Walter and his father agreed that as the heir he could use this title; but as it happened, he was to have little time to use it, for less than two weeks later on New Year's Day 1809, James Grimston died, quite unexpectedly.

Walter noted that his father's hearse was drawn by six horses, and followed by seven mourning coaches, each with four horses. The pulpit and the clerk's desk at St Michael's church were put in mourning. Black scarfs, hatbands and gloves were provided for eight pall bearers, two medical attendants and Mr. Gape, vicar of St Michael's. There were also black hatbands and gloves for 32 tenants, 22 labourers who acted as 'underbearers', and six footmen. Twelve black cloaks were provided for 'mourners, two mutes, and one plume bearer'. Walter thus became Viscount Verulam and Baron Dunboyne in the peerage of Ireland; Baron Verulam in the peerage of Great Britain; and Baron Forrester of Corstorphine in Scotland. It was a singular honour to hold peerages in all three countries.

After his father's death, Walter saw himself as a great 19th century figure. His manner was as pompous as his language was verbose. He lived in great style, both in his beautiful Palladian mansion at Gorhambury, and at 42

Grosvenor Square, maintaining two households of liveried servants, and entertaining lavishly. At both houses he undertook large-scale building programmes, without apparently giving any thought to the cost. He ran two horse-racing establishments, both of which lost him a great deal of money, and also spent large sums on elections at St Albans. Walter and Charlotte were to make Gorhambury into one of the fashionable houses of the day; they were also the proud and devoted parents of a large family. The following pages will attempt to explore and to depict various different aspects of Walter Grimston, and of life at Gorhambury during the early years of the 19th century.

The Public Life: Parliament

In May 1812 a shocked country learned that the Tory Prime Minister of England, Spencer Perceval, had been assassinated in the House of Commons by a man with a grudge against the government. Perceval's position as Prime Minister and that of his government in general had been weak and precarious. The man appointed to succeed him was Charlotte Grimston's half-brother Robert Banks Jenkinson, later the 2nd Earl of Liverpool, who was to enjoy an unusually long period of office from 1812 to 1827.

Walter had first spoken in Parliament during Perceval's premiership, at Jenkinson's request. Walter needed much persuasion before he did so, 'being fearful beyond measure that my total want of habit in public speaking will prevent me doing the cause justice, or myself'. Cecil Jenkinson, Charlotte's full brother, then wrote to him, saying how delighted Robert 'would be if his brother-in-law brilliantly and independently situated should undertake to do it'. Walter was to second an address 'as a friend of the King' on the first day of the session, and after he had rehearsed his speech countless times with Charlotte,he went through his ordeal successfully.

In 1815 Walter became the Earl of Verulam, an honour which he achieved in a rather amusing manner. On 3 August 1815, Charlotte wrote to Lord Liverpool:

> My dear brother,
> As it is very generally said that at the termination of the great struggle which this country has been engaged in [with Napoleon], that there will be a considerable promotion in the peerage, I cannot let pass this opportunity of requesting most earnestly that you will secure Lord Grimston's being included in it, and obtain for him the dignity of an earl. I am sensible that he has no claim to this favour from any public service, but, already being a peer, a considerable landholder, and the representative of an ancient and respectable family, and also having been a steady supporter of the present administration, it appears to me not impossible, that you might obtain this favour for the husband of your only sister, and I feel that it would be so great an advantage to my children that I am induced to make this application to you. Believe me my dear brother, your very affectionate Charlotte Grimston.

Lord Liverpool replied to this appeal in a letter to his brother-in-law, written on 6 September:

> Charlotte wrote to me some time expressing her anxious wish for the sake of her family that in the event of any promotion in the English peerage you might be advanced to the

rank of an earl. I had an opportunity of speaking to the Prince Regent on the subject before he left London, and he assured me that he should have great satisfaction in including you in the promotion which is intended to take place. I should be obliged to you therefore if you would let me know which you would wish to be your title in order that I may lay it regularly and officially before the Prince Regent with some others which are before him. I beg my love to Charlotte.

Walter immediately took up his pen to reply.

I feel very gratified and very thankful too for the kind manner in which you have answered Lady Grimston's request. I so well know to what I must attribute my advancement in the peerage that I shall always feel how much I owe to you, to the connection I have formed with Charlotte and to the kindness of the Prince Regent in complying with our wishes at your desire. I should wish my title to be Verulam.

And so it was in this way that Walter and Charlotte Grimston became the Earl and Countess of Verulam. Charlotte herself was triumphant: coronets were painted on all the carriages, on the footmen's chairs, on the porcelain and engraved on the table silver – on everything, in fact, where they could serve as a reminder of the family's new status.

In 1821 Walter was appointed Assistant Cup Bearer for the Coronation of George IV, As Prince Regent, the latter had married Princess Caroline of Brunswick in 1795. Although she bore him a daughter – Princess Charlotte – he found her distasteful and refused to live with her. He tried to get a divorce, and offered her an annuity of £50,000 a year to renounce the title of Queen and live abroad, but she refused. Public opinion was strongly on her side, but Walter supported the King, believing the scandalous stories about Caroline. He referred darkly to the 'depraved and disgraceful manner in which the Queen passes her time'. During the debate on the royal divorce, which was held in the House of Lords, Walter attended daily. The feelings of the common people on the matter ran high, as he himself found, for after attending one such session, he found himself 'annoyed by a madman coming into my room in Grosvenor Square. I got a sword he had with him from him, and had presence of mind enough to secure myself from his displeasure and resentment. I wish I had had more, and had detained him'.In 1821 George IV was crowned without his Queen. However, Caroline was determined to assert her claims. On the morning of the coronation, she was turned away from the door of Westminster Abbey, which caused 'an uproar amongst the lower orders'.

Walter's sisters Harriot and Charlotte came up to London to see the coronation, and took charge of Walter's little girls for the occasion. Charlotte wrote a vivid account of the day.

London was in a complete hustle the whole night the bells rang. At twelve o'clock the guns fired and at two, and numberless persons proceeded towards the Abbey at three o'clock. At an early hour the Queen made an attempt to gain admission, but having failed she returned to Cambridge House and for a short time there was a strong appearance of riot amongst the lower orders of people. Several windows were broken in Grosvenor Square ... But peace was restored in less than an hour and the numberless efforts which were made to amuse the people succeeded in keeping them in good humour and in creating great popularity for the King. At about one o'clock we carried my brother's two little girls to see a balloon go up. The day was most beautifully clear and fine and we had an excellent view of it from Lady Holland's. The two children were delighted. My brother was desired by the King to act the part of Assistant Cup Bearer to Lord Abingdon. The Champion was performed by the young Dymoke, hardly of age, who having spent his whole life at sea, was not, until he claimed his right of serving, a practiced horseman, but by laudable exertion he acquired sufficient knowledge of the art to perform his part in a very becoming manner. The Duke of Wellington who rode by his side as Constable whispered to him at the proper time to throw down the Gauntlet. Lord Angelsey supported him on the other side and shewed the most perfect grace in the management of his horse. The Duke of Wellington appointed his second son Lord Charles, a beautiful boy, of about 10 or 11, to be his Squire, and the admiration this affectionate appearance gained must have been highly gratifying. The Duke also acquired great popular favour by backing his horse quite into the stable for the amusement of the people without doors. The Lord of the Manor of Haydon who claims the right of presenting the Napkin to the King, after he had washed his hands before dinner, was not ready to perform the office. Lord Gwydyr, therefore, desired my brother to give it. When the proper person presented himself, Lord Gwydyr told him that he had been too late and that Lord Verulam had officiated for him, he answered he was shocked to have given Lord Verulam the trouble. 'Sir', said Lord Gwydyr, 'Lord Verulam has not had any trouble but you have lost a great honour'. He however begged to have the Napkin as his fee, which was accordingly put into his hand.

In the evening there were fireworks in Hyde Park till a very late hour and the day passed off almost without an accident. The manner in which the Duke of York did homage was particularly admired, there was an honest tenderness in his manner and an appearance of sincere affection when he gave the kiss which drew from the beholders loud acclamations. It was said that the Duke of Gloucester was in bad taste upon that occasion.

The parts of the coronation which gave Walter the most pleasure occurred when he saw 'the galleries all filled with women in their handsomest attire, and the area filled with nobles and knights and squires in their different costumes. The next most remarkable sight was the commencement of the procession, all sides of the houses in the vicinity being fitted up as galleries for spectators, and filled with well dressed people, expressing with loud huzzas and clapping of hands their loyalty ... The Abbey was grand and imposing beyond all words, the most beautiful part of the ceremony was when on the crown being placed on the head of His Majesty the peers all put on their coronets'. The central figure of the day, George IV, must have presented an amazing spectacle in white kid trousers and loaded with jewellery. The occasion was said to have cost the country £400,000.

Although the Queen was not present in the Abbey, the King's current mistress, Lady Conyngham, was very much in evidence. Gossipy Aunt Charlotte Grimston recounts in her diary the tale that Lady Conyngham was not satisfied with the position she was given and 'she complained of being so much behind the King that he would get a crick in his neck by looking at her'. A wit of the day depicted the royal lover in the following lines, which Charlotte copied into her diary:

'O, place me not there', the Marchesa exclaims
'And what fault's in the seat, which your ladyship blames?'

'I'm not forward enough, 'tis a scandalous thing,
And I vow that I'll sit on a par with the King.
Would you have it appear to ev'ry beholder
That he cannot look at me, but over his shoulder?
What avails it my hair with his jewels to deck,
If in gazing he catches a crick in his neck?'
The Colonel replies 'The arrangements are made,
But your Ladyship's wishes must still be obey'd,
For my part, I thought you well plac'd, as 'tis said,
That your first wish in life is to turn the King's head'.

Queen Caroline died a few weeks later on 7 August. Another entry in Charlotte Grimston's diary tells of 'the disgraceful conduct of Her Majesty's attendants' and of the mob riots which followed the funeral. The Queen's friends had a silver plate affixed to her coffin which read 'The injured Queen of England'.

The silver inkstand which George IV used to sign his coronation documents is at Gorhambury. It was left to Charlotte, Walter's wife, by Dr. Ireland, the Dean of Westminster, who in his turn had been bequeathed it by Lord Liverpool. With the inkstand there was also a table given to the Dean by the Countess of Liverpool. The whole bequest was valued at £35.

In the 1831 election Walter's son, young Grimston, who was now 22, contested one of the two seats for the Borough of St Albans, but he was not elected. The following year brought many important Parliamentary debates, in which Grimston's father played an important role. Walter attended debates on the Roman Catholic Relief Bill, which he called the 'odious bill'; he also became intimately involved in the negotiations over the second Parliamentary Reform Bill. On 7 May, along with the Duke of Wellington and many other Tory peers, Walter voted in the majority against the second Reform Bill. The genial King, William IV, was strongly in favour of it, however, and this caused a conflict of loyalties for Walter and others like him between their loyalty to the monarchy and their fears that the Reform Bill would bring about a revolution. When a third attempt was made to introduce the Bill, once again the House of Lords refused to pass it.

Great indignation was expressed in London. The mob smashed the windows of Wellington's house and tried to drag him from his horse when he rode through London. Wellington appealed to Walter for help, and asked him, as a close friend of the King, to negotiate with him. William had proposed creating extra peers to ensure the passage of the Reform Bill through the House of Lords, an idea which alarmed the Tory peers almost as much as the Bill itself.

On 16 May, Walter attended a Levée with the King, and noted in his diary that he had 'had an audition with His Majesty'. Later that evening the two were together again at 'a great and very magnificent dinner given by H.M. to the Jockey Club'. When Walter returned home to Grosvenor Square that night he recounted to his wife the conversation which had taken place with the King. Charlotte considered it to be of such importance that she wrote it down

THE UPSETTING OF THE REFORM COACH.

at Walter's dictation. Her account was subsequently altered and amended by Walter himself and these additions are shown in square brackets thus:[].

> Lord Verulam having requested a private audience of His Majesty waited upon the King after the Levée this day. He was most graciously received and began the conversation by expressing his thanks for His Majesty's condescension in admitting him again to express his gratitude for His Majesty's own firmness in resisting so destructive a measure as the creation of peers for a particular purpose. The King replied 'Lord Verulam, it is my duty to grant interviews to peers of the realm [and if it was not my duty it would be my inclination] when they wish to communicate with me. In your particular instance I wish to hear your opinions and communicate with you thinking you a dispassionate and practical man, and knowing from early association and old friendships much regard for those [persons] allied to you. Moreover I am very desirous to learn distinctly the opinions of respectable and well-intentioned persons upon subjects of that importance. Lord Verulam, I frequently argued with my mother, the late Queen Charlotte, who contended with the King the Catholic Relief Bill would be a breach of her coronation oath [being passed by both branches of the legislature]. In this I differ from her, but I decidedly think and feel that to destroy the power of one branch of the legislature for any particular purpose and for a bill brought forward by one set of men would be a flagrant violation of my coronation oath [and additional only by the other]'.
>
> Lord Verulam then repeated his thanks to His Majesty, and begged to add, that not only himself but several other peers and very influential members of the community were willing to sacrifice much of their feelings and opinions concerning the Reform Bill and to assist His Majesty as much as in their power lay, that they felt for the difficulties the King was placed in. The King replied that such feelings and support and conciliation were the most likely means of solving the difficulties by which we are surrounded, that he thanked God his health and spirits were greatly supported, that when a man firmly resolved to act as his conscience and duty direct, he may only with calm and confidence ask Providence for the results.

On the next day, Walter found himself in a dilemma. 'The state of politics bore me to death and I see no way of extricating the country from the disasters which threaten it' he wrote. He had been resolutely against the Reform Bill and had now done his best to persuade the King to have a change of heart on the subject, but this morning he had received 'an extraordinary letter from Sir Robert Taylor by H.M.'s order asking me to join in a declaration in the House of my having withdrawn my opposition to the Reform Bill'. The 'extraordinary letter' reads:

> I have received the King's Commands to acquaint your Lordship, with reference to what has passed between His Majesty and you, that all difficulties and obstacles to the arrangement in progress will be removed by a declaration in the House of Lords this day from a sufficient number of peers that in consequence of the present state of things, they have come to the resolution of dropping their further opposition to the Reform Bill so that it may pass, as nearly as possible, in its present form.

Walter immediately called on the Duke of Wellington, who he found had received a similar 'extraordinary letter' and after discussing the matter with Wellington, Walter replied, saying that he would comply with the royal request. He preserved a copy of his reply:

> I received your letter too late yesterday to answer it before the meeting of the House. In the audience which His Majesty was pleased to grant me I told His Majesty that I was ready individually to make every sacrifice of opposition to the Bill in order to extricate His

Majesty and the country from the dilemma in which they are placed. I should however make myself a party to the measure which I still think is striking a fatal blow against the monarchy if I made a public disclosure of my dropping all further opposition to it. I shall keep my word with His Majesty, and I trust that will be sufficient.

The Duke of Wellington, realising that matters were so serious that it might result in civil war, had decided that it was best that he and the other Tory peers should abstain from voting. The Bill was passed and received the King's Assent before the end of 1832.

The family had always been on close terms with William IV. When young Edward Grimston was seriously ill in 1825, Charlotte asked the King to lend her his carriage to take Edward to London! According to Edward himself, Sir William Knighton, the King's secretary, wrote to say that 'Mama might have the King's carriage whenever she chose to take me to London and Papa and I go up in it on Tuesday ... The faster the carriage goes the easier it feels, so we shall go up rather quick ... in two hours and 20 minutes'.

Not all the favours which the King showed Walter and his family were of so minor a nature, however. Just before Christmas, 1834, Walter received a private letter from Whitehall, handwritten and signed by Robert Peel, who had been Prime Minister since November.

> My dear Lord Verulam,
> I must not take credit for myself for an appointment, which mainly originated at the personal wishes of the King, but I hope I need not assure you with what great satisfaction I acquiesced in those wishes. I refer of course to the appointment of a Lord of the Bed Chamber, which the King told me that he knew you would gratify him by accepting. Believe me, dear Lord Verulam, most truly yours Robert Peel.

Walter replied by return of post:

> My dear Sir Robert,
> I beg to express my most humble acknowledgement for His Majesty's gracious intentions towards me, and at the same time to thank you for the very kind manner in which you have communicated his wishes. I shall feel infinite gratification in accepting the honour of being attached to His Majesty's Household ...

However, Walter had received no definite instructions as to what he should do, where he was to attend, and so on. With Christmas almost upon them, Charlotte began to 'fuss' for him. There is a draft of a letter in her handwriting which she thought her husband might send to the King:

> I have received through Sir R. Peel an intimation of Your Majesty's gracious intention of appointing me one of Your Majesty's Lords of the Bed Chamber. I beg most gratefully to acknowledge Your Majesty's condescension and kindness towards me and to assure you that I shall have the greatest satisfaction of serving Your Majesty as one of your personal attendants ...

She drafted another letter to be sent to the King's private secretary, Sir Herbert Taylor:

> His Majesty has been most graciously pleased to appoint me one of his Lords of the Bed Chamber, which has been very kindly communicated to me by Sir Robert Peel, assuring me at the same time that it has been done entirely in consequence of His Majesty's direction. I cannot say how much the latter circumstance has gratified my feelings and how willingly I accept the offer of becoming one of His Majesty's personal attendants. I

am at a loss to know how I ought to proceed on this occasion. Whether I ought to intrude myself on His Majesty at Brighton, whether I ought to write my thanks, or whether I ought to attend at St James's on the first day a Court is held. If I was to set off for Brighton I should get there on Xmas Day which would not perhaps be a fitting or convenient day for me to appear. If I ought to write I enclose a letter which I beg of you to present, if not to put it into the fire, and I shall certainly be in London on Friday and Saturday when the newspapers inform me His Majesty will be at St James's.

Whether or not these letters were actually sent, on 10 January 1835 Walter was sworn in as one of the Gentleman of His Majesty's Bed Chamber. The appointment would have given him prestige, but above all else, it would have brought him a salary. In the previous reign, the 12 Lords of the Bed Chamber each received £1,000 per annum. A fixed income of this kind would have done much to ease Walter's financial situation; but sadly he held the post for only a short while, for in April 1835 Peel's government fell, and Walter lost his sinecure to a Whig.

The Public Life: The Social Whirl

From the beginning of their married life, Walter and Charlotte had entertained on a lavish scale. In June 1816, for instance, Charlotte gave a magnificent 'assembly' at their house in Grosvenor Square to celebrate her husband's new peerage (see above). Between 'three and 400 distinguished friends' were entertained. A contemporary report of the occasion is written almost entirely in superlatives. 'The grand entrance hall and staircase were lined with exotics, and a variety of odoriferous flowers, which shed a rich perfume. The superb suite of drawing rooms, five in number, presented a scene of splendid magnificence not to be excelled; the richness and elegant taste displayed in the furniture and drapery, together with the brilliance of the chandeliers, lustres, &c., were the admiration of the company. The centre drawing room was appropriated for dancing; the carpet being removed, the floor was elegantly chalked in various emblems ... at half past eleven o'clock dancing commenced, the first dance ... was the "Waterloo", a new favourite ... The company was alternately supplied with the rarest ices and refreshments during the night. A table, in the form of a horseshoe, was laid in an anteroom, which was well supplied with cold fowls, hams, tongues, wines, &c' ...

In the same year Walter and Charlotte were 'of the party' at Buckingham House when Prince William Frederick of Gloucester married his cousin Princess Mary, one of the many daughters of George III. Three years later, after calling in at Ashridge, where the Verulams and Walter's sisters Harriot and Charlotte were amongst the guests, the Duke and Duchess of Gloucester made the first of many visits to Gorhambury. Aunt Charlotte Grimston gives an account of the event in her diary. 'From Ashridge ... we followed Lady V. to Gorhambury'. Their brother had already gone on ahead to 'prepare for the reception of their R.H. of Gloucester'. The weather was 'intolerably wet'. The Duke and Duchess 'arrived at about six. My brother's keepers preceded the Duke's carriage through Pré Wood and up the Park. There was a band of music on the portico which played 'God Save the King' when the carriage stopped. The Duke and Duchess walked round the shrubbery before dinner. The Herts Band played during dinner and in the evening in the hall. After dinner the Duchess sang in a pleasing manner and Lady Verulam played on the organ and a duet on the harp with Mrs. Martin. The Duchess said to my sister on taking leave that she had liked her visit so much she should be very happy to repeat it. Lady Salisbury, Lady Fanny Talbot, the Dowager Lady Liverpool, &c., &c., were at G.'.

This was the first of very many visits, the Duke often coming to shoot and the Duchess very happy to spend her time with Charlotte and the children. There were many days like the one of which Walter wrote in his diary 'after a magnificent day's shooting round the park ... in the evening we had the projected Charades, which all the women & some of the men had been working at during the morning. I have seldom, if ever, seen anything better done, & considering the time for preparation it was marvellously good. The first word was 'novice', 'no' being exemplified by a young lady refusing a young gentleman in favour of another, who in his turn is rebuked by the young lady's parents, and she because she will not obey is sent off to a convent. The lover is driven to despair, and addicts himself to vicious courses, which is shown by a drinking and gambling party in which he stabs himself, thus exemplifies vice, and the whole is made out by the young lady taking the veil. The last view was the prettiest I ever saw, and the girls looked very well having chosen their dresses as nuns with excellent taste. 'Humbug' was the next word enacted'. Sadly, he does not tell us how! Walter added that 'their Royal Highnesses expressed great pleasure, especially the Duchess, to whom it was new'.

Writing years later, one of Walter's daughters had this to say about the Duchess of Gloucester:

> She must have passed the dullest youth, surrounded as she was by form and etiquette; she did not marry her cousin the Duke of Gloucester till late in life, and had never visited in any private house till after her marriage, when she came with him to Gorhambury. She remained a great friend to my father and mother till her death, and was always very kind me and my brothers and sisters; many were the presents she lavished on us, which we treated with all the carelessness of children. One in particular she gave me when I was nine years old. It was a watch of red enamel with pearls on either side which I should have been whipped for destroying recklessly as I did.

Guests would breakfast in the Great Hall at about half past ten, and shooting would begin at noon. If there were not too many guests, breakfast might take place in the Library, where the eating tables were often folding ones, so that they could easily be put up and taken down.

Walter once commented in his diary on 'the quantities of pheasants feeding quietly in the park little suspecting the tragedy that awaited them'. The sport which he was able to provide for his royal guests was, as he himself put it, 'most excellent'. However, he was often secretly critical of their shooting skills. One weekend, with three Dukes, of Gloucester, York and Wellington staying – who were privately referred to by their host as 'the Dukes, Royal and Hero' – Walter made the comment in his diary that 'gentlemen who shoot in *battues* should learn how to shoot, otherwise they wound pheasants and waste powder'. On another occasion in 1827 when the party included Prince de Polignac, the French Ambassador; Prince Leopold of the Belgians; Lord Salisbury and the Duke of Gloucester, the host's comment at the end of a day's shooting was 'Never saw the game more abundant, or the gunning worse'. Fortunately the shooting was better next day 'for the nerves of the party were better strung'.

It was usual for the largest weekend shooting parties to take place after Charlotte's annual New Year party held at Grosvenor Square. After three full days of shooting, the whole party would move on to Lord Bridgewater's house, Ashridge, for another *battue*. The women and children would drive over to Ashridge for the day and return home in time for dinner.

Each evening after dinner, the party would play simple card games. If the Duke of York was staying, the choice always fell on whist. The children would stay up late, and dance while their mother played the fiddle for them. Charlotte also sang duets with the Duchess of Gloucester, and as she grew up, Katty, the eldest Grimston daughter, also sang. There was always music when Charlotte was around, and the guests were often carried away and joined in too. In 1824 Prince Leopold was staying; Walter describes how he was playing cards, 'Charlotte sang and the Prince joined in with good voice and much taste.' On another occasion there was 'music triumphant! Lady V. at her music with Sir Gore Ouseley till I was quite tired of it!' On some occasions there was livelier entertainment, as in 1823 when the Duke of Gloucester joined in 'a foolish romping game with the young party, and ... under a misunderstanding, took the liberty of saluting Miss Paget, which highly offended her and some of the ladies. He did not know much of this at the time, but on its being talked about, he was hurt, and explained fully that he thought it was part of the game and was told to do so!'.

Not surprisingly, with such eminent guests, we find Walter paying his cook four guineas a week in the 1820s, an enormous sum for the time. The chief requirement he made of his cook, it would seem, was he should be able to 'dress turtle excellently'. Walter often referred to the cook as his *Maître d'Hotel* and, considering the number of guests he often had in the house, this would seem an apt description. At one time, however, Walter asked Mr. J.S. Story, his solicitor and agent, to investigate the running costs of the kitchen. He suspected that the cook was extorting large sums from the butcher and grocer in order to keep the profitable Gorhambury trade. 'I find the consumption of grocery in my kitchen prodigious' he wrote to Story. However, the investigation found that the cook received nothing beyond a present at Christmas, which was quite a normal custom.

Nevertheless, Gorhambury was not immune to servant problems. In 1824, for instance, the kitchen maid was detected in embezzlement, and there was a great row with the cook; Charlotte intervened, but with unfortunate results – '*ergo*', wrote Walter, 'I am in want of a cook'. Many of the other servants detested the butler, and yet Walter himself found him 'an excellent upper servant, his cellar keeping appears excellent'. A laundry maid created absolute panic in the household by developing a high fever, which Charlotte feared (wrongly, as it turned out) was infectious. The 'fool of a footman' got so drunk 'he could scarcely sit on the dickey' (the footman's seat on the carriage). The head gardener was 'so stupid' that Walter found him endlessly 'provoking'! Later in the year, matters had not improved. The footman had left, the poor laundry maid had died. The girls' new governess, Miss Parry, was 'ill-tempered' and 'showed want of conduct with her presumption'. The nursery maids were quarrelling with the *maître d'hotel*. In consultation with the butler, Walter drew up 'some regulations for the servants' hall, which I propose they shall in future abide by, or go'. This hall was at that time the enormous room with the coved ceiling, which is situated below the yellow drawing room.

1824 may also be cited as an example of the sort of life which Walter and his wife led in the 1820s. It began with one of Charlotte's great balls at Grosvenor Square, 'and a very pretty ball it was' he wrote. They did not go to bed until four in the morning. Walter 'rose late with a headache and was surprised to find the house all set to rights as if no ball had taken place, for which I give great credit to my servants. They must have sat up all night'. Next we find him paying a visit to the Duke of Wellington at Stratfield Saye. He arrived from London in time for breakfast, and found there his usual shooting friends – the Duke of York, Prince Leopold, the Marquesses of Hertford and Salisbury, Lord Palmerston, Mr. Arbuthnot, Sir John and Lady Shelly, and Count Lieven. The sport was excellent. Accompanied by Prince Leopold, 'who seemed to know a good deal about Old Masters', Walter examined Wellington's collection of pictures, which seemed to him disappointing after his own at Gorhambury. Nor did he like Stratfield Saye itself: he considered it 'unfit for his Grace's residence – the soil is too wet – the surrounding country not pleasant'.

However, he wrote enthusiastically 'oh! what a blaze of beauty!' when he beheld the glittering scene at a party held at the Duke's town residence of Apsley House in Piccadilly soon afterwards. That year the Duchess of Wellington held two music parties, both of which were attended by Walter and Charlotte. They heard 'Pasta, Rossini, Colbran, Romonor'. Giuditta Pasta was a Jewish opera singer, who had studied in Milan and had had a great success in Paris as well as London. At the second musical evening the King was present to hear 'Rossini at the pianoforte ... beautiful!' It is not surprising with Charlotte's love of music to find that the children's musical education was not neglected. Young Grimston accompanied his parents to hear Rossini and Angelica Catalani, another Italian singer. That spring Walter engaged a Mr. Lord to teach his daughter Katty to play the harp.

As always, Gorhambury saw many visitors that year. Among them were the 'Abercorn boys', who came to stay with the Grimston boys for the holidays. Walter noted that his daughter Emily, only nine years old, had fallen in love with one of them. 'Her dear little heart is gone to Abercorn' he wrote. Another guest at a Gorhambury party in the summer greatly attracted him. 'If I was young,' he wrote, 'I should decidedly fall in love with Lady Caroline Lamb, her singing is delightful and she is one of the most unaffected agreeable young ladies I have ever chanced to meet'. Perhaps therefore it would have gratified Walter, if he could have known that in 1971 Gorhambury would be the setting for the filming of Robert Bolt's production *Lamb*, the story of Lady Caroline's life?

The previous year Walter had become Lord Lieutenant of the County of Hertfordshire – a honour which, like his peerage, had come to him mainly through his wife's efforts. In June 1823 he noted that he had had 'accounts from Lady Verulam that Lord Salisbury was very ill and that she had made application to Lord Liverpool for the Lieutenancy in the County of Herts in case of his death'. Charlotte was definitely quick off the mark; Lord Salisbury was not yet dead. This was in fact the second time that she had written to her brother on the subject, for as early as February 1818 she wrote that 'I have reason to think Lord Salisbury's health is declining, and therefore the vacancy may not improbably take place in a short time, although it may be postponed for some years ... I hope I am not doing an improper thing in mentioning our wishes to you ... I can venture to affirm that he [Walter] would fulfil his duties conscientiously, and his residence being in a central situation, and possessing I believe the largest landed property in the county, &c. ...' When Lord Salisbury finally did die, Lord Liverpool acceded to his sister's request, and proposed Walter's name to the King. Walter was pleased, but he was far more reticent about the honour than his wife, who 'became annoyed that my appointment as Lieutenant of the County of Herts has not been Gazetted [announced in the newspapers]'. He wrote that she 'faggs' her brother 'to enquire why I am not Gazetted; she is very impatient'.

Walter proved to be a conscientious Lord Lieutenant, even missing the Newmarket Races when duty called. In 1824 we find him going into the City to buy a turtle for his 'entertainment to the judges on their circuit at Gorhambury', a task which fell to him in his new position. He also borrowed some plate from the silversmiths Rundell & Bridges 'for the same purpose' and thus loaded set off back to Gorhambury, his 'poor little victim the turtle' riding in the carriage with him. The reception went very well, he wrote subsequently, and the judges enjoyed their turtle.

In the autumn of 1824 he and Charlotte stayed at Lord Hertford's house at Sudbourn for a shooting party, on their way to Newmarket. They passed somewhat uncomfortable nights, the bed being, Walter wrote, 'decidedly too small for so large a pair'. However, he enjoyed his stay, for there was 'a hot sea bath in the house' of which he made use every day. At Christmas the house was full as usual, with the Gloucesters, the Clarendons, the Dowager Lady Salisbury, Lord and Lady Frederick Beauclerk, Mr. Sebright, his son and two daughters from Markyate, and Mr. and Mrs. Fremantle all staying. There was the usual Christmas dinner of venison for family and staff alike. 'It rained cats and dogs' all day. The party 'played whist for the Duke' and a game called 'snip snap' for the Duchess. In his diary, Walter asked once more that God should 'continue his protection'.

The Private Life of the First Earl

In 1819 Walter Grimston began to write a daily diary. It is a most remarkable record. He starts off by telling the reader that 'This book commenced on the first of January 1819 and will at least be a correct remembrancer of some things which passed during the time of which it treats. I do not mean it to sing my praises'. His diary offers us a surprisingly frank narrative of his personal life. Much is revealed about his thoughts and his character. It shows him to have been a deeply religious country landlord, something of a hypochondriac, with 'troublesome and frequent headaches' for which he was leeched and cupped almost weekly. After his wife and children, sporting pursuits were the great love of his life; hunting, racing, shooting. His life revolved around his estates at Gorhambury, Pebmarsh and Messing, and around the other country houses of the great, but above all amid the glittering world he had created at his London residence, the intimate friend of princes, dukes and earls. The pattern of his life was regulated, however, by the sporting calendar; Gorhambury for him was no more than a perfect backcloth for his thoroughbred horses, his strutting pheasants and his grazing deer.

He was devoted to his stately, clever wife, but it is amusing in the context of modern family planning to find how the appearance or non-appearance of what Walter invariably referred to as 'X' every month dominated his relationship with Charlotte. He makes observations such as 'On this day Charlotte expected X which did not arrive'. He leaves home for a few days and returns some days later to find that 'my dear Charlotte tells me that X is not yet arrived'. Once again he went away for a few days, returned again and this time records gloomily 'From the reports I hear I sadly fear my dear Char. is again in a family way as X is not yet arrived but as she is nursing [a baby] it may probably be some little irregularity and I pray God it may'. Four days later comes the entry 'passed the evening tête-a-tête with my dear Char. It would have been more comfortable if X had arrived'.

When Charlotte was proved to be pregnant – which frequently was the case – it often seemed to result in bickering between husband and wife. Walter refers to her coldly, no longer his 'poor dear Char.' but 'Lady V.' or even 'Lady Verulam'. During one pregnancy, he noted that after he had ridden to Hatfield 'to confer with Faithfull [the schoolmaster] about the boys' return to school' he was 'questioned, cross-questioned, and at last scolded by Lady V. In the evening got sulky, went to bed, shook hands with Lady V. and slept very ill'. Every month it was the same; the behaviour of X ruled his life. 'Alas! I am almost sure my poor dear wife is again with child, but God's will be done'. A week later: 'To my infinite delight Charlotte woke me to say that X was arrived. Thank God for this and all his mercies'.

Walter and Charlotte's first boy was born in February 1809 at the Grimston London establishment of 42, Grosvenor Square. Charlotte was unable to feed the baby, and the family's St Albans' doctor, Thomas Rogers, found a poor young woman, living with her mother and sister, who had just had a child of her own. Rogers arranged that this young woman should leave her own child in the care of its grandmother and should travel by coach to Grosvenor Square to feed the Grimston baby. Walter promised her 'a large gratuity' if all should go well. He was concerned for the well-being of the baby left behind, so Dr. Rogers arranged that milk from the Gorhambury farm should be provided; as the nursing mother's 'younger sister will walk to Gorhambury for some every morning, and as the child feeds remarkably well', he felt that his master should have no further cause for concern. To walk the two and a half miles out to Gorhambury and back again in bad February weather with poor shoes and by bad roads certainly merited 'a large gratuity' for the family, quite apart from the benefit of the life-giving mother's milk for the baby.

The child was named James Walter after his father, and was at first called Walter in the family: however, as he grew up he was generally known as 'Grimston'. In November 1809 Charlotte began a diary of her child's progress.

> November. Thurs. 9th. My dear little Walter cut his third and fourth teeth thank God without any suffering.
> December. Tues. 5th. My dear Walter cut his sixth tooth thank God without any illness. The weather very beautiful.

Charlotte found herself much tied to Gorhambury, and to the care of her baby. She recorded her gardening activities, the planting of hyacinths, roses and tulips around the house. On Walter's first birthday she wrote 'My dear little boy completed his first year this day. May God grant him many happy returns of it and above all make him a pious and good man'. The following year, on 18 April, she noted that 'at four o'clock on this morning, I was taken ill, and at eleven my dear little girl was born'. This was Katherine, immediately 'Katty' to her adoring father. Coming so soon after Walter, it is not surprising that she was a delicate baby. Her brother meanwhile was having trouble with his teeth; when they consulted the King's physician, Sir Henry Halford, he ordered that Walter should be weaned, much to Charlotte's distress.

In celebration of little Walter's third birthday, the servants had a dance in the evening. His mother noted that he was 'thank God, in perfect health and everything my heart could wish him to be'. Her third child, another boy, who was christened Edward Harbottle, was born on 2 April 1812: Charlotte described him as 'a very fine boy. May God graciously accept my humble and hearty thanks for so great a blessing'. Life continued on this pattern, with babies arriving almost annually. Henry Luckyn was born in 1813 and christened on 19 February at St Michael's; but on 7 May the following year, the happy diary she had kept so meticulously ends suddenly on a tragic note.

> On this day I had the severe misfortune of losing my dear little Henry. He breathed his last at about 12 after an illness of a week. None but a mother can conceive the anguish of

such a loss. Religious feelings and the blessings still left in my three darling remaining babes are a solace to even such a blow as this, though the regret and pain is most acute'.

At Gorhambury today there is a marble figure of a sleeping baby boy. One is bound to wonder after reading Charlotte's diary, whether it is a figure of her little Henry Luckyn on his deathbed?

As we have already seen, the north wing of the house had been built on between 1788 and 1790, and an upper story was now added to form extra nurseries. There seemed no doubt that this provision was necessary. Emily, a second daughter, had been born the year before in 1815, and another son, Robert, arrived in 1816. There were now five little Grimstons.

Charlotte had a 'perfect horror' of red hair, and was much distressed to find that two of her daughters were born with 'carrotty locks'. She tried everything to alter the colour; Katty's head was shaved twice, and later on both girls had their heads deluged in a preparation called 'Rowland's Macassar Oil'. Whether this really had any effect or not is unknown, but the girls' hair began to lose its brilliant tinge and by the time the eldest girl, Katty, 'came out', she had auburn hair, which was considered acceptable.

Grimston and Edward had their earliest lessons at home from Mr. Thomas Henderson. After this, Charlotte reluctantly allowed them to board at Mr. Francis Faithfull's school at Hatfield, which was also attended by the Cecil boys. 'The Reverend Mr. Faithfull is a good schoolmaster, able to preach a good sermon' wrote Walter in his diary. However, it was 'never a very pleasant excursion' for Charlotte when she had to take them back to school, and if she heard during term-time that one or the other had 'stomach pains' or 'the ear ache' she was off in her curricle at once to see them. In the holidays, Mr. Henderson, now taking clerical orders at Oxford, was engaged as a holiday tutor. He supervised lessons, took them swimming in the Pondyards, coached them in cricket which they played in front of the East Portico, and in wet weather, played billiards with them.

Katty, the eldest girl, was always delicate, and suffered some serious illness in 1816. With Robert still a baby, Charlotte had her hands full: Katty was sent to live with her aunts Harriot and Charlotte at Berkhamsted Castle, where they nursed her back to health. This visit inculcated in her a love of painting, as she watched the two ladies at work on their miniature portraits and water-colours. This was not the only occasion on which Walter's sisters helped their sister-in-law with her large and growing family: the children were frequently sent to stay either with them, or with their great aunts Frances and Charlotte Johanna, according to the time of year that the many confinements of their mother took place. The same year in which Katty was ill, and while little Robert was still in the cradle, another baby (Charles) was born.

Charlotte was a devoted mother, and constantly worried herself with fears about the two little boys away from her care at school. When Edward caught measles, one of the Gorhambury house-guests, Lord D'Acre, 'made himself an enemy in Lady V. by joking about the measles which he thinks nothing of.

Lady V. sillily violent afterwards with *me'*, her husband recorded with astonishment. Poor Lady Verulam. This was during her ninth pregnancy; she was no doubt feeling more edgy and apprehensive than usual, for she had already lost one child, and the sick boy, Edward, was always a favourite of hers. The baby she was carrying was born on 29 July 1820, and named Mary Augusta Frederica. Her godfather was the Duke of Gloucester, and her godmothers the Duchesses of Gloucester and Dorset, the latter being Charlotte's half-sister.

In 1823 young Grimston went to Harrow. At first sight Walter thought 'the accommodation for the boys very bad' but Mr. William Drury, Grimston's housemaster, assured him that 'parents see these things with different eyes from the boys themselves'. Walter was a tender-hearted father, and the thought of 'my boy being so uncomfortable' made him 'rather out of spirits'. However, when Charlotte visited the school and saw the accommodation 'she did not think so ill of Grim's room' as Walter had given her reason to suppose.

There could be no New Year's Ball at Gorhambury in 1825, for Charlotte was once more 'largely pregnant' as Walter put it. Grimston, Edward, Robert and Emily, however, all attended a 'delightful ball' given by Lady Cowper at Panshanger, and sat up very late. Katty did not go, since her governess had suggested that late nights were bad for her weak constitution. This sensible suggestion, although implemented, met with no thanks from Katty's father, who noted in his diary that 'It is curious how ill-judging Lady Katherine's governess has been about this said ball'. Early in January the family set off for Grosvenor Square, where Charlotte was to give birth. Emily, Katty and Mary were packed off to stay at Berkhamsted Castle with their aunts. 'I trust in God he will give my dear wife a safe delivery' Walter wrote; in the event Charlotte had such a quick delivery that the baby – another daughter, who was to be named Jane – was delivered by a servant called Mary Gosford before the doctor had arrived. Jane's godfather was the Duke of York, the Regent's brother.

With the children growing up, Walter found himself in ever deeper financial waters. Snow, his banker, who had previously been 'so accommodating', wrote him 'an unpleasant letter' in January 1826. The girls were now at their most expensive age: the cost of 'bringing them out', which involved parties, dinners, ball gowns and all sorts of incidental expenses, was overshadowed by the ominous thought of the dowries they would need should they become engaged to be married. In addition, Walter had undertaken a series of expensive alterations at Gorhambury, both to the house and to the gardens, which will be more fully described below. However, it is undeniable that all these expenses were as nothing, as we shall see, besides the enormous sums consumed by Walter's leading passion – the Turf.

In 1827 Walter thought for a while that some of his financial problems were to be solved. In September Charlotte's mother, the Dowager Lady Liverpool, died suddenly. While Walter and Charlotte were both sincerely distressed by this, they naturally expected a legacy of some sort would be coming to them.

However, when Walter attended the funeral on 10 October, he noted significantly in his diary that his brother-in-law Cecil Jenkinson was perhaps 'somewhat less distant in his behaviour to me'. Something had happened between Charlotte and her brother; there had been a family quarrel. As time went on, Charlotte became increasingly irritated with her brother 'who has not yet sent her any account of her mother's will'. Walter wrote to Cecil on the subject, and in reply 'received a very cool letter ... enclosing a copy of Lady Liverpool's will, under which he proposes to acquire all her personalty [personal fortune]. Horror!!!'. On the recommendation of his solicitor, Mr. Story, Walter decided to take an 'opinion' on the will; in fact he took not one opinion but three, from Sir William Tindall, Lord Broderick and Dr. Lushington, all of whom agreed – that, as Walter put it bitterly, 'Cecil must walk over the course without opposition'.

In 1828 Lord Liverpool died at Hawkesbury. He had suffered a paralytic stroke in 1827, but had seemed to be on the road to recovery when death intervened. Walter and his sons Grimston and Edward attended the funeral, of which he wrote 'Few were there except the paid servant of the undertaker. The greatest statesman of the age went thus to the grave. Lord Liverpool [the dead man's son], Lord Verulam and two sons, Sir W. Boothby and two sons, Mr. Holford, Mrs. Willimot, Major & Mrs. Chester. Alas! no opening to reconciliation took place at this awful ceremony. On the contrary, [Cecil Jenkinson] maintained a harsh, unbending demeanour. I thank God I did not feel animosity. I would have rejoiced in again seizing his hand but it was not proffered'. On the way back from the funeral Walter had the happy thought of calling in at Hatfield, where they were received kindly by Lord Salisbury. He gave the boys 'five very fine carp' which were 'put into the dickey of the phaeton and travelled well to Gorhambury' where they were immediately popped into Brick Kiln Pond. When the Prime Minister's will was read, again Walter and Charlotte's expectations were dashed.

Four years earlier Walter had already become so worried about money that he had hastily drawn up his will. He found that he was 'made miserable about it, which not having looked over for years, I find I would, had I died suddenly, have left dear Lady Verulam what her poor father called her long ago – comparatively a beggar. Lost no time in altering it. Very uneasy all day, and headache in the evening which lasted all night'. Comparatively a beggar? It was an interesting statement. Prior to their marriage, Walter's father had commented on the comparative amounts to be contributed to the young couple's income by himself and Charlotte's father. 'Should Lord Liverpool be prevailed upon hereafter to act up to his proposal for the convenience and comfort of his daughter, I will readily comply with it, and exert myself to meet him half way; but if not we must stand as we are, Lord Liverpool at £300 per annum and I at £2,200, which on the face of it does not appear to do us discredit'.

Walter poured out his anxieties to his wife. 'Dear Charlotte was so kind I quite hate myself for ever having so far forgotten to make her comfortable in the event of my death. I trust however I have now done so, though I am aware that my fortune will have a greater burthen attached to it for this [present baby on the way] and for younger children's maintenance. Grimston must be prudent and if possible and if compatible with his happiness marry a woman with money'. Upon thinking it over, Charlotte became alarmed 'lest my will should be rendered abortive by not being legally executed'. It was, Walter commented, 'as if she thought me about to die'. Early next morning, after a sleepless night for both of them, he galloped down to St. Albans to ensure that 'Mr. Story gets the will quickly and properly finalised'.

Chapter Twelve

Two Portraits

Before we return to Walter and Charlotte themselves, however, we may
pause to meet Walter's uncle, the Reverend Harbottle Grimston, and his
unmarried sister, Frances Cooke Grimston. Both were important members of
the family. Born in 1752, Harbottle was destined for the church from an early
age. He became a Doctor of Divinity, and later, in April 1788, his father gave
him the living of Pebmarsh in Essex. This living had come to the Grimstons
through their inheritance of the Luckyn family lands, and the family
continued to present incumbents there until the pastoral reorganisation
scheme of the 1970s. As we have seen already in Chapter 8, William Grimston,
James Grimston's second brother, had been left the Bucknall estate at Oxhey
on condition that he took the name 'Bucknall'. His uncle, John Bucknall, in
making this bequest, specified that if William did not leave an heir – which
was to be the case – then the property should go to the next brother, who was
Harbottle, with the same proviso, that the name 'Bucknall' should be
adopted. Thus Harbottle Grimston became Harbottle Bucknall.

A shy man, he remained a bachelor. He wanted to marry very much, but
found great difficulty in expressing his feelings to any young lady he wished
to approach on the subject. A story is told, for instance, of his odd behaviour
on one such occasion. Harbottle owned a dog, named Wolf, of whom he was
very fond: thought him a splendid creature. Harbottle went to the young
lady, and asked, stuttering, whether she would 'like to have my dog Wolf?'
Puzzled, she replied that she would not dream of taking his favourite animal
from him. Harbottle then tried to explain his real intentions, which came as a
great shock after this curious way of broaching the subject! Not surprisingly,
he was rejected.

During the years that he was at Pebmarsh, two or three of his five sisters
would often stay with him there. The girls had inherited red hair, and must
have been conspicuous on their walks round the village. Late at night,
Harbottle would go about his parish and take note of those who sat up late
burning candles or lamps in their cottages: he would severely reprimand them
by name from his pulpit the next Sunday, for keeping late hours. After he
changed his name to Bucknall, he had occasional lapses of memory and
signed the register 'Harbottle Grimston'; once at least he signed himself
'Harbottle Pebmarsh'! He started a Bible Association in his parish in 1814,

whereby poor people could buy Bibles and prayer books cheaply by subscribing only a penny a month. The accounts of this Association are still in existence at Pebmarsh. Harbottle also founded a Sunday School, and did not confine himself to instructing the children in religion: he also taught them to read and write. The cost of the books, the small salaries of the teachers, and the maintenance of the schoolroom were all met by voluntary contributions, augmented later on by a legacy Harbottle was to make to the village.

Towards the end of his life, Harbottle deteriorated both physically and mentally, and he became a great trial to his family and his parishioners, who were sincerely attached to this kindly if eccentric man. In Walter's diary of 1 March 1819, he noted that he 'Went to Essex. Found Mr. Bucknall very much debilitated.' However, on the very next day we read that 'Mr. Bucknall insists on walking from Pebmarsh to Messing', doubtless intending to view the family property there. It was a journey of at least 13 miles, and it is not surprising to discover that the stubborn old man 'appeared very weak after his walk'. The next year, Walter found Mr. Bucknall 'much more infirm', and by 1821 he had to be nursed by his two spinster sisters, Frances and Charlotte Johanna Grimston, at their home in London. On 10 December 1821, Walter 'found my aunts in a woeful state … quite worn out with nursing Mr. Bucknall'. By the end of the month, he noted that he had 'administered comfort to my aunts, in their distress on Harbottle's account, who appears to have totally lost his intellect, but I should think likely to linger on some time'. And linger he did: death did not come for him until 28 January 1823, at Richmond in Surrey, where the sisters had bought a small country cottage which gave their demented brother privacy and seclusion.

Whilst dealing with his uncle's financial affairs during the latter's last months during 1822, Walter happily noted in his diary that he had 'found his uncle Harbottle's accounts in a prosperous state, having no less than £8,000 in his banker's hands'. When he heard of 'poor Harbottle's death by express from Richmond', Walter went to London 'to make as many arrangements as I could in poor Harbottle's business, found nothing of consequence at Snows [the bankers] excepting a very large balance … Opened a box of Harbottle's in which we found an account book that gives us a good insight to the property he has left. It will amount to a very large sum' he wrote expectantly.

However, Walter was in for a shock. After the funeral, which took place at Oxhey church on 5 February 1823, the reading of the old man's will took place, and Walter was tremendously disappointed to find that Harbottle left his possessions to be divided amongst his five sisters, and nothing at all to his nephew, who was, however, appointed as executor. Walter even had to find £555 out of his own pocket to make good dilapidations to the rectory at Pebmarsh. He was deeply disappointed, and wrote pained and resentful letters to his nephew Thomas Estcourt, and to his aunt Frances, who, with her sister Charlotte Johanna, had nursed Harbottle in his declining years. 'My dear Fanny', Walter wrote:

13. Medallion head of a Roman Emperor (Julius
Caesar?) from the portico of the Tudor Gorhambury.
(9 ins. diameter.)

14. A portrait bust of Pope Clement XIV (Ganganelli),
who received James Bucknall Grimston in audience;
the work of the sculptor Christopher Hewetson.

15. (*above*) Berry Hill, near Dorking, Surrey, the home of the Walter family. A pencil drawing, very possibly the work of Harriot Grimston (née Walter).

16. (*below*) Oxhey Place, Hertfordshire, willed by John Bucknall, brother of the 2nd Viscountess Grimston, to his nephew William Grimston.

17. (*opposite above*) Miss Charlotte Grimston, sister of the 1st Earl of Verulam; a lithograph from a drawing by I. Jeffroy.

18. (*opposite below*) A water colour drawing of Gorhambury as she knew it by lady Katherine Grimston, eldest daughter of the 1st Earl of Verulam (reproduced by permission of the Marquess of Salisbury).

1. (*opposite above*) The Gorhambury fire engine, purchased by the 1st Earl of Verulam.

2. (*opposite below*) Varennes, the 1st Earl's most successful racehorse, with William Corringham, the head groom: in oils by Bristowe.

3. (*above*) James Walter, 2nd Earl of Verulam as a boy.

4. (*right*) Lady Katherine 'Katty' Grimston, later Countess of Clarendon: a pencil drawing by H. Hawkins.

25. (*top left*) Lady Emily Mary Grimston, later Countess of Craven: a pencil drawing by H. Hawkins.

26. (*below left*) Lady Mary Augusta Frederica Grimston, later Countess of Radnor: an engraving by H. B. Hall after a portrait by John Hayter.

27. (*below*) The Hon. Charles Grimston, fourth son of the 1st Earl of Verulam, a pencil drawing by H. Hawkins.

I hope I dare not suffer a disappointment, which I ought not at this moment to feel (having long known the outline of Mr. B.'s disposal of his property) betray one in to any expression of unkindness, or anything which might make you, or Charlotte, suppose I should repine at the duty that has been imposed upon me, but you must allow, that it is an irksome task, to act as sole executor to a man, who has disinherited one. He gives the strongest marks of his confidence, and at the same time inflicts the severest punishment he is able. The consolation I have is, that I neither have, nor will deserve it, but I cannot help feeling that my children have some reason to complain, as I do, and as you might, that for generations, the same inexplicable line of conduct has been pursued, which has reduced the family from the highest rank among the rich nobility of the county, to one of comparative poverty. But let me not be misunderstood; if you and Charlotte had received the whole of poor Harbottle's large fortune for *your joint lives*, I should have been delighted. I acknowledge your prior claim, and should have applauded the disposition. I should not have thought it wise to have given a share of it, even for a life interest, to the married ladies [his other aunts], though perhaps his natural affection for his sisters might have induced him to do so, and ought not to be too severely scanned; but I think it absolutely unjust to give it them in perpetuity, it is enriching Estcourts, and Hales and Wardes, at the expense of Grimstons. And now my dear Fanny, that I have told you what I think upon this subject, I must congratulate you on the extent of the share you will possess, I wish most ardently it had been a half, instead of a fifth, and you shall never hear another angry or disappointed word escape my mouth about it.

Miss Frances Grimston replied to her nephew's letter with understanding and tact:

I most sincerely grieve at the subject of your letter and do most truly admit the justice of your complaint, but for our poor brother's past errors I can only repine and lament that his want of judgment in the distribution of his effects has deprived you of your natural expectations and caused you a cruel disappointment. I am confident that if he had been less mysterious about his affairs all his life, he might have understood the seeming injustice of enriching other families to the detriment of yours hereafter. For my *own personal* concern, I am very much satisfied that he made his arrangements as we find them though so different from your conjecture and previous statement. For your sake I wish he had allotted a larger sum to my disposal with better judgment and if it amounted to a tithe that I wish you, I think you would not have been disappointed. I wish I could assist in relieving you from the troublesome business that you are now engaged in, your labours would be joyfully shared by your most truly affectionate Aunt F. Grimston.

It was Frances Cooke Grimston (who was given the second name Cooke after her grandmother Jane Cooke, wife of the 1st Viscount), who kept the valuable records of the Grimston family which are so useful for the historian of today. Frances was born in 1757 and lived to the great age of 90; thus she outlived the whole of her own generation of the family and almost the whole of the next. She was thus well-placed to record, as she did, the dates of births, marriages, deaths, and any other details of her family and friends, in a small red-covered notebook.

She was a woman of remarkable strength of personality: at the age of 81 she set in motion the building of a new house for herself, near the ancient site of the nunnery of St Mary le Pré, not far from Bacon's Pondyards. The book in which she kept her accounts for the building work also contains a loose sheet of paper from a letter to her sister Susanna Warde:

> When I began my building I was in great affliction. I considered that if I did not enter into
> some occupation to divert my mind and oblige me to exert myself with some weighty
> concern, it would naturally increase upon me, & I should become an annoyance to myself
> and everybody belonging to me. From Lord Verulam's affectionate kindness [her nephew
> Walter], he assisted me, and though in the first instance, I proposed only to throw away a
> few hundreds in building a *cottage*, it is now become a habitable mansion, which with
> humble gratitude to almighty God I am now enjoying in health and surrounded by him
> and his young family, who evince their kindness to me in every act of attention and seem
> pleased with everything I do at the Pré, with these happy impressions I ought to be
> thankful and satisfied.

This letter is dated 1842. Frances had begun work on the Pré in 1838. The
'great affliction' to which she referred was undoubtedly the death of her sister
Charlotte Johanna the previous year: the two unmarried sisters had lived their
lives together, shared the care of their brother Harbottle, and Frances missed
her very much.

Even if Frances's handwriting was not quite as steady as it had once been,
her brain was acute and active despite her advanced age. A Mr. Wright was
responsible for carrying out most of the building work. For the two years from
July 1838 to August 1840, she noted 'accounts settled' as £4,139. In January
1841, there was a thunderstorm which necessitated repairs to the roof costing
£50, added to which was the cost of a tarpaulin 'for covering the roof £7'. Bills
for further work after 1841 amounted to £1,908.2s.4d. The cost of building the
stables and a hothouse between 1841-7 came to £533.9s.4d.

In 1839 we find her purchasing furniture for the house: chimney pieces,
card-tables, looking-glasses, kitchen furniture, flower-stands, a pestle and
mortar, a 'Pembroke table', a dining-table and a bed for a servant, all of which
came to £790.2s.3d. Frances was determined to have a beautiful garden at her
new house, and spent £1,609.11s.0d on gravel, plants, shrubs, paving, seats
and 'a virenda'. In all, it would seem that the old lady spent £9,037.4s.11d. on
the Pré – a dramatic investment in a project undertaken to stop her brain
declining into self-pity and introversion. From the papers which survive, it is
clear that Frances became, indeed, a little carried away by her building
activities, and had to turn to her nephew Walter for assistance. Walter was
sympathetic to his aunt's difficulties, but he himself, as we shall see, was
extravagant by nature and had no money to spare. However, he came up with
a plan; that Frances should hand over the whole of her property and fortune
to him, and he would pay her in return a 'large annuity' of £1,512.9s.6d.
yearly or £756.4s.9d. half yearly. This annuity was continued after Walter's
death by his son. Just before her own death, Frances wrote to her
great-nephew releasing him from 'his debts' to her. 'Be assured', she wrote, 'I
do this with the greatest pleasure and on mature reflection'.

The Pré House has been let as an hotel since the mid 20th century, but still
belongs to Gorhambury. It was built on the foundations of an old inn, and the
cellars have places for the storage of wine and beer. After Frances's death, the
house was altered and added to in the 1880s by the Toulmin family, who lived
there for many years.

Frances wrote her will in her own quaking hand, despite her great age. Her sight was failing, for the writing is very large and occasionally she writes one line on top of another. It reads as follows:

I, Frances Cooke Grimston, request to be buried in the same vault in which my sister Charlotte Johanna Grimston is buried, in St Michael's Church, St Albans. I will and direct that my personal property shall be disposed of in the form following. I bequeath to my sister Mary Hale Charlotte's work box studded with gold beads, the bracelet of my three sister's hair linked together to my sister, the Viscountess Grimston's legacy to me. [This refers to Harriot, the 3rd Viscountess]. I bequeath to my great-nephew Robert Grimston £1,000; I bequeath to my great nephew Charles Grimston £1,000; I bequeath to my great nephew and godson £10,000 in the three per cent Consols. I bequeath to my niece Harriot Grimston, as much, and her choice of, any of my plate. I do appoint my great nephew the Earl of Verulam my residuary legatee and do also appoint him sole executor to this my last will and testament to which I put my hand this 26th day of November, 1845.

Her great nephew noted her death in his diary on 3 January 1848 – 'Aunt Fanny's death at 12 at night'.

As well as the £10,000 in three per cent Consols, it will be noted that Frances left all her remaining estate to her great nephew, the Earl. It was thus the main branch of the Grimston family which ultimately benefited from the legacy which the Reverend Harbottle Bucknall had made to his sisters.

"The Great Aunts"

9. *A sketch by William, Earl of Radnor, grandson of the 1st Earl of Verulam, of two unnamed Grimston 'great-aunts'. They could be Frances Cooke Grimston and her sister Charlotte Johanna, or Harriot and Charlotte Grimston, sisters of the 1st Earl of Verulam (reproduced by permission of the Dowager Countess of Radnor).*

Chapter Thirteen
The Pleasures of the Turf

Walter had had turf mania since early manhood. Before he married Charlotte, he lived for the most part in Grosvenor Square, keeping his horses, however, at Gorhambury, together with the servants he felt were needed to look after them. When he was 25 his father felt it was necessary to write to Walter on the subject of his extravagance.

> A report prevails among the servants at this place [Gorhambury] that you pay board wages to your servants notwithstanding they live at Gorhambury and have always done so; and, in confidence, I have been desired to enquire of you this fact to prevent, if it should be so, such an enormous imposition and extravagance. From motives of delicacy, I have never wished to look into your expenditure, but it would show a very blameable indifference did I not hint to you that I think the expenses of your stable much beyond common means, and I am induced to observe this with much feeling and reluctance by the appearance of an additional groom yesterday who claimed the conduct of your horses. *Nil nimis** is a good maxim: I hope you will take the quotation in the friendly manner it is meant and believe me to be your most affectionate father G.
>
> [* A proverb from the Latin author Terence, literally meaning 'don't be extravagant']

The 1820s were the years of Walter's greatest achievements in the world of racing. His newly-built stud farm at Gorhambury, his stable yard at Newmarket, his thoroughbreds – all were flourishing under the control of his stud trainer, William Corringham. In his diary, Walter described himself as being 'very well pleased with the appearance of things'. On fine mornings he would take a gallop in Gorhambury park with his stable boys, and would watch them 'sweat' the fillies. All the names of his racehorses began with the initial V. They included Varennes, Vates, Vapor, Varga, Vanillas, Vaurien, Veterinarian, Vittoria, Vittelina, and Verbena. However, he had many other horses – Sporus, his prized 'Rubens filly', Philip, his own 'nag', who carried him about Gorhambury and St Albans; and Gallipot, 'as slow as a top'. Walter's racing colours were white and black, with yellow down the seams and a black cap.

In 1820 at the Hoo Races, which were held annually on Lord D'Acre's land at Kimpton Hoo, Walter's horse Veterinarian won the Maiden Stakes, and later the same year won twice at Ascot. Walter proudly described the horse as 'my three-year-old, the subject of some envy to the Gentlemen of the Turf'. The following year was to be even more successful. At the Hoo Races, Veterinarian came in second for the Cup and was entitled to 'double stakes', while at Newmarket Varennes won the Gold Cup Race, which brought Walter the prize of 100 guineas. He decided to have the horse painted, and by December a Mr. Bristowe, a painter from Eton whose work Walter had admired, was engaged to paint Varennes. This picture, showing the horse with the stud trainer William Corringham holding his bridle, and Gorhambury in the background, still hangs in the house today as a reminder of those extravagant days when life seemed to revolve around racing. There are also two silver-mounted inkpots, made from Varennes' hoofs.

It is sad to read in Walter's diary a month later, in January 1822, that 'Corringham committed suicide...The poor man was well and in spirits at 4 o'clock yesterday when he showed off the stud with great good humour and pleasantry. At 10 he rushed uncalled, unprepared, into the presence of his God'. The guests to whom Corringham had shown the horses included the Duke of York, the Duke of Wellington, the Duke and Duchess of Gloucester, and Lord and Lady Londonderry, who were present as part of a large house-party down from London for the shooting season. With this party taking place, it was considered singularly bad timing on Corringham's part to make his sudden departure. Eventually the Coroner was to bring in a verdict of accidental death – a verdict which permitted the unfortunate man's body to lie in holy ground. Could it be that Corringham's hard work and devotion as a trainer had received too little recognition? He had written his master what Walter described as 'a capricious foolish letter', to which he admitted to himself he had replied 'angrily'. At Ascot, although the horses were all in good condition, Corringham himself had been 'in a foolish jealous humour, without the slightest foundation'.

Greatly upset by the whole affair, Walter decided on the spur of the moment to sell his horses. He went off the next day to Tattersall's, the major horse dealers in the country, to see 'about receiving some horses for sale on Thursday next' and gave orders to his servants 'for clearing out all the nags, some to Tattersall's and some to Newmarket'. However, when he went again to Tattersall's on 13 February, he found to his annoyance that 'not one shilling had been bid for any of my horses. *Provoking.*' He found himself going about 'trying to dispose of my horses without success'. Despite this attempt to cut down his stable, he had by no means lost interest in racing, for in the same diary entry he notes that he had 'named Sporus for the Cup at the Hoo to the surprise of the knowing ones'.

Eventually the clouds lifted; some of his horses were taken by Lord D'Acre and others were sent to Newmarket, where Walter was in the process of establishing a new yard under Colonel Synge, who came from Exning in Suffolk. In April he entered several horses at the Hoo Races; first 'Vapour began the amusements of the day by winning the County Stakes, beating seven others' and then, just as he had foretold to the 'knowing ones' in February, 'Sporus won the Gold Cup'. Finally, Vapour won the Maiden Stakes; all in all, it was not surprising that Walter and his family went home highly delighted. At Newmarket shortly afterwards, 'Sporus won his match against Antigallican', and in June he sold the horse to a Mr. Peel. Although the year had started so badly, and Charlotte was once again pregnant (with their ninth child), it was now proving to be one of unusual gaiety – and extravagance. At the Derby there was 'an amazing assemblage on the racecourse. I think even London must appear deserted. H.R.H. the Duke of York won the Derby, which delighted everybody who did not lose upon the race'. After dinner Charlotte and Walter went to 'His Majesty's party at Carlton House, where everything was magnificence and splendour. After Carlton House, to Devonshire House, where the Duke had a grand party and some capital music'. It seems extraordinary to find that three of the Grimston children – little Grimston, Edward and Emily – were invited to the royal Carlton House party; delicate Katty could not go. 'My three children looked very nice and appeared delighted with their evening entertainment' Walter wrote proudly. Poor Charlotte, once more 'in her present situation' was not able to attend all the functions of the season.

Walter considered his to be a 'well-regulated family' but the children kept amazingly late hours and ate far too much rich food. The high living and the perpetual social round upset his own digestion, and if he found it gave him stomach upsets, what can it have done to the children? Walter often notes that he was feeling 'headachey and uncomfortable' and in such circumstances, he would summon 'Minors the cupper to take some blood from my back'.

His appetite for the social whirl was undiminished by such problems, however. That year, at an 'excessively hot' Ascot, Walter was a guest, with the Dukes of Rutland and Portland, of the Duke of York. 'It is impossible to say how obliging the kind H.R.H. the Duke of York made himself to all his party. The Duke is fond of whist, and plays rather too deep to give me amusement, so I retired to my room about half after 12'.

Walter took a particular interest in the welfare of his little stable boys. In December 1822 he ordered 'great coats for my racing stable boys', and noted that he had 'walked down to St Albans to ask if Mrs. Orme had considered of my enquiries for a man who could teach my little racing boys to read and write'. She recommended one Mr. Monk, and two days later he was engaged as schoolmaster for the stable lads. He was the son of the parish clerk of St Michael's, and lived in Oaken House in St Michael's Street. He was a bootmaker by trade, and we find receipts from him for boot repairs amongst the Gorhambury accounts. Having found his schoolmaster, Walter regularly made enquiries of 'my little school at the racing stables and found it going on very well; the boys attentive; bought some spelling books for them'. Mr. Monk was paid 12s.6d. a week.

It was at about this time that we find a groom by the name of Cotton has appeared in the Gorhambury stables. The Cotton family connection with the racing world was to be of long standing. Another family which was to be closely associated with the business were the Nashs. Walter noted that Charles Nash, 'a great acquisition', had been installed at his Newmarket yard. This family later moved to Gorhambury, where a son, Henry Nash, became coachman. It was from him that the second lodge on Gorhambury Drive – 'Nash's Lodge' – acquired its name.

When Walter's financial affairs became catastophically entangled in the 1830s, it was to Richard Cotton that he wrote, to tell him of his decision to give up his Newmarket racing establishment. On 2 August 1835, he wrote:

> I grieve to say that it is become absolutely incumbent on me to give up my racing establishment. Many circumstances have contributed to this, but the great defalcation in the payment of my rents has principally caused the necessity. I cannot inform you of this without at the same time acknowledging the faithfulness with which you have served me for so many years and the right you have to expect from me a retiring pension. There are other things to attend to, which we must consider of, when I come down to Newmarket in October. In the meantime I shall advertise my horses for sale ...'

Cotton wrote his master this very sympathetic reply:

> I cannot express to your Lordship my feeling in reading your letter of yesterday to find you are necessitated to give up an amusement that you are fond of and am still more at a loss to find words to express my gratitude to your Lordship for the benevolence you have always shewed towards me and my family and trust and hope something may turn up for the future support of a large and young family. I am glad to say the horses are well except now and then a cough but nothing of consequence. I am, my Lord, your dutiful servant, Richard Cotton.

He added, however, 'I will thank your Lordship to send me some money'. The small well-worn personal account book that Walter surely kept folded in his pocket shows that Cotton had received £100 every two months. The same pocket book reveals that in 1845 – ten years later – Cotton was still in his employ, now living at Gorhambury, but receiving only £50 every two months.

Walter's love-affair with the Turf, however, was in reality far from ended. Not quite two years after he had found it essential to give up his Newmarket racing establishment, Walter made a startling offer to the Hertfordshire Hunt Dinner Committee, in a letter to their chairman:

> A report has so long been prevailing that Lord D'Acre wishes to discontinue the races which he has for many years kindly allowed to take place in his park at the Hoo, that I cannot but suppose that there must be some foundation to it. If this is correct, I beg to offer Gorhambury Park for the purpose. This year I have not had time to put it into that order for racing, which I shall endeavour to do for future occasions. At the same time I wish to state that I do not make this offer unless it is clearly understood that Lord D'Acre wishes the races to be discontinued at the Hoo.

Flat racing under under Jockey Club rules had long been established in Hertfordshire since the early years of the 18th century – it had taken place at Barnet, at Lord Melbourne's Brocket Hall, and at Nomansland near Wheathampstead as well as at Lord D'Acre's Kimpton Hoo. The type of racing which Walter, however, proposed to institute at Gorhambury was steeplechasing. It is probable that this idea was first put into his mind through his acquaintance with a well-known trainer, Thomas Coleman. Coleman's version of steeplechasing was not in the modern form, the jumping of hurdles, sham brooks and artificial fences, but held over hedges, ditches and streams in open country. Before 1830, there had been some races across country, and one small sweepstake had been held in Leicestershire.

GORHAMBURY RACES—

10. *A scene at the races in Gorhambury Park, May 1844 (reproduced by permission of the Illustrated London News)*

ETCH IN THE PARK.

St ALBANS GRAND STEEPLE CHASE,
— March 8.th 1832. —
PLATE 1. PREPARING TO START.
The Turf Hotel, with the Horses and their Riders going to the field, preceded by G. Osbaldeston Esqr. Umpire and Mr Coleman Clerk of the Chase.
DEDICATED TO THE GENTLEMEN OF THE St ALBANS STEEPLE CHASE, BY THEIR OBLIGED SERVANT, J. MOORE, and Published at his Picture Frame Manufactory, West Street, 87 Martins Lane

11. *Horses and riders competing in the St Albans Steeplechase assemble outside Thomas Coleman's Turf Hotel, in 1832.*

According to the account of Walter's son Robert (a great racing man himself), it was Coleman who first developed the sport of steeplechasing on a large scale, and it was at Gorhambury that the first major steeplechases were held – the forerunners of the Grand National. According to Robert Grimston, the idea of steeplechasing had originated from some officers of the 1st Life Guards, who were at dinner in the *Turf Tavern*, and they commissioned Coleman to put their ideas into execution.

Coleman had already achieved success as a trainer and as a jockey when he took a lease of the *Chequers* public house in the middle of Chequer Street, St Albans. He pulled that house down and replaced it by a new one, the *Turf Tavern*. Later this was renamed the *Turf Hotel*, and after a visit by Queen Victoria (when she stopped to change horses), it was renamed once again, this time becoming the *Queen's Hotel*. At the back there was a spacious yard, around which Coleman built enough loose-boxes to house 40 horses. On one occasion, William IV's pack of staghounds were housed there, and the whole retinue of men, horses, hounds and deer made the Tavern their headquarters for a fortnight. The inn was pulled down in the early 1980s.

Coleman had long been acquainted with Walter Grimston as a patron of the Turf, and for some years he had been permitted to exercise his horses in Gorhambury park. It seems likely, therefore, that it was he who first suggested the idea of Gorhambury Races. It does seem remarkable that Walter was happy to offer to make the park available for a full-scale race meeting over two or three days, with the inevitability of lavish expenditure on entertaining royalty and other wealthy friends, at a time when his financial resources were so strained. Lord Melbourne, the former Prime Minister, had found to his cost just how expensive such an undertaking could be when he had allowed races to take place at Brocket Hall.

Nevertheless, the scheme went ahead. There could be no doubt that, putting aside the question of the cost, Gorhambury provided an ideal setting for such an occasion, with its well-drained parkland and its beautiful surroundings. The construction of the course involved the removal of some standing timber and some building work, of stands and so on. The first meeting took place on the 22nd and 23rd of May, 1838. In those days, Gorhambury's distance from London made sure that the attendance was select. Walter's guests included leading members of the Jockey Club, his royal racing friends, as well as many of his own relatives and friends. The Gorhambury races were a success from the start. They were held in May, between the Newmarket Second Spring Meeting and the Epsom Derby Meeting, at a time when the old oaks and chestnuts in the park where in the full beauty of their fresh spring foliage. There could have been few more beautiful race courses in the world. The track was an oval, left-hand, course, about two miles in circumference, finishing with a straight five furlong, 136 yards, which formed the course for the Two-Year-Old Race, which, according to Robert Grimston, was the leading feature of the races. This race was held on each day of the meeting, and Walter's entrants for it included Maid of Orleans and Robert de Gorham. There were also races for 'gentlemen riders'; Lord Glamis, afterwards the Earl of Strathmore, rode his maiden race at Gorhambury. Invariably, Robert Grimston notes, Thomas Coleman was there in all his glory wearing a blue coat with brass buttons, a buff waistcoat, a white necktie, and 'kerseymere' breeches and gaiters.

The success of the steeplechase delighted the townspeople of St Albans. The hoteliers (who charged a guinea a bed), and the shopkeepers all flourished on the influx of visitors. However, not everyone was happy with the new institution. It was Walter's intention that the race meeting should always be held on a Tuesday and a Wednesday, to allow Monday for the final erection of refreshment tents, betting booths and so on, thus leaving Sunday free. Despite these laudable intentions, he did not escape criticism. The Rector of St Peter's church, St Albans, the Reverend H.N. Dudding, wrote to him on 29 April 1844:

My Lord,
I do not believe that you, your Lordship, are acquainted with the following facts which
have been brought to me on credible authority. In your Lordship's park, booths were put
up on the Sabbath Day preceding the races. There was drunkenness with fighting in the
park on the Sunday in the year 1842. The publicans of St Albans consider Sunday as one
of their best day. I do not believe that your Lordship as Lord Lieutenant (the *Custos
Morum*) of the County is aware of these things. I believe them to be facts, which are
currently reported here. As a minister of God, I respectfully draw your attention to them.
If they are not facts I trust that the cause which has induced me to write will hold me
excused in your Lordship's sight.

Walter replied as follows:

Sir,
I should be sorry if I thought that through my means the Sabbath was desecrated in the
park at Gorhambury and I am confident that no such circumstances have taken place but
that some officious person has misrepresented the case to you. The races have been put
off to Tuesday on purpose to avoid interfering with the Sunday. In respect of
drunkenness and fighting I don't believe a word of it, for the liquor would not have been
brought up the Sunday to get ready before the assemblage of the races on Tuesday nor
have I ever seen the people there before Tuesday morning.

He added cuttingly:

You are mistaken very much in supposing that I am *Custos Morum* [guardian of morals] of
the county. I would give up the Lord Lieutenancy sooner than undertake that task. I am
Custos Rotulorum [guardian of the archives] but not *Custos Morum*.

By 1844 the railway had come to Watford, making Gorhambury more
accessible to the race-lovers from London. They rode or took coaches from
Watford to Gorhambury. According to the *Illustrated London News* of May that
year 'the sport, the fashion of the company and the courteous attendance of
stewards and their officers to their respective duties – everything was in
keeping with the established character of the meeting'. During the eight years
in which the races were in existence, Walter consistently headed the list of
winners. The last steeplechase at Gorhambury was held in 1845: that autumn
Walter died, and an extraordinary chapter in the house's history was closed.

Chapter Fourteen

Daily Life at Gorhambury in the Early 19th Century

Building Activities

Apart from the large groups of guests who assembled every May for the races, Walter and Charlotte were constantly entertaining. The great shooting parties they held were very popular with the royal Dukes, who would arrive with their servants, loaders, coaches, wagons, dogs, guns and other paraphenalia and stay for long weekends several times during the shooting season between November and the end of January. The principal guest rooms are on the south side of the Great Hall, on the balcony level, with east-facing windows. This suite of rooms gives the visitor a great feeling of height, for 38 steps must be climbed from the level of the Great Hall to reach them. From the windows, the view is magnificent, particularly in the early morning. Here, standing almost on a level with the great acanthus-leaf carvings of the stone capitals which top the enormous Corinthian columns, one feels the grandeur of the architecture. The eye sweeps down to the Ver valley and up again, over towards Childwickbury. Other rooms used for guests were on the same level, on the west side of the Great Hall. These rooms have charming curved walls. From these rooms, the view is still very beautiful and little changed from that seen by Walter's noble visitors. The eye takes in the ruins of the Tudor Gorhambury beyond the gardens and wood plantations. In the evening the red low sunsets of winter would have provided a splendid spectacle for those returning from a day's sport.

Beautiful it might be, but from the point of view of those who had to keep Gorhambury running, it was singularly ill-planned. If one stands on the attic landing and peers down the 88 steps of the stone back stairs which lead to the basement far below, one can only speculate how many times the aching feet of servants must have trudged up and down those four dreary, dismal flights from top to bottom. From early morning until late at night, every day, the servants carried wood and coal for the fires, and water for washing and cleaning purposes. They had to empty the chamber pots, clean and fill the oil lamps. Long after their master's family and guests were asleep, the servants would struggle up, candles in hand, to sleep for a few hours on their thin mattresses in the stark bareness of their attic rooms, only to rise again at 4.30 the next morning, to set the great rooms to rights before the guests came down, to burnish and black-lead the grates, to polish the brass surrounds, to lay and light the fires in time for the first guest to rise.

From the earliest days of his marriage, Walter had intended to make alterations to Gorhambury – but not with any idea of making life easier for his servants. Charlotte was as interested in the plan as he was himself. In 1810 they drove over together to see Lord and Lady Bridgewater at Ashridge. 'We looked over the new house' Charlotte wrote, 'which promises to be a magnificent building. The architecture Gothic, some faults are to be observed which will make the rooms less comfortable than they might be. The library will be dark, and the drawing room, 50 feet in length, has but one fire place and that at the end'. They admired the 'carving in wood and stone done in Ld. Bridgewater's own workshops' and noted that there were 'quantities of people differently employed'.

Of her own home, she records that 'the veranda on the west front was finished and the library inhabited for the first time' on Sunday, 23 September 1810. Prior to this, all the windows on the west front would have followed the sash pattern of the other rooms, and originally there were no open casements in the library which led on to the terrace, and thus down to the garden. The only entry to the garden level up to this time had been by a spiral staircase which ran down to the lower corridor at ground level.

It may be recalled that young Grimston laid the foundation stone of the new nurseries in 1816; work on the north wing was still progressing in the mid 1820s. The architect was William Atkinson, and the contractor was Thomas Martin of 12 George Street, Portman Square. Additional bedrooms for the family were being added over the original passage that connected the main block to the north wing, and over the north wing itself other rooms for servants were being built. The rooms for maidservants were on the first level and manservants were on the upper level. The two levels were completely isolated from each other, even being served by separate staircases, to prevent any communication between the two.

Charlotte had further ideas about improving the house. In 1825 Walter noted that she was 'quite full of the improvements she is about to make at Gorhambury. Mr. Atkinson's plans examined and re-examined'. The proposal under discussion was the complete demolition of the south wing. One reason for this drastic step was that as the kitchens and bakery were situated there, smells from them could permeate into the dining room; Charlotte may also have felt it would be more practical to have all the service areas located together in the north wing. The distance of the kitchen from the dining room did not seem important. The room which, with its fine wagon ceiling, Sir Robert Taylor had intended to be 'Lord Grimston's business room', opening out of his dressing-room, was now to become the new dining room. The room originally intended for that purpose became a reception salon for Charlotte's assemblies, balls and musical evenings. In the same year Charlotte also put in hand alterations to the gardens: in December 'Mr. Gilpin arrived to look over the flower garden and grounds' and two years he was still hard at work at Gorhambury.

By March 1826, the south wing was almost gone. Walter commented that 'the wing being nearly down now opens a pleasing prospect towards Pré Wood, and I think improves very materially the appearance of the house, which I think will be infinitely better by this measure of Lady Verulam's'. As before, some material from the south wing were used in the additions being made to the north wing. Lime was burnt and bricks manufactured at Gorhambury, and this drew complaint from some local lime-burners, who claimed this would cause them hardship. The site of the lime-burning and brick-making activities was in a wood on the estate, known today as Brick Kiln Wood.

The following year, Walter found it necessary to make very strong complaints to the builder about the chimneys in the new rooms. Even before the rooms were completely finished, the chimneys seemed unsatisfactory. Walter recorded that he was 'in a great passion against Martin the builder for having totally neglected his duty in the building flues in the new part of the house into which they admit smoke, so of course fire would take the first opportunity to follow'. He wrote in strong terms to Martin, complaining of 'the culpable negligence ... in the driving plugs into the chimney, displacing the pargeting and making such a hole, that if the room had been finished we should have been ignorant of any danger existing till the woodwork caught fire, and my house, together with some of my family, fallen a sacrifice. It is quite enough to frighten one, when one sees the danger one has escaped, and is aware that in all the other chimneys of the new building the same may exist. Indeed, I have reason to think it does exist in our own bedchamber and in the room inhabited by my little girls ... I speak of what has given me serious cause for alarm, and has rendered what I thought would have been a comfortable convenience to me and to my family, the reason of distrust and disappoint-ment'. Later events showed how right he was to be uneasy about the chimneys' construction. A week later Walter found 'smoke still in our bedrooms' and in anger he 'got some mortar and plastered up some holes in the flue myself'. He also bought a fire engine. The boys 'took it to try it out to the Pondyards with the great chance of damage to it, which I disapprove' he wrote.

Work was simultaneously in progress at Grosvenor Square, for immediately upon his marriage, Walter had begun spending enormous sums of money on improving his town house. In fact, he completely rebuilt it at his own expense. In August 1815 he wrote to Lord Grosvenor's agent to ask for 'indulgence' as to the terms of his lease 'in consequence of the great expense I have been at, in rebuilding my house from the ground'. He asked for an extension of his lease, but the request was refused. In 1815 accounts from Thomas Martin show that £12,902.4s.7d was spent on 'sundry work' at Gorhambury and for 'erecting house and offices at Grosvenor Square'.

Early in 1828 Lord Salisbury showed off 'his improvements, repairs and amendments in the garden and house' at Hatfield to his neighbour. Walter was extremely impressed. 'His hydraulic machine, called the *Ram*, extremely clever', he commented admiringly. He may also have been impressed by the interest and personal involvement which Lord Salisbury took in his estate, for from this time onwards Walter spent more time at Gorhambury, going through the rent rolls and working long hours in the room called 'the Den' which housed his steward, Pocock. This closer involvement with his steward led him to suspect that something was wrong – 'Pocock's conduct so strange and his habits so improper'. Pocock was dismissed, and investigation showed so much to be amiss on the estate that Walter wished he had decided on this step sooner, adding philosophically 'but regrets avail nothing and I must correct his disorders as well as I may'. He installed John Purrott as Pocock's replacement, but everything was now intended to be much more under his personal control. He found considerable neglect on his farms in Hertford-shire; the situation on his Essex estates appeared less desperate. At least he received the Messing rents 'very prosperously'.

In 1829 work began on the new approach road to the house. It was to be cut from Gorham Block past the site of the Roman theatre, which at that time still lay undisturbed under the ground. The drive joined St Michael's Street almost opposite to St Michael's Church. This road-making operation was an expensive business, and came at a time when work on the south wing demolition, the enlargement of the north wing, and Mr. Gilpin's improve-ments to the garden, were all under way.

The Gorhambury Game Preserves

The head keeper at this time (the 1820s) was Joseph Card, and his second-in-command was William Bowra. There were others besides them, all of whom had their special responsibilities. As well as breeding pheasants and keeping down the rabbits and hares, they had a large herd of deer to look after. Card was principally in charge of the deer, killing them in due season and distributing the necks and haunches of venison, and selling the skins and horns. From 1829 onwards Walter kept a list of people to whom he wished to send venison in very much the same way in which his descendants would keep lists of those to whom pheasants were to be sent. Portions were sent to doctors, old servants, tenants, the Mayor of St Albans and anyone else who had been of assistance to the family during the year. The 1st Earl sent venison to the Sheriff for the Assize Dinner and to the Judges, and also to all his uncles, cousins, sisters, aunts and brothers. He provided two haunches and two necks for the Mayoral Dinner and 2 haunches for the Gorhambury Cricket Dinner, two necks for the 'Ploughing Match', two haunches for the Gorhambury Audit Dinner but only one for the Messing Audit Dinner.

In 1821 the Earl wrote out some 'Regulations of Gorhambury Park':

The Park, that is the deer, is to be put under the care of Card, but without any perquisite whatever, as perquisites always lead to distrust and dissatisfaction, both to master and servant. For the additional trouble this will give him he should have an additional allowance of £21.16s.3d. and as I am anxious he should not be taken out of his business as head gamekeeper he may give an additional allowance of £5 per annum to the shepherd, whom I observe always assists him. The skins, horns, etc., must all be taken care of, and accounted for. No fee must be demanded for venison sent out. The number of the deer will be very much diminished, and the fawns which are not to be kept must be killed before they run.

This additional allowance for Card seems extraordinarily high for the times. The skins of 'stall fed bucks' were sold to a Mr. Rich of Watford, who gave Walter 'the same as he does Lord Essex, Clarendon, &c. &c. for them'. Mr. Rich also bought venison from Walter in 1822 at 16 guineas a buck.

Joseph Card must have had some education, for there survive his own lists of recipients of venison, written in a good round hand. He was a faithful servant, and would miss even the special Christmas dinner for the family and staff at Gorhambury in order to keep a watchful eye on the game and deer. His basic wage was £14.8s.9d. paid every three months. Under-keepers received £13.2s.6d. every three months. It is sad to relate that their wages were always paid late.

Although Walter never entirely abandoned game preservation, any more than he ever completely gave up his racing stables, in the mid 1830s his financial difficulties forced him to cut back in this area. As we have seen, he was extremely short of money at this time owing to his extravagant spending on his sporting and building activities, and to the cost of 'bringing out' his daughters. He wrote many letters personally to his tenant farmers, inevitably starting with such phrases as 'I am quite miserable at being obliged to write to you upon such a subject' or 'I must entreat you will exert yourself to pay up your arrears of rent'; 'Nothing but necessity should induce me to trouble you in this way … It is impossible for me in any comfort to leave London, my bills almost all unpaid, and with scarcely anything left to meet current expenses. Be assured I write this with the greatest regret …'.

In return, he received friendly letters from his farmers explaining their problems. Thomas Saunders, who farmed at Hill End Farm, wrote 'I will give you the reason for becoming in arrears … the produce of the farm about 3 loads of wheat per acre and about the same of quarters of barley. Oats have proved very bad'. 'The corn makes no money' wrote William White of Wood End Farm. The enterprising Samuel Smith of Sopwell Farm offered to pay his rent with hay! Frederick Gough of Cunningham Hill Farm thanked his landlord for the understanding he had given him in the past. 'Accept my Lord the warmest thanks of a grateful heart. By your allowing it [the rent] to remain so long it has given me the means of getting my farm in a good state of cultivation'.

Walter found himself searching desperately for ways to economise. He had even borrowed money from his aunts Frances and Charlotte Johanna, and was often late paying them the small amount of interest they charged him. This did not greatly concern them, since they intended that their money should go to him ultimately, but it worried him very much. In January 1834 he wrote to his steward Purrott:

> I can no longer incur the expense of game preservation to the extent I have heretofore done, the only question in my mind is how I can give it up with the least hardship to those who have faithfully discharged their duties, while I have employed them, my sons not caring much about it. The additional expense produced by the New Game Act, and the increase of poaching fostered by beer shops, the facility the predators have for lurking

comfortably near the scene of their exploits, together with every means of escape, have brought me to this determination ... I mean not to allow any further issue of pheasant food, any more night watching, or assistance to the keepers ... The clothes for all the keepers must be stopped, but I shall allow them their salaries during this year, in return for which I expect they will keep trespassers from Pré Wood, the park, and its immediate vicinity, as it would be unpleasant to have people shooting just under one's nose. Card will not have the additional allowance he now has as Gamekeeper, but his salary must be revised as Park Keeper. Park Wood, Birch Wood, the Furzefields may be given up entirely, and in respect of the fine stock of game contained in them I expect that a considerable quantity shall be brought to the house, of which an account may be sent me'.

When Lord Verulam died in 1845 the herd of deer was sold. Joseph Card became obsessed with the idea that this meant the end of his employment at Gorhambury. In a fit of great depression, the poor man shot himself in Pluck's Bushes, where his body was found by a young keeper called White. In later years when the deer were re-established, White was put in charge of them, for it was to him that Card had passed on his knowledge of the subject.

Charlotte Grimston at Home

While Walter occupied himself principally with sporting activities at Gorhambury, Charlotte Grimston had more varied interests. Amongst these was the school for girls which had been established by her dead mother-in-law Harriot in 1781. As early as 1811 we find Charlotte referrring to the school in her diary. She noted that she had heard 'my little school girls say their catechism' and that she had paid the schoolmistress her salary. The school was for the daughters of estate workers, and was housed in the old parish room (which stood on the site now occupied by the present one), to the left of the entrance to St Michael's churchyard. As well as receiving religious instruction, the girls were taught reading, writing and arithmetic, and special emphasis was placed on needlework. Lessons in this skill were given in the afternoons by a St Michael's woman, Mrs. Newell; there are still Newells living in the parish today. When Harriot started the school there were only 12 pupils; there were now between 18 and twenty.

The schoolgirls were responsible for marking all the Gorhambury linen – sheets, pillowslips, towels and table napkins – with the initial 'V' for Verulam. This was marked with red cotton in fine cross-stitch, with the date when the linen was purchased embroidered beneath the 'V'. Often a coronet was added, also embroidered with exquisitely tiny stitches. The girls also hand-sewed Charlotte's fine cambric camisoles, her petticoats and her knickers, and faggot-stitched and lace-edged her flannel nightgowns. Even when Charlotte was a very old woman she still visited the school from time to time. She would make a special point of talking to any girls who had embroidered a garment for her, inviting them to sit in her carriage while she spoke to them. She usually made a present of half-a-crown to any particularly industrious girl.

The schoolgirls were provided with a uniform, consisting of a frock made of warm brown 'Coburg', which was a kind of cashmere, worn with a round 'tippet' of white linen. Over these dresses they wore blue checked aprons, and on their heads they had small caps of white mull muslin with a brown ribbon tied under the hair at the back and another on the top of the head, and covered by a white straw bonnet with brown ribbons. On Sundays, when they all went to church together and 'were heard the catechism', they wore special red capes for the occasion. This description is close to that given by Harriot's accounts for 1781. It is likely that these girls were also responsible for making horse-cloths for Walter's colts and fillies. He noted that 'he had the horses up from the stud in new cloths, which I make at home for half what they cost made by the saddler'. After 1877, when the present school at St Michael's was built, Charlotte's school for girls became the infant school.

Charlotte had artistic tastes – we will hear more about her love of music a little later – but she was also a talented artist. In 1819 we find Walter buying her 'French brushes' and *l'encre d'or*; on another occasion he had to wait *'en attendant'* while his wife was 'putting on her bonnet and putting by her painting materials' before they could go out together to pay calls. Perhaps influenced by the illustrations her sisters-in-law were undertaking to Francis Bacon's *History of King Henry VII*, Charlotte began to illustrate *The Memoirs of the Court of Queen Elizabeth*. There are four enormous volumes, each measuring 20 inches by 15 and about three and a half inches thick. They are bound in cream vellum with a two-inch classical design richly tooled in gold around the borders, on the front and back and down the hand-sewn spine. Two clasps of gilt keep each volume shut. The inner linings of the covers are of cream moiré silk; here again the framing is tooled in gold. The edges of each volume when closed are gilded and purfled. The title page, which was also designed by Charlotte, depicts Gorhambury from various angles. In the centre, surrounded by elaborate curlicues, is her dedication, written in black and gold ink:

MEMOIRS OF THE COURT OF ELIZABETH
illustrated with drawings by Charlotte, Countess of Verulam
To
JAMES WALTER GRIMSTON, EARL OF VERULAM
these Memoirs of the Court of Queen Elizabeth illustrated by a few portraits and coats of
arms are most affectionately and respectfully dedicated by Charlotte Verulam
Gorhambury, January 1830

Her title page says that there are 'a few portraits and coats of arms'. This is a considerable understatement for there are hundreds of them, all exquisitely painted. Each page consists of one of the original pages of the *Memoirs* inset in the same careful way as in her sister-in-laws' production. Each page is bordered with flower designs, and while Charlotte may have made use of stencils in some cases to do these, she has added tiny supplementary details, such as the shading of petals and the veining of leaves, which could not be shown by a stencil. Most of the borders are undoubtedly her own freehand paintings of flowers. The book also contains many portraits, and to produce these she must have had to undertake considerable research. Charlotte also depicted the Tudor Gorhambury and the modern house on porcelain plates, as well as Verulam House and the homes of her four married daughters.

 A most interesting record from Charlotte's day, which may also have been her work, are the perspective representations of three of the large state rooms, showing the positioning of the pictures in each room. These pictures were mounted on card, the edges were gilded with gold paint, and a handle of ivory and black enamel was attached. Above each picture a number was neatly written, and on the reverse of the board against each number the title of the picture was given. The visitor could thus hold the 'fan' in his hand and identify the pictures he saw before him. For the family's historian, these 'fans' have a special interest, for they show us the furnishing of these apartments at that time. The picture of the Great Hall, for instance, shows that there were originally two niches on either side of the door to the Library. In the niches stand two tall blue and white jars, part of a garniture of about 1680. These niches were later filled in, to give more wall space for hanging pictures. We can also see the elegant classical balustrading to the gallery which was put there when the house was built, and which was later changed for the heavy ironwork which is still there today.

 In the painting of the yellow drawing room we can see the fine pier glasses given to Walter and Charlotte by Walter's aunts, Frances and Charlotte Johanna. There in position is the great carved curtain pelmet which was later broken into pieces and left in the stables and attics, to be finally restored to the yellow drawing room only in 1971. The room is furnished in 'blue and gold' exactly as Walter's sister Charlotte recorded it to be in her diary. Many pieces of furniture which are still at Gorhambury today can be recognised. In the Library we can identify the 'cheap' busts which Charlotte and Walter bought from an Italian who 'happened to call' one day in 1823, as well as the bust of Pope Clement XIV by Christopher Hewetson which Harriot's father had brought back from Italy. The harp which Charlotte and her daughter Katty played at evening parties can be seen. The Library was painted in white and gold.

 Charlotte may also have painted some exquisite miniature portraits of her children. Looking at their little faces, so charmingly painted, it is little wonder that their parents doted on them. The four girls wear white lawn bonnets, gophered, with minute blue forget-me-nots fringing their faces. Their dresses are white with the low, scooped neckline of the period that reveals their plump shoulders, cupped with tiny bunches of flowers. Katharine (Katty) and Mary wear pink coral necklaces and have reddish hair, while Emily and Jane are fair. The five boys are equally attractive, and Grimston's miniature has a twist of his reddish-brown hair preserved in the reverse of it. Edward, Robert and Francis have brown hair, while Charles's appealing countenance is fringed with fair curls.

Chapter Fifteen

The End of an Era

The Deaths of Walter and Charlotte

It was on 17 November, 1845, that Walter Verulam reached the final post in life's race, as he would have put it. For him spring did not return. Never again would he feel the pounding hoofs beneath him, or hear the race resound around his park. Never again would he hear the cracking whips, the strident horns, or the chatter of the bookies on a green May day. No more would he watch the crowds in their gay holiday attire enjoying themselves. The thrill, the colour, the smell of the turf – all disappeared like the hot breath of his racing horses into the November mists of his Gorhambury woodlands.

He had added five codicils to the will he had made in 1833, one at the marriages of each of his children. There was to be a sixth and final one, which his daughter Emily wrote at his dictation a month before his death. Walter was able to sign and affix his seal to it. There is a touching reference to his valet:

> The poverty shown by my banker's pass book will fully explain why I have not lavished presents upon my servants and friends in legacies, but I am fully aware that Grimston will appreciate those who are most deserving amongst the former and be kind as far as convenience will allow him to the latter. I have therefore added this small codicil to my Will that nobody may think that I have neglected or forgotten them. I request to add that my servant Pulham has been very attentive to me.

His children were all with him at the end, except Charles, the black sheep of the family, whose story will be told more fully below. With this most kind and lenient of fathers, they had all spent a happy youth –hunting, beagling with their own pack, swimming, playing cricket. For Walter, thinking as he must have done of them all, perhaps especially of Charles, the words of that great philosopher who, nearly 300 years before, had also lived at Gorhambury, would surely apply:

> The joys of parents are secret, and so are their griefs and fears: they cannot utter the one, nor will they utter the other. Children sweeten labours: but they make misfortune more bitter: they increase the cares of life, but they mitigate the remembrance of death.

Walter's 'dear Char.' had a further 18 years of life left to her. During the winter she lived at Gorhambury, going up to stay at Grosvenor Square each February for the London Season. Bob, her unmarried son, lived with her and travelled up and down from Hertfordshire to London as she did until her death.

One of her son Edward's daughters, named Charlotte after her grandmother, recalled her well, for she often stayed at the Grosvenor Square house.
Little Charlotte remembered that her grandmother would rise at noon, and
take breakfast in an anteroom adjoining her bedroom. Every day she had a
hot Sally Lunn, a boiled egg, coffee with candy sugar, and then grapes or
strawberries and cream. She ate no luncheon. Even in old age, Charlotte was
still methodical, and each Tuesday her house-books were brought to her for
inspection. She paid for the outgoings recorded in these books from her long
silk sovereign-purse-bag, which was fastened by a ring at the top, and would
often say to little Charlotte 'look in the end and see if you can find a little piece
of gold'. All through her life, Charlotte Verulam had loved highly perfumed
flowers, and her granddaughter remembered her rooms as always scented
with by such flowers as narcissi or wallflowers.

Towards the end of her life, when staying at Gorhambury, Charlotte lived
in the yellow drawing room, using it as a bedroom and living-room combined.
They put up a big four-poster bed at the opposite end of the room to the organ
for her. She became very stout and walked with the aid of a stick. Little
Charlotte had vivid memories of her grandmother's death. She had been sent
for to stay at Grosvenor Square; as soon as she arrived, her grandmother gave
her a special diamond pin. That night all the Grimston relatives arrived. Little
Charlotte went to bed. At about two in the morning she was woken by her
father, who said that Grandmama would like her to play the harmonium for
her. The little girl put on her dressing gown and ran down to the anteroom
where the harmonium was, and by the light of a single candle she played for
what seemed to her to be a very long time. At last her father came, and told
her to stop playing and go back to bed. She walked back through the drawing
room, and was horrified to find it full to capacity with relations. The next
morning she was told that Grandmama Charlotte had died in the night.

Music triumphant, right to the end, as Walter would have said.

Walter and Charlotte's Children: A Brief Summary of Their Lives

James Walter, 2nd Earl of Grimston

By choosing Elizabeth Joanna Weyland for his bride, Grimston had done
exactly as his father had hoped he would – chosen a woman with money.
Elizabeth was the only daughter of Major Richard Weyland of Woodeaton
House, near Oxford. Her father was a distinguished soldier who had fought
in 84 engagements with the French in the Peninsular War, and had narrowly
escaped death on one occasion when the rim of his hat had been shot off.

Grimston and Elizabeth were married in September 1844, and Walter had
lived long enough to get to know his daughter-in-law. Her portrait, painted
by R.J. Swinton when she was 25, shows a gentle lady. Her dark hair, parted
smoothly in the middle and draped on either side of her face, is bound in a
narrow band of black velvet. Her dress of grey striped silk is embroidered
with brown ruching. Over her shoulders she wears a blue India shawl with a

red border. In her hands, which are clasped in front of her, she holds a pair of white gloves, and she wears a bonnet with broad grey ties. Swinton painted her standing in a country scene of foliage and trees. Grimston was 'very much pleased' with this painting, and agreed that he too should sit to Swinton, which he did in 1851. Elizabeth's portrait must have been a long time in Swinton's studio, for he was not paid for it until 1856, although it had been started six years earlier.

In all probability, illness prevented her giving the artist regular sittings, for it was said in the family 'Poor dear Elizabeth, think of her having all those children and suffering from hay fever all the time!'. She was also asthmatic, which made her a semi-invalid. She seldom left the house from the autumn to the spring, and did not involve herself in giving great country-house parties, as her mother-in-law had done. During the spring and summer she suffered badly from hay fever, and she would sit shrouded in towels, steaming her head over a bowl of hot water and Friar's Balsam. One of her granddaughters recalled how very gentle she was, and what a tremendous ascendancy she had over people despite her quiet ways.

In 1846 Grimston's aunt, Harriot Grimston, died and left him her fortune, including the large legacy which had been left to her and her sister by Richard Glover (Chapter 12 above). Grimston also benefited from the will of his great-aunt, Frances Cooke Grimston, when she in turn died in 1848. It thus seemed that the financial problems of the family were no longer as acute as they had been in his father's day. However, it seemed that as soon as the Grimstons were financially solvent, they immediately spent. For almost 20 years Gorhambury had been relatively free of workmen, and yet within two years of acquiring his windfall, Grimston was embarking on new schemes and alterations. In 1848 the balustrading of the main stairs, and that of the hall gallery, which was of a classically simple design, was replaced with heavy black cast iron, more to the current taste. It is strange that Elizabeth, who generally preferred light furniture, should have approved of this ugly ironwork, but on this occasion she fell in with fashion. The work was carried out by Armstrong and Smith of Pimlico, and the architect was William Burns of 6 Stratton Street, London.

Some of the work which was undertaken was certainly necessary. The roof of the Portico needed to be reconstructed. The heavy pounding given to the stone and marble paving of the Great Hall by two generations of feet tramping over it had made the floor uneven, and it had to be relaid. Other changes reflected the apparently hereditary interest in building. The bottom flight of Taylor's original spiral staircase which had descended to the basement was removed, and a new straight flight was made to descend northward from the first floor to the ground floor level of the large north wing. Here new living rooms were arranged, opening westwards to face the garden. To light the stone passage, Grimston bought some 'bracket lamps' which burnt oil. Another entrance hall was formed at ground level, with an entry from a new projecting porch; the old family entrance under the Portico could now be kept shut. The bill for this work was £2,190.8s.0½d. The architect's bill was only £140, which Grimston felt to be very moderate. On 12 April 1848 he noted in his diary that they had 'got into our rooms at Gorhambury'. Grimston made one of these new rooms into another library, which he called his 'Brown Study'. On the top of one of his bookcases, he put one of the mottoes admired by Sir Francis Bacon – *MONITI MELIORA* – the best is yet to be. Grimston was a classical scholar, a bibliophile, a numismatist, and something of a geologist as well.

One of his granddaughters recalled him in her own old age. He was, she said, 'very wise, very well read, and very good'. Her own mother, who came from a rather cynical family, the Grahams, was very struck by him. She said she had 'never met anyone so good' as her father-in-law. It is plain that his own brothers and sisters were devoted to 'Grim'. There are many instances of his kindness to others. In 1840, he had been riding in Hyde Park when he saw a boy throw himself into the reservoir there. Grimston immediately leapt from his house, plunged into the ten feet deep waters, and brought the boy to the surface. The latter was half-drowned, but Grimston managed to revive him and took him to the gatekeeper's lodge. When he had recovered enough to speak, the boy told his rescuer that he was a 'parish apprentice', and had suffered so much from the severity of his master that he had become tired of life. During very bitter winter weather when his estate workers were working on the drive, clearing snow or mending holes, Grimston would personally take hot rice puddings to warm and sustain them.

In 1848 there was a short cessation of spending on the house. In a letter written on 6 June, Grimston told his sister Katty Clarendon that 'our works at the house are not to go on at present from prudent motives, but we are building a cottage at the old garden for the gardener, and as soon as we leave [for London] next week a roof and a small colonnade around the dairy will be constructed'. Charming Garden Cottage, looking like something from Beatrix Potter with its pretty porch, still stands by the red-walled gardens laid out by Francis Bacon. The colonnade around the dairy forms an attractive feature of the 19th century gardens.

Grimston's wife, Elizabeth, had her own ideas on furnishing, and as her mother-in-law Charlotte was now almost permanently resident at Grosvenor Square, Elizabeth could feel free to change things at Gorhambury as she wished. She did not like dark furniture, particularly mahogany, nor the drab colourings which Charlotte had introduced 30 years earlier, and which at that time had been in the best possible taste. In 1849 Elizabeth purchased a 'suite in walnut with green velvet cushions' for the Library from Charles Hindley & Sons of 134 Oxford Street, London. This was only the first in a series of purchases – between 1849 and 1853 she spent £988.0s.6d. at this shop alone. Hindley's agreed to take the furniture which Elizabeth wanted to replace in part exchange. Six mahogany chairs covered with needlework went for 5s, two armchairs from the same set for the same sum. Hindley's gave a pound for a mahogany sideboard, 15s for a further eight mahogany dining room chairs, while the sixteen drab and gold chairs which Charlotte had been so pleased with fetched £3.5s.0d. Elizabeth purchased enormous lengths of flowered glazed chintz for curtains, bed-hangings and chair-covers. Some of this chintz with a striped pattern was used to make loose covers for Hepplewhite chairs, covering them down to the floor and completely concealing the wood. A new chimney piece was purchased for the dining room, in a fine marble rococo design, which is still there today.

Three years later it was decided that the Library should be redecorated. It was probably last done in 1806, when a Mr. Godbolt painted and gilded it at a cost of £19.17s.0d. The paintwork at this time was white. During the winter of 1851 the bookcases here and in the little anteroom leading from it to the yellow drawing room were combed and grained in imitation of satin wood. Grimston's diary does not give the name of the craftsmen involved. The Library was to keep this style of decoration until 1960, by which time the paint was flaking badly. The bookcases were stripped, revealing pine shelving with oak facings, and traces of gilding on the carving. In 1960 it would have been an extravagance to have the bookcases repainted, and therefore the bookcases were left as natural wood, and the carving picked out with fresh gilding. The walls were painted pale green. The anteroom remained in its shabby flaking state, and it is only recently that it has been beautifully restored by Paul and Janet Czainski. It now looks as it would have done in Grimston's day, except that the bookcases have been removed and the walls painted a very dark peacock green, which forms a superb background for two Monnoyer flower paintings.

To consolidate the Gorhambury estate, Grimston bought enough land to give him possession of almost all the area between the existing boundary of the estate and St Albans. To give just a few examples, in August 1853 he heard that 'the Freehold Land Society had sold Verulam Hills, &c., for the enormous sum of £9,460, exclusive of timber. One lot to me, ten acres for £1,030. Copyhold!!!' he added with obvious satisfaction. In the following year he obtained all the Verulam Hills estate, bought for him by Elizabeth. On 13 March 1854 he noted in his diary that he had 'heard from Elizabeth that Mr. Adams would take what he gave for Verulam Hills, and she was willing to purchase with her own fortune'. (This land was sold by the estate in 1931, to the St Albans Corporation).

Grimston also bought Westwick Farm at Leverstock Green in November of the same year, 'in a dreadful state as new purchases always are'. The following January he bought 'fields of Lomax (at Childwick) about £1,217'. In 1857 he purchased 'Great Cell Barnes for £5,850, being £650 under my limit'. The number of land purchases was so great that a new map of the estate had to be drawn up. On 24 September 1860, Grimston noted that he had looked at the new map at his agent's house – this agent was another Mr. Purrott, living at Maynes Farmhouse on Gorhambury Drive.

The Second Earl was also responsible for the construction of not a few new estate buildings. In 1855 a site was chosen near Bacon's Pondyards for the construction of two new cottages. These were sold by the estate in the 1970s. A new lodge and new gates were erected at St Michael's. On 14 June 1857 Grimston noted that 'Mr. Parsons says he can make a good thing of lodge and gates for £700'. The knapped flint stonework on the lodge was done by a Mr. Thomas at a cost of £21.5s.0d. The lodge gates cost £75. These attractive gates were removed to make a wider entrance possible during the later years of the Sixth Earl; they are now utilised in the garden. The stables at the stud were converted into three cottages for estate workers, and the cottages at the Temple were enlarged. Grimston's diary provides proof that these latter are of 18th century date, for on 18 April 1870 the Earl recorded that he had seen a piece of wood uncovered during the alterations on which was written the words 'Bilt [sic] by Grove, October 8th, 1787'. There are some interesting reminders of Gorhambury's history incorporated into these cottages. Some of the statuary came from the Tudor Gorhambury, and the 3rd Viscount installed the chimney piece from that house in one of the cottages. In 1957 the 5th Earl had it removed to the Great Hall of Gorhambury, where, fully restored, Sir Nicholas Bacon's motto – *MEDIOCRIA FIRMA* – can once more be read. It is even possible that the Temple cottages cover the site of the medieval house built by Geoffrey de Gorham. In 1871 two cottages – nos. 35 and 37, St Michael's Street – were built, again of knapped flints, and in 1874 a new farmhouse was built at Kettlewells.

Like his parents, Grimston was interested in extending the benefits of education to the children of the 'lower orders of society'. In 1851 the Rector of St Michael's, the Reverend B. Hutchinson, wrote to the Earl about education, and referred to Monk, who had been installed as the teacher of the First Earl's stable boys in 1824. Mr. Hutchinson commented that 'Monk, the school master, deserves great credit for the improvement of himself and with a short sojourn at one of the training schools he might be made a really efficient master, but if he were much improved, he would require more than the 15 shillings a week. The school mistress is an excellent person, but inefficient. At the same time, we could not supply her place with a better at the small salary of eight shillings a week'. It is probable that the Earl was willing to increase the salaries paid to the school teachers, for he undertook to 'build a new school room without delay'. This school was the forerunner of today's school at St Michael's, and was built in 1876.

In thanking Lord Verulam for his generosity, Mr. Hutchinson referred to the 'model cottages' which Lady Verulam wished to build. These cottages were paid for from her own fortune and were named 'Elizabeth's Cottages'. They are situated in Blacksmith's Lane on the left-hand side as one approaches it from St Michael's Street. Today they mostly house retired people from the Gorhambury estate.

Grimston was interested in silviculture. He took delight in planting trees, and pruned the young saplings himself. He liked to keep a record of the growth of the trees. In September 1853 he 'looked at some of the young cedars in the park, which have made good shoots'. The following January he recorded that he had 'got up the cedar in the garden and cut off its second leading shoot – a hard job'. This would have been one of the cedars planted in his father's day, which are today so impressive. Grimston measured the cedars annually, and noted that they grew about two inches a year. In 1868 one of these cedars was about 10 feet and 11 inches tall – now they have an average girth of about 22 feet! These cedars are magnificent specimens, and complement the classical architecture of the house to perfection.

It was Grimston who 'showed Bogue where to plant the Wellingtonias in front of [the] house' in 1874. These form a great avenue today, which frames a spectacular vista down to the valley of the Ver from the east portico. The soil at Gorhambury nurtures fine trees. Besides those already mentioned, there are a catalpha tree, a tulip tree and a great ilex. There are ancient Spanish chestnut trees which have grown into unbelievably twisted and fascinating shapes. The great 'Kiss Oak', now hollow, but still with a girth of 23 feet, is said to have been there in the days of Sir Nicholas Bacon. An improbable legend has it that the Earl of Leicester kissed Queen Elizabeth in its shade. Whether the story is true or not, the old oak was a particular favourite of another Grimston who loved trees – the Sixth Earl. Of him, and of his great-grandfather the Second Earl, it can be said:

> He that planteth a tree is a servant of God,
> He provideth a kindness for many generations,
> And faces that he hath not seen shall bless him.

Elizabeth Verulam was concerned with the welfare of mothers less fortunate than herself. She started the St Albans Maternity Charity, its object being 'to assist respectable married women in procuring the services of a properly trained and certificated midwife, during their confinement'. Those eligible for this charity had to have 'resided within three miles of the centre of St Albans for one year'. A woman was not eligible if her husband was 'in receipt of wages exceeding one guinea a week'. A midwife was appointed at an annual salary of £65.

The Countess's kindness to individuals is still recalled today by the descendants of Jesse Sears, who in 1867 was a gardener at Gorhambury. He lived at one of the Temple cottages, and he and his wife Emma had 13 children. After one of the births, Emma became very ill with 'white leg'. Elizabeth took the new baby into the nursery at Gorhambury until its mother was well again. When the baby went home, Elizabeth gave the child a small black japanned chest, which is still a prized family possession.

Lady Maud Hastings, the third child of Grimston and Elizabeth, who was born in 1857, recalled her youth at Gorhambury in her old age to the 4th Countess of Verulam. She considered that the family had kept up an unnecessarily large establishment. The family was always secretly struggling to make ends meet, yet it never seemed to occur to her parents to reduce the army of servants who waited on them. Every month there was acute depression when the wages had to be paid and the housebooks dealt with. After each windfall of money left to them, the first action of the couple was to engage another couple of manservants in livery. She recalled that there was never enough money for tickets for the theatre or the opera, but always it could be found to give big parties. The family resorted to some strange tactics; Elizabeth Verulam instructed Garrard's, the jewellers, to melt down a Queen Anne silver toilet set – basin, jug, etc., – to make an extra dozen spoons and forks for dinner parties. A credit note has been found from Garrard's, for the purchase of 'one washing basin, one ewer and cover, and two soap boxes' but it has no reference to their being melted down.

Among the accounts for the year 1873 are licences for '18 male servants ... at 15s each' and licences for 'six horses or mules at '10s 6d each'. There are also licences for six carriages and for 'armorial bearings for three carriages; each one is authorised to wear and use armorial bearings, and to have the same painted, marked, or affixed on to any carriage'. The first coachman to serve Grimston and his family was Henry Nash, who received £37 a year and a cottage – 'Nash's Lodge' which may be seen on Gorhambury Drive. The second coachman was George Cotton, who came to Gorhambury from Newmarket in 1850 (where his father had been stud groom). His wages were £21 per annum, rising to £34.2s.6d. when he was promoted to first coachman in 1859. Cotton married Caroline Collyer, one of the many housemaids at Gorhambury. In February 1850 her wages were £13.13s.0d. a year.

In 1827 the First Earl had expressed great concern about the safety of the chimney flues in some of the new bedrooms being built for him by Thomas Martin. How right he proved to be: in 1855 there was a fire in the servant' wing, which fortunately the servants were able to 'allay quickly'. Grimston's valet John and a housemaid called Ellen were each given £6 for their efforts in quelling the conflagration. A very much more serious fire took place in 1863, on 31 October. It was caused, according to Grimston, by 'an overheated flue which set fire to some woodwork on the roof'. He himself had just left the town hall in St Albans and was about to join a shooting party when the news of the fire was brought to him by the family's doctor, Dr. Drage. The small fire engine which his father had bought for such occasions was unable to dowse the flames, but 'the St Albans County engine and fire brigade were on the spot first, joined almost immediately by the borough engine and brigade and the Hemel Hempstead fire brigade'. Grimston wrote later 'Providentially the kitchen wing alone is burnt and no one hurt. The coolness of Eliz. and Harriot [one of their daughters] beyond praise. The furniture of the house itself is uninjured. The show of feeling quite touching'. It was market day in St Albans and the farmers flocked to Gorhambury. 'The park was thronged with persons anxious to aid and quench the flames'. Less altruistically, crowds assembled in St Albans to gaze at the burning mansion in the distance. The servants' rooms, their bedding and clothing and Grimston's own dressing-room were completely destroyed. 'Many people called to offer kindnesses' he noted. 'We accepted Salisbury's and sent governess, tutor and five children to Hatfield'. Happily, the house was insured, and Grimston wrote with satisfaction that 'Royal Exchange offers £3,100 compensation'.

In 1852 and again in 1858 and 1859 he was gazetted as a Lord-in-Waiting. He represented St Albans in Parliament in 1830 and the county of Hertfordshire from 1832 to 1845. Grimston was Lord Lieutenant of the County from 1846 to 1864. In 1871, he set in motion a scheme for the restoration of St Albans Abbey, and became Chairman of the Restoration Committee. (Later the wealthy lawyer, Sir Edmund Beckett, later Lord Grimthorpe, came on to the scene and took the lead in the restoration.)

As early as 1856 when he was 47, Grimston began to notice 'a lack of power in my knees'. He weighed 14 and a half stone. He consulted Dr. Drage, his family physician from Hatfield, who sent him to Dr. Burrows of Cavendish Square, London. 'He pronounced that it was gout flying about me, and nothing, he thought, organic'. Three years later, still suffering from discomfort, Grimston consulted another specialist 'who said my failure in knees was a failing of power and he expected to cure it'. However, the lameness increased, and eventually Grimston could no longer play his favourite game of cricket.

Lord Verulam's lameness and heaviness continued to get worse: eventually he needed a Bath chair to get about. One day he narrowly escaped death when a chandelier crashed down on the empty chair. It was for his benefit that the lift was constructed in the lower hall at Gorhambury, whereby with the use of ropes, he could haul himself up to the first floor. He endured his disability for many years with great patience and died at the age of 84 in 1895. Elizabeth had predeceased him, dying in 1886, aged 61.

> Like leaves on trees the race of man is found
> Now green in youth, now withering on the ground
> Another race the following spring supplies;
> They fall successive, and successive rise.
> (Homer)

Robert Grimston

The Grimston boys were not cossetted: they were brought up to be spartan and tough. They were encouraged to take part in outdoor sports such as swimming, cricket, coursing and boxing. The fine character of Robert, the third boy in the family, was plain from an early age. When he was nine Walter wrote of him 'He has a peculiarly affectionate manner which I suspect indicates a heart too perceptible for the rough of this world. God grant it may never give him an undue portion of pain'. Even as a small boy, he seemed 'old-fashioned', and his father thought how 'droll' Bob looked riding his pony. If he felt that he had been unjustly accused or punished he would say 'It ain't justice and it ain't truth'. He used the old form 'ain't' for 'is not' right to the end of his life. This keen sense of justice and truth, and the steady determination which he himself called 'obstinacy' were the strong features of his character. He would take delight in saying 'as obstinate as a Grimston'. He thought 'obstinacy' in fact to be 'the greatest virtue'.

When he was at school at Harrow, Bob was head boy of Mr. Benjamin Kennedy's house. Charles, Bob's younger brother by two years, was in the same house. Charles was not as serious and well-disciplined as his elder brother. When both boys left Harrow at the same time, in 1834, his housemaster wrote of Bob 'It is my sincere and very agreeable conviction that his conduct will be at all times a credit to himself and gratify your Lordship'. But of Charles, Mr. Kennedy wrote 'I cannot but lament that the moment of Mr. Charles Grimston's leaving my house should have been preceded by any unpleasant circumstance ... His conduct has given pain to myself and Mrs. Kennedy ... We do hope that in his new career his conduct and success may be all that your Lordship can desire'. Of the nature of the 'unpleasant circumstance' which preceded Charles's departure from Harrow, and of his 'conduct and success' thereafter, more will be found below.

Bob Grimston was an all-round sportsman, but cricket was his favourite game. Today the name of Bob Grimston is still venerated at Harrow for his cricketing skills. It is strange that he, to whom Harrow cricket owes so much, was not in the Harrow eleven. According to their cricket history, he was 'next out'. After Bob left the school, he continued to coach the boys in cricket. He taught them to play in a manly, honest manner, and the boys were all greatly influenced by this gentle, kindly, but determined man. He did not like the then new overarm bowling, and did not advocate its use. He took his involvement with Harrow cricket very seriously, and there was one occasion when he could not bear to watch a match between Eton and his own team, for fear they might disappoint him. During the game he stayed in a nearby churchyard; a mounted groom brought him news of the state of play throughout the day. On another occasion when Harrow lost a match, it has been said that he arrived back at Gorhambury riding in a hearse!

He also excelled in sport during his time at Christ Church, Oxford. John Ruskin, who was a fellow undergraduate, described him as 'a man of gentle birth and amiable manners, and of herculean strength, whose love of dogs and horses and especially of boxing was stupendous'.

Like his elder brother Grimston, Bob was a great walker, and thought nothing of setting out to walk from his London house to Gorhambury at a steady four miles an hour. He freqently walked from Gorhambury to Lord's Cricket Ground, playing cricket there and then walking back to Gorhambury in the evening. This was a distance of perhaps 20 miles. Lord's at that time was practically in the country, with open ground to the north and west. Should Bob come from London to stay at Gorhambury, he sent his servant by train, but he always walked.

Bob Grimston was not a great scholar, but whatever he undertook was done with great determination. He studied law, but did not feel suited to it as a profession. He virtually abandoned it to devote himself to the then new enterprise of electric telegraphy. He joined the Board of the Electric Telegraph Company in 1852 and became connected with the International Telegraph Company. His idea of testing tensions to which cable on the seabed was subjected overcame what had until then been an insuperable obstacle, because undulations in the seabed caused cables to break.

As he walked along the newly-built approach road to Gorhambury on a hot day, Bob Grimston was struck with the idea of providing shade for walkers along it, and planted the lovely line of red chestnuts which still flower in May and June there today. They are still known as 'Uncle Bob's umbrellas'. When in a bad year some died, they were replaced by Bob's great-great-nephew, the 6th Earl of Verulam, in the 1960s.

Wherever he went, Bob Grimston's strange clothing made him conspicuous. He did not like change and enjoyed his own peculiarities. He wore clothes cut after the fashion of a Methodist minister. He could only persuade his tailor, Mr. Poole, to make them as he wanted, on the condition that he never revealed who made them! His hat, which had a four-inch brim, was always worn on the back of his head. When he hunted he wore exactly the same clothes as usual – no pink hunting jacket for him – and his hat was tied on with a broad black velvet band. He hated jewellery, never wore even a watch chain, and disliked what he called 'flash conceit' in anything. Bob had no trace of his father's 'Turf mania', but he loved hunting. He hunted regularly with the Rothschild Stag Hounds in Buckinghamshire. He kept his stud all summer at Golders Green and in the winter at Leighton Buzzard. He had six horses.

He started life with the fixed determination never to be dependent on his family. He lived quietly, never marrying, alone with one servant called Payne, always 'cutting his coat according to his cloth', and never indulging in pleasures or luxuries that he could not afford. In later years the great success of the telegraph companies made him well off.

His handwriting was large and clear, and every word was to the point. Writing to Lord Salisbury in 1857 on the subject of his possibly standing for an election at St Albans he wrote 'My mind is made up. If you reckon upon my moving you will only disappoint yourself. Get new pipes to play on, the old ones are worn out'.

Bob Grimston died suddenly sitting in his chair at Gorhambury. He was 68. The Harrow cricket ground was enlarged as a memorial to him, by the purchase of outlying land. A Harrow master, E.E. Bowen, wrote a long poem to 'R.G.'. One verse reads:

Well played. His life was honester than ours;
We scheme, he worked, we hesitate, he spoke:
His rough-hewn stem held no concealing flowers,
But grain of oak.

Charles Grimston

Charles was the good-looking fourth son of Walter and Charlotte. Like his elder brothers, Charles went to the house of Mr. Benjamin Kennedy at Harrow, where he was terribly unhappy. He had not been, it would seem, a spoilt child, for there was at least one occasion when his father found it necessary to discipline him with a whipping. 'Charles very naughty and whipped for the first time' Walter noted in 1823 when his son was just five years old. It was very distressing for his parents when they were asked to removed him from Harrow. According to Mr. Kennedy, Charles was 'rude to and terrorised the maidservants' and now he had ducked a cousin of Kennedy's in the pond. Robert Grimston, then 18, and in his last year, told of the occurrence in a letter home, written on 26 July 1834:

> When you hear what Charles has done I do not think that you will be so annoyed as by the vague report that you will have heard. Kennedy has got a cousin of his in the school called Distin and Charles and this other boy have always been wrangling together and Charles the other morning with the assistance of young Milbank ducked him while bathing. Distin told Kennedy of it and said that Charles was always bullying him – now Distin is as big as Charles and a great deal older and besides the other morning they had a round or two together when some other boys put a stop to it: Distin wanted to fight it out but Charles said that he would rather not go home with black eyes. Kennedy complains that the boys have cut Distin. Very few ever spoke to him before and still fewer will now, and as several fellows have threatened to lick Distin for his share in the business, and Mrs. Kennedy is very much frightened about her cousin, they have sent him home, so there is no chance of Charles getting into any more trouble about him, except that I believe he is to be flogged for having ducked Distin. All the boys think that Charles is used very hard in being flogged – Several of them went into Kennedy to expostulate, the truth is that if he had not been a relation of Kennedy's nothing would have been thought of it'.

Charles, aged 16, also wrote home:

> I think that Kennedy cannot have represented the matter fairly to you from the letter you sent to Bob and as Bob is writing to you now about it I shall not tell you the story. The boy whom the row is all about is now put into Coventry by the school: that proves what they think about it. I remain your affectionate son C. Grimston. I wish you had come down here as it is not fair of Kennedy writing such a letter to you as he seems to have written. I hope you have now forgiven me.

This letter does not seem to have softened his parents towards him. Charlotte wrote off immediately to the soldier Duke of Cambridge to ask about the possibility of Charles joining a military establishment run by a Captain C.C. Trott in Hanover, which was under the Duke's patronage. His mother wrote that Charles was a 'very amiable and well-disposed boy, but certainly idle and fond of amusement'. She considered it desirable that he should be 'kept strict and well-looked after'. The Duke sent her the prospectus of the military academy, but did not think that Captain Trott would 'have the means of exercising a sufficient degree of discipline over a boy so wild and fond of pleasure'. However, William IV had made the promise of 'a pair of colours in one of the regiments of guards' when Charles had been one of the pages to Queen Adelaide, and so it was into the Coldstream Guards that Charles went, with the rank of Captain, and for three years he served with them in Canada, returning in 1842.

However, from the time of this incident at Harrow, nothing ever went right for him. There was a petty affair over a debt of five shillings for the purchase of a pipe when he was at Brighton in 1836. In 1844, in company with Lord Caledon, he was in trouble with the police, accused of having taken a soldier from their custody and of being abusive. Charles insisted that he was rescuing the soldier from the civil power with the best of motives. In spite of his father approaching the Duke of Wellington, who gave all the advice and help he could, there was a public trial and Charles was fined. This was seen as bringing dishonour to the regiment, and to the family.

Charles married against the wishes of his parents, and the name of his wife is never mentioned; she is always just 'Mrs. C. Grimston' in family letters. The worry of the trial had preyed on his father's mind: perhaps it just as well that he did not live to know that Charles became bankrupt, lost his land at Glen Moidart in Scotland and began to drink heavily. His brothers took him in hand, and with the wife of what his mother called 'his wretched marriage', he was put in what Charles himself referred to as 'Dr. McAllister's madhouse in Skye'. Charles wrote to his brother Grimston's solicitor, George Nicholson:

> If you and my brother think I am mad they are much mistaken, but I hope that they are aware of the character of the place that they are about to consign me to; it is true that there are many foolish things that I have done which may lead them to that conclusion, and that it would be better for me to be placed under restraint, but for God's sake, do not let me be placed in a house where I may never see my friends again and where Lord Macdonald's brother William committed suicide ...'

Nicholson sent the pathetic appeal on to Grimston. 'Pray', he wrote 'what answer shall I give to it? I have recently remitted your brother £5, for I found that he had not a farthing, and began to fear that he would raise means in some way or other to get to England, if he found that I wholly neglected him.'

It is a sad picture which emerges from the letters which Charles wrote from Strathaird to his brother, always via George Nicholson. He wrote of the poverty, starvation and typhus fever which was affecting the little town in 1852; on another occasion he wrote touchingly that he had found a piece of woodstone which he intended to keep for 'Grim'. 'It is not very large but it is prettily marked. Lord Salisbury's island Rhum they tell me is full of it, I wonder he does not work it. My arithmetic goes on very well. I work at it very hard, and hope that it may turn out of some use to me'. He begged again and again to be allowed to come home for a short time, 'to see you all, and then you would be able to judge for yourselves if I am fit for anything, and I trust in God not to disappoint you, pray take it into your consideration, and I shall wait anxiously for your answer'. His mother refused. Charles replied humbly 'pray do not be angry with me for the longing homesick feeling which I cannot subdue'. He then asked that his sister Mary, Lady Folkestone, should receive him at Longford. Mary conferred with her mother, and her reply reveals the true reason for her harshness towards her son. 'It is his wretched marriage – when he took that irrevocable step, that *must* for ever separate him from his family'.

Ultimately Charles and his wife left Skye. He was a very sick man; he had a skin eruption and a badly ulcerated leg, and also suffered from heart spasms. They went to live in a small, damp cottage in Edinburgh, probably acquired with the money that his great aunt Frances had left Charles in her will. In 1855 Charles was discharged from bankruptcy. The 2nd Marquess of Salisbury wrote in October of that year to suggest to Grimston that as there was a vacancy in the adjutancy of the 4th Middlesex Militia during an interregnum of commanding officers, that Charles might be suitable for the post. 'It has the merit of permanancy...there is a good deal of work as your brother knows which...he is perfectly capable of performing. I believe him to be perfectly steady'. This offer came too late, for the following year, Charles was dead at the age of forty.

In the diary of his brother Grimston, there is an entry for 26 April 1876, which reads 'Notice of Mrs. Brown's death and burial, near Blindwell, Millbrook. Widow before of my brother Charles, s.p.'.

Edward and Francis Grimston

Edward Harbottle Grimston and his younger brother Francis Sylvester Grimston both entered the Church. After Edward had taken his M.A. he became the Rector of the living owned by the family at Pebmarsh, like his great-uncle before him. Francis who according to his father was 'destined for the cure of souls' became Rector of another family living, at Wakes Colne in Essex. The brothers married two sisters, Frances Horatia and Catherine Morier, the eldest and fourth daughters respectively of Mr. John Morier.

Lady Katherine Grimston

Katty, as she was known in the family, was a very gentle, delicate and sensitive girl, a particular favourite with her father. She was presented at the Court of St James in April 1828, when she was 18, an occasion described by her Aunt Charlotte. 'This day ... Katharine was presented. I pray anxiously that the vanities of this world may not destroy in her those seeds of goodness, which now make her the delight of my life'. After her presentation, her mother chaperoned Katty to balls, sometimes accompanied by Katty's younger sister Emily, only 14 at the time. Several young men were considered to be eligible for her hand. There was 'Young Trotter', the son of Sir Coutts Trotter, who proposed to her the month after her presentation. Katty liked him very much, a fact which reassured her father, who 'wanted to be kind to my dear child and walked and talked with her' to ascertain her feelings about Trotter. He found her 'very reasonable upon the subject of Mr. Trotter's proposal'.

Nevertheless, it seemed to be taking some considerable time to sort matters out. Walter noted that Katty - and perhaps even more her mother - were 'considerably discomforted by the unsettled state of the Trotter affair' when he returned from Newmarket. Accordingly, on the following Sunday Sir Coutts Trotter was invited to lunch at Grosvenor Square to discuss marriage arrangements. However, after these discussions, the conclusion was reached that 'the alliance would be so very moderate, the father coming most unwillingly to the post', that 'Young Trotter' was rejected.

The unhappy suitor was overwhelmed with grief. He continued to call at

Grosvenor Square. Walter wrote that 'Poor Trotter called and was miserable
... I wish he had better parents or that they understood how to conduct
themselves'. Katty herself was more upset about the outcome than her father
had anticipated; in fact she was inconsolable, although Walter wondered
whether perhaps 'what she felt was more pity for poor Trotter than love'. He
himself certainly pitied the young man. 'How unenviable is Trotter's lot. He
loses his love, and learned of the worthlessness of his parents, also he
discovers that the attachment shewn to him by his father was pure
selfishness'. He thought Trotter 'a very nice young fellow, and if circumstances admitted I should like him for a son-in-law, but I should abominate his
connections'. On both sides of the proposed match there was little money –
perhaps Katty's lack of dowry came as a surprise to Sir Coutts. Seeing the
young couple together at a ball some time later, Walter realised that his
darling daughter was 'not comfortable, still desperately in love'. As he so
often did when perplexed, Walter wrote a little prayer in his diary. 'Most
humbly do I wish that it would please God to send me a little more prosperity
that I may be enabled to bring up my family in the situation in which He has
been pleased to place them'.

Another suitor for Katty's hand was Lord Frederick John Monson. Walter,
who had already heard 'a very good report' of the young man, went round all
his friends, to his sister Harriot, to his old aunts Frances and Charlotte
Johanna, to get their opinion of the proposed match. Poor Katty, not
surprisingly, became more and more uneasy as the time approached when
Lord Monson was to call. To ease the situation, Walter invited the Revd. Lord
Frederick Beauclerk, the Vicar of St Michael's, a keen huntsman, and an old
friend of the family, to dine at Gorhambury. According to Walter's diary, Lord
Frederick 'in a very good-humoured and ... gentlemanlike manner took off
much of the awkwardness' of the occasion. Even so, the fond father could not
but note that 'Poor Monson's manner is very good but alas his figure and size
make me tremble for him'. Katty did not take to him at all.

She was a great favourite with the Cecils of Hatfield, and a close friend of
Fanny, Lady Salisbury. (Today there are still several of her watercolour
drawings at Hatfield.) Katty and her brothers had often taken part in the
theatrical entertainments at Hatfield which Lady Salisbury loved to arrange.
In 1833 Katty played the part of 'Rowena' in *tableaux vivants* based on Sir
Walter Scott's 'Waverley' novels. This came about after a visit to Hatfield by
Sir Walter's daughter and son-in-law.

Lady Salisbury, when she was Fanny Gascoyne, had met her future husband
at Gorhambury; now, she was asked to vet the latest suitor for Katty's hand.
He was John Foster Barham, who had been M.P. for Stockbridge, and was to
represent the constituency of Kendal from 1834 to 1837. He was four years
younger than Katty, and was the son of John Foster Barham of Trecwm,
Pembroke, and Stockbridge, Hampshire, by Lady Caroline Tufton, daughter
of the 8th Earl of Thanet. Lady Salisbury was invited to Gorhambury and
described the course of events in her diary:

November 11th [1833]. Went to Gorhambury to meet Mr. Barham who is coming down on trial for Lady Katharine.

12th. The lover expected all day but in vain.

13th. He arrived at breakfast having been delayed by the fog the day before – 6 hours between London and Barnet – and obliged to sleep at St Albans. He acquitted himself very well today in his very awkward and difficult position. He is not good-looking, nor the reverse: tall, with small eyes and a reddish face, and rather tigerish in appearance. I see no fault at present in his manner or conversation: and at least he had the rare merit of being desperately in love.

14th. She is favourably disposed, and will not be able to hold out long against the pressing entreaties of her family, and the persecution of her mother to give him a final answer.

15th. A letter from Emily Grimston saying Katty has finally consented. I hope it may be for her happiness; it is a leap in the dark. I regard her as lost to me – he is a Whig, and will probably avoid associating with us as much as possible.

Katty was married to John Barham two months later at St George's Church, Hanover Square, on 14 January 1834, by the Dean of Salisbury. A newspaper report under the heading 'Marriage in High Life' noted that 'The bride was attended at the altar by her three sisters and five brothers. After the ceremony, the Countess of Verulam gave a breakfast in Grosvenor Square to the Dowager Marchioness of Salisbury, Lady Cowley, Mr. and Lady Catherine Cavendish, &c. The happy couple afterwards left town for Gorhambury'.

Mr. Barham was thought to be a kind and excellent man, but 'either from a fall he had just before his marriage, or from some hereditary taint', symptoms of insanity emerged, even during the honeymoon. For a long time, Katty managed to conceal this from her family, but 'the birth of a dead child a year later completely turned John Foster Barham's brain'. He became more and more violent towards her, and one day his fury was so great that Katty sent for her eldest brother Grimston, who arrived just in time as 'Mr. Barham had knocked her down and was standing over her'. Grimston saw to it that Barham was placed in 'a private asylum'. Lady Salisbury went to see Katty soon afterwards on 5 May 1836. Her diary tells us that she 'went to sit with poor Lady K. Barham after this shocking calamity. Her self-possession and strength are wonderful. He is in confinement and it is hoped may not live'. Katty dined at Hatfield on 6 July, and Lady Salisbury noted that there was 'no change in Mr. Barham'. The next year in May, however, she was able to write 'heard of Mr. Barham's death – a great blessing'.

This tragic story was the stepping-stone, however, which led Katty into a happier second marriage. Katty's sister Emily tells us that '[Lord] Clarendon's mother told me that when her son, having just inherited his title from his uncle, was returning from Spain, where he had been minister,[he] wrote to her saying that he wished as soon as possible after his return to marry, but as his uncle had left everything he possibly could away from him, he would not be able to marry a penniless bride; he therefore begged his mother to let him know whether there were any young ladies that would suit him, having some grist to bring to the mill. His mother ... ended her letter by saying: "And your old friend Katty Grimston has just become a widow". Clarendon's answer to that was "Many thanks for your information. I shall certainly look after my old friend Katty Grimston"'. No sooner did George Clarendon arrive in England than he posted down to Gorhambury, and, says Emily, 'it was evident what would be the result, and my darling Kit was a very happy woman'. The unfortunate Barham had at least left his widow the benefit of considerable wealth.

It seems possible that Clarendon had hoped to win Katty's hand at an earlier date, for amongst the family letters is one signed merely 'C' from Darmstadt in Germany, sent four years before Katty married Barham. The letter is addressed to Katty's father. Was it from George Clarendon – the handwriting resembles his closely?

> I am anxious to hear from you again particularly about Katty. It is a critical time of her life. I should have much confidence in her own good sense – and hope she will please herself and be happy. However, I must say the last batch or two of beaux I saw, did not inspire me with much respect. I hear some better specimens have appeared lately. Tell Katty, I visit her sometimes when she is not aware of it, if she ever feels anybody giving her a little pinch when she is looking at the wrong beau, or doing anything wrong, it is me – if she wants any proof I can give it to her – I even remarked how she was dressed at both balls at Gorhambury as well as Ashridge and elsewhere. Let her dare to criticise it if she will. Above all give her my best good wishes and love. C.

George Clarendon and Katty (now more generally known as Kitty) Barham were married in June, 1839. They went to live at the Clarendon family seat at The Grove, Watford. George certainly made his wife happy, as shown by her lively chatty letters home to her family, written whilst she was accompanying her husband on various ambassadorial missions. Lord Clarendon was to have a distinguished political career, and Kitty was very willing to involve herself in it. He was Lord Lieutenant of Ireland from 1847 to 1852 and afterwards Foreign Secretary for a number of years, being one of the most influential holders of that office at a time when Great Britain was at the height of her prosperity.

Lady Emily Mary Grimston

Walter and Charlotte's second daughter was a beautiful, petite girl, as light-hearted as she was dainty. As we have already seen in Chapter 11, Emily had fallen in love with Claud Abercorn, a friends of her brothers, at the age of nine. For a long time Walter expected the romance to lead to marriage, but Abercorn appears to have been an indecisive fellow. During the London season of 1832 he sent a pony every day for Emily to ride in the park. At the this time her father considered 'Emily's position with Lord A.' to be 'critical'. However, he seemed to blow hot and cold. One evening Emily and her family went to the Opera and 'Abercorn came too; but he went away almost immediately to the Duchess of Bedford's box. Poor little Emily quite uncomfortable'. However, the same evening the party went on to Lady Grantham's house; 'A. followed and late in the evening got Emily to sit by him'. At the same party, another young man was paying some attention to

Emily: he was Lord Craven, a friend of Emily's eldest brother Grimston. Walter noted that he 'talked somewhat seriously to E.', but summed up the evening as being 'upon the whole a bad one'.

From this point on, Walter's enigmatic diary entries relating to the matter shed little light. Were Abercorn and Craven rivals for Emily's hand? Could she herself not make up her mind between them? The very next day 'Lord Abercorn came and insisted on Emily's riding out', and the day after 'Lord A. breakfasted with Grim and had some conversation with him'. Lord Craven was still very much on the scene, however, for later the same month (March), Walter wrote 'A very disagreeable day. To the Opera. Abercorn and Craven came into the box together, the latter stayed until the end and handed E. away'. Abercorn had his revenge on his rival next day when he sent his pony over for Emily and 'the young ones all rode together, and were gratified with all the circumstances of the day'. Two days later 'the young ones rode to the races and had a very jolly morning. Abercorn paid great attention to Emily and gave me much food for contemplation'. However, it was Craven who 'lent Emily his horse' to use at Gorhambury. It is plain that Walter favoured Abercorn of the two, but his dilatory behaviour was infuriating. On 1 May the angry father wrote in his diary that he could not but think 'Abercorn has used us all ill, and long to tell him so, but have promised patience'.

Three years later William Craven was finally successful in winning Emily's hand. Lady Salisbury noted in her diary for 28 July 1835 that 'Emily Grimston's marriage to Lord Craven announced at last. I am glad to hear of it'. Emily's great-aunt, Frances Grimston, wrote in her notebook of family events 'Emily Grimston was married in the Drawing Room at Gorhambury to the Earl of Craven, this 5th September 1835'. The yellow drawing room at Gorhambury, with its blue and gold furnishings, and the organ which had belonged to Emily's grandmother Harriot to provide the music, would have been a perfect setting for a wedding on a mellow autumn day.

The day was not a happy one for Katty, Emily's elder sister, who had given birth to a dead child four days earlier. Lady Salisbury wrote in her diary:

> September 5th. Went to Emily Grimston's marriage at Gorhambury ... They were married in the house by the Dean of Carlisle, about 30 people present and a breakfast to the county afterwards. I was heartily glad when it was over – nothing so melancholy as a wedding when one considers the chances for its turning out ill: and how often both parties may wish in vain those awful and irrevocable words then said, unsaid. I saw poor Katty, inconsolable for the loss of her child, and crying night and day in the midst of the festivities around her. Perhaps in another year her sorrow may be turned into joy and Emily's ...'

Lady Mary Augusta Frederica Grimston

Walter and Charlotte's third daughter had been named Mary after the Duchess of Gloucester, Augusta after the Duchess of Cambridge and Frederica after the Duchess of York. To judge from an engraving made from a painting of her by John Hayter, Mary was a handsome girl. Her dark hair was parted in the middle over a high forehead and curled in ringlets to her shoulders, and her beautifully shaped neck is reminiscent of that of her great-grandmother, Mrs. Walter.

At Queen Victoria's coronation in 1838, Mary, then 18, was one of the eight unmarried daughters of peers who bore the Queen's train. Among her father's papers is a poem about these trainbearers, with one verse about Mary:

> There (theme for poet's praise!)
> With swan-like throat, and clear majestic eye
> Verulam's stately Mary glided by:-
> And with her quiet gaze
> Fix'd smiling in the scene which she surveyed
> The soldier Anglesea's bright Adelaide.

The verse on Victoria herself is as follows:

> Young were they all – and fair –
> But thou, Victoria, held'st thy fitting place,
> As amongst garden-flowers the lily's grace
> Blooms with royal air,
> And from that lovely various group, apart,
> Dids't stand, and gently look the Queen thou art.

Mary Grimston married Jacob Pleydell Bouverie, a son of the 3rd Earl of Radnor, by special licence at St Michael's Church, St Albans, in September 1840. In time she and her husband became the Earl and Countess of Radnor.

12.   The Grimston coat of arms.

Epilogue

Like a mature vine in need of pruning the Grimston chronicle must of necessity be broken off. Another volume would be needed to complete the full history and so what follows is the merest fragment of the endeavours of later heads of the family.

The courtship of James Walter, later third Earl of Verulam, with Frances ('Fanny') Graham of Netherby was unusual; he had long admired her, indeed had proposed marriage to her, but had been rejected in favour of a handsome dark-haired Scot, the Mackintosh of Moy. It was cruel that the Mackintosh should die of pneumonia within a year of marriage, leaving Fanny pregnant. Had the child been a boy, Grimston history would have been different, for Fanny would no doubt have felt it her duty to remain with the Mackintosh family in Scotland. However, the child was a girl (christened Eva). After some persuasion by Mackintosh's sister Mary, Fanny returned to London and once more met James. After some further persuasion, she came to Gorhambury as James's bride, and bore a further six daughters and a son.

The Third Earl was something of an inventor. One of his more memorable inventions was a non-drip tap, patented under the name of 'Ye Tippe Toppe Tappe'. Later in life when corpulence had confined him unwillingly to a wheelchair, he maintained an element of independence by inventing a motorised wheelchair powerful enough to outpace his attendant footman.

The Third Earl died in 1924 and was succeeded by his son, James Walter, always known as Jim. The Fourth Earl had a brilliant academic and sporting career at Eton and Christ Church, Oxford. He went bald early in his 20s and when he rowed in the Boat Race a spectator was heard to say 'Who is the old man in the Oxford crew?'. In 1909 he married Lady Violet Brabazon, a statuesque Irish beauty, whose family, the Earls of Meath, live at Killruddery, a magnificent house with a famous garden near Dublin.

The Fourth Earl was an entrepreneur, starting numerous companies in England and abroad. He was one of the two founders of what was to become a major non-ferrous metal empire. He drilled for oil in South America, and in Southern Rhodesia purchased a large acreage of virgin bush which within 30 years had been transformed into farms which formed the largest tobacco growing unit in the world. All seemed to be going well, but the Fourth Earl had not foreseen the crash of 1929 and the slump which followed it. He found himself needing cash at a time when any asset could be bought for a song. In

1930 Gorhambury, its contents and the majority of the estate were put up for sale but no acceptable offer materialised. In 1931 the majority of the farmland was sold, the house was closed up and Jim, Violet and their four sons went to live in Hampstead. However, the family did not lose interest in Gorhambury during what was to be a five-year exile, and in 1934 the archaeologist Mortimer Wheeler was asked to undertake the excavation of the Roman theatre of Verulamium which lies on Gorhambury land. (It has remained on public view ever since).

The Fourth Earl was able to move back to Gorhambury in 1936, but within months of the return Violet died suddenly at the age of fifty. Although she had been châtelaine of the house for only a few years, she catalogued and restored order to the contents of the house. Many notable discoveries were made in the course of this procedure, including seven early quartos of Shakespeare's plays, which were loaned to the Bodleian Library. Violet recognised sacks of dirty broken glass in the stables as the remains of the enamelled glass from Bacon's day. The panels (recreated by experts from the Victoria and Albert Museum) are now prominent amongst the treasures at Gorhambury.

Two years after the declaration of the Second World War, Gorhambury was requisitioned by the War Office and was used by branches of the Intelligence Services for the rest of the war. The Victorian wing was left for the family, securely bricked off. It was in this relatively small and somewhat dismal area that the Fourth Earl continued to live, with his sons, his daughter in law and his young grandchildren. His two younger sons, Brian and Bruce, both awarded the Distinguished Flying Cross, were killed in action. Furniture which had been sent to a storage warehouse in order to make room for the War Office was destroyed in an enemy air raid. Gorhambury's stables were accidentally burnt to the ground by our own troops.

In 1949 the Fourth Earl died in a motor accident and his elder son, James Brabazon, also known as Jim, became the Fifth Earl of Verulam. He formed the bold resolution of restoring the decaying fabric of the house, now almost 200 years old. The stone which had been used to face the main block of the house had weathered badly by the end of the 19th century, and was in a very poor state by the 1950s. With the aid of a substantial grant from the Historic Buildings Council, every existing facing stone was replaced by a new Portland stone, with the exception of the 'Coade stone' capitals which top the numerous columns. This restoration was begun in 1956 and continued for ten years. The roof was relined in copper, all the pictures were cleaned and restored as necessary, and the main rooms were redecorated.

The Fifth Earl, who had never married, died in 1960 and was succeeded by his brother John, under whose supervision the restoration was completed. Jim and John were both great men, but their interests and successes were in completely different spheres, the exception being their mutual love of Gorhambury. It is thanks to such enduring feeling for the house and estate that Gorhambury stands secure today as the home of the Grimston family.

GORHAMBURY, 1967.
W.Bryson.

13.   Gorhambury's newly-restored portico in 1967. A pen and ink
drawing by W. Bryson, butler to the 6th Earl of Verulam.

Appendix One

The Three Wives of Edward Grimston, 'The Ambassador'

Edward's first wife was called Alice; unfortunately her surname is unknown. A manuscript which belonged to the parish church of Eye in Suffolk has an obscure entry which perhaps refers to her. It reads as follows:

> *Obit venerabilis feminae quodam uxoris E Grimston ab infanti excellente ducissa postea generose magnifice Margarete Reginae que etiam et virtutibus futi indata obiit 1456*

It thus seems possible that she was a lady of the court.

We know much more about Edward's second wife. There is a copy of the marriage settlement, dated 26 September 1459, between Mary, daughter of Sir William Drury by Katharine Swynford. We may note here that although Katharine herself was descended from the marriage of Sir Hugh Swynford and his wife (another Catherine), the family had an interesting connection with the royal house of Lancaster. After Sir Hugh's death, his wife (Katharine's grandmother) married John of Gaunt, the Duke of Lancaster, and became the ancestress of the Tudor and other royal houses. Edward Grimston had eight children by this second marriage.

Mary Grimston died in 1469 and two years later Edward married for the third time. The bride on this occasion was Phillip [sic], daughter of John, Lord Tiptot, and widow of Lord Roos. There were no children by this marriage.

Appendix Two

Anne Grimston's Father, Sir Nathaniel Bacon of Culford, 1585-1627

Sir Nathaniel Bacon of Culford occupies an important position in the history of English art. He came from that extraordinary Bacon stock, which produced so many artistic and erudite people, being a grandson of Sir Nicholas Bacon, the builder of the Tudor Gorhambury, by his first marriage to Jane Fernley. Little is known of his life until 1613, when he began to court Jane, Lady Cornwallis (mother of the Anne of our main story). Before her marriage, she had been Jane Meautys, daughter of Hercules Meautys (a relative of Sir Thomas Meautys) and at the time of Sir Nathaniel's courtship of her she was a young, attractive and rich widow, with one son – Frederick Cornwallis – whose portrait hangs at Gorhambury.

At first Jane was suspicious of Nathaniel's intentions, and she told Mr. Parr, the Rector of Palgrave, Suffolk, that she thought it was her fortune that had attracted him to her. 'I confess by several circumstances I shall find my fortune to be the chief motive'. However, Nathaniel's parents, who were anxious that his suit should prosper, also wrote to Mr. Parr, telling him to assure Jane that it was for herself and not for her money that he courted her. Finally she gave in and the two were married the following year. Nathaniel's parents settled the estate of Culford on him, together with an income of £1,000 a year.

In November 1613 he wrote to tell his wife that he was going to Antwerp to study painting. His only surviving writings are his letters to Jane. In these he says little about painting, except for an occasional passing reference, as in one letter where he asked her 'bid thou John Fenn to send my colours as soon as possible'. On another occasion he asked her to send more 'masticott'.

It has now been proved beyond doubt that it was this Nathaniel and not his half-uncle, Sir Nathaniel Bacon of Stiffkey, who was the amateur painter referred to by contemporaries. In 1907 Prince Frederick Duleep Singh clarified the matter once and for all in an article in the *Burlington Magazine*.

On 7 March 1618 Lucy, Countess of Bedford, a friend of Jane's wrote to implore her to buy any Holbeins in the possession of Sir Nathaniel's father, who was 'like to die'. She had heard that he had 'some pieces of Holbein's which [the Earl of] Arundel I am sure will try all means to get'. Nathaniel was asked to 'prevail with his brother to whose share I conceive they will fall'. Nathaniel did her this service and was thanked for his help.

Art historians today consider that Sir Nathaniel studied in Italy, and although this seems a valid supposition from the evidence of his paintings, there is nothing in his letters to substantiate it. On 29 November 1613 he stated that he was about to depart for Flushing, so he clearly visited the Low Countries.

Nathaniel Bacon was knighted at the coronation of Charles I, in 1625: his wife, who until then had always signed herself 'Jane Cornwallis', now began to use 'Jane Bacon'. At this time we find Sir Nathaniel promising Lady Bedford flowers for her garden; however he warns his wife that he had better not be 'too free an offerer to a free taker'.

He writes affectionately of his three children. His eldest was a daughter, Jane, who died as an infant and was buried at Culford. His son, Nicholas, born in 1617, lived until 1660 but died unmarried. Anne, the youngest, was to play a part in our Grimston saga, marrying firstly Sir Thomas Meautys and secondly Sir Harbottle Grimston (see pedigree, p.17). There is a charming letter from Nathaniel to his wife, written from their home at Redgrave when the children were small: 'Our children are well, and little Nick has cast his coat and seemeth metamorphosed into a grasshopper. Jane is a very modest maiden, and is wholly taken up with travelling by herself, which she performeth very handsomely, and will be ready to run at your command when you return. Thus with my best love and prayers I leave, resting always and only yours, Nath. B.' The children are represented on Sir Nathaniel's marble monument in Culford church.

In 1624 Nathaniel first showed signs of ill-health, and apparently suffered pain in his teeth. He died three years later, aged 42, on 1 July, probably from consumption. He was buried at Culford where a marble bas-relief was erected to his memory. Oval in form, the features bear some resemblance to his great self-portrait which still hangs at Gorhambury. On the slab a palette and brushes are shown. The monument's inscription describes him as a man of 'great modesty, of most plain and single heart, of an ancient freedom and integrity of mind, loyal to his Prince, a lover of his country, and a great sufferer for both'. In his funeral certificate it says of him that 'he was endowed with many excellent virtues besides his endowments of nature. He was a great lover of all good arts and learning and knew good literature'. Edward Norgate spoke of him as his 'dear friend Sir N. Bacon ... a gentleman whose rare parts and generous disposition, whose excellent learning and great skill in this and good arts deserve a never-dying memory'. Speaking of the colour pink 'which is a colour so useful and so hard to get good', Norgate observes that Sir Nathaniel had succeeded in making one so good that 'P. Oliver making proof of some that I gave him, did highly commend it, and used none other to his dying day; wherewith and with Indian Lake he made sure expressions of those deep and glowing shadows in those histories he copied after Titian, that no oil painting should appear more warm and fleshly that those of his hand'. He gives the recipe for Sir Nathaniel's 'brown pink', which may be found in Dallaway's notes to Walpole's *Anecdotes of Painting*.

Sir Nathaniel's work attained the perfection of a master. Walpole observed that his 'manner and colouring approaches nearer to the Flemish School'. Indeed the works of Snyders and Cuyp come readily to mind when one contemplates his two still-life pictures at Gorhambury, the earliest English still-lifes painted. His 'Cook Maids' with dead birds and animals are painted with much skill and lustre of colour, and he incorporated a curious technique by including the shadowy figure of the gamekeeper in the background. One of the two 'Cook Maid' paintings – the better of the two – came by inheritance through Nathaniel's daughter Anne. The other, less good, was purchased for Gorhambury during the lifetime of the Fifth Earl of Verulam in the 1950s.

The artist's great self-portrait is also at Gorhambury. Painted in a style reminiscent of Van Dyke, Sir Nathaniel gives us an insight into his interests and way of life. He is shown dressed as a gentleman of fashion with a gay sporting hat and a little 'tumbler' dog beside him. A sword hangs next to an artist's palette. There is a painting of Minerva, goddess of the arts and of war. Nathaniel holds a drawing, and in front of him an atlas lies open at a map of the Low Countries. Beside it on the table are several large volumes and two further sheets of paper, the upper one bearing a diagram of perspective lines to a vanishing point. Beside the self-portrait hangs a painting of his wife Jane in profile. It is perhaps his most delectable work, reminiscent of Pollaiolo's 'Profile of a Woman' in the Museo Poldi Pozzoli, which Nathaniel may have seen if in fact he did study in Italy.

The monument erected to him in Culford church is undated, but he was certainly dead by 2 July 1627, for on that day Sir Thomas Meautys wrote a letter of condolence to his widow. A translation of the inscription on the monument was made by the Fifth Earl of Verulam: 'Traveller! Behold! This is the likeness of Nathaniel Bacon, Knight, wearing the Royal Bath, whom, when practice and observation had made him most learned in the history of lineages – the same, Behold a thing so wonderful! in the expression of the same Nature alone taught with the brush to conquer Nature with Art. Thou are destined sufficiently for our eyes. Fare thee well!'.

In the Ashmolean Museum in Oxford there is a small, strange landscape painted on copper, given to John Tradescant, the famous botanist, by Sir Nathaniel Bacon.

Appendix Three

The Expenses incurred at the Funeral of Sir Harbottle Grimston, the Second Baronet

	£	s	d
To the searchers		5	0
Four flambeaux		18	0
Paid the groom's bill for the line of four horses expenses on road to Gorhambury	1	16	0
To Mr. Cole five guineas	5	7	6
More to him the forfeiture to the poor for burying in linen	5	0	0
To the bearers	2	0	0
To the clerk	1	0	0
To Joseph Carter for his work at the vault		10	0
To Robert Bradwine for his work there		10	0
To the sexton		2	0
To Mr. Reeves the apothecary his bill	11	0	0
Paid for making Mrs. Mantor and petticoats [sic]		8	6
Paid Mr. William Bennett's bill	11	7	0
To Mr. Lee in lieu of mourning for his children	4	0	0
To Mr. Reeves the apothecary for his attendance in the Master's sickness	3	4	6
To the hosier his bill	3	16	6
To the saddler his bill	3	0	0
Paid for making five 'mantors'[?mantles] and petticoats for the maids	1	15	0
To Mr. Hobart his bill	10	18	0
Paid for the black gown, cap and slippers	3	0	0
To Mr. Wiseman his bill for probate of the will	2	6	0
To Edward Downes his bill for charge of the horses	4	14	7
To Mr. Page his bill the charges at Gorhambury and other things on the road	3	11	6
To Sir William Luckyn in lieu of mourning for his children	4	0	0
To Mrs. Smith in lieu of mourning for her children	4	0	0
To the mercer his bill for crape	23	14	0
Paid for James (Mr. Grimston's footboys) and Jack's black coat	2	5	0
Paid Mr. Saunders the herald painter his bill	32	0	0
To Mr. Pennice the woollen draper his bill	270	0	0
To Mr. Sherl the tailor his bill	25	0	0
To Mr. Smithsby the woollen draper his bill	247	13	0
To Mr. Russell his bill for the coffin etc.	64	0	0
To the Gentlewomen for making up the gowns and mantors[sic]	6	19	0
Paid for wax candles	5	2	0
To the coachmaker his bill	55	0	0

Note: the item 'To Mr. Russell his bill for the coffin etc.' was

	£	s.	d.
	810	4	0

made up as follows: For a large double coffin, covered with
velvet, and set off with the best work, with his coat of
arms, all the hinges chased and silvered, with a large leaden

coffin, and preserving his body	30	0	0
For the use of a velvet hearse	5	0	0
For the use of ten fine cloaks for gentlemen	3	0	0
For the use of 17 cloaks for servants	3	8	0

For a man and horse going into the country to hang the

church	1	0	0
For a piece of diaper		10	0

The room where Sir Harbottle lay, hung deep, and the floor
covered; 12 silver sconces, six silver

candlesticks, and six black stands	7	10	0
For two latches and putting them on		3	0
For three mourning sconces	12	0	0
For my attendance and trouble	2	0	0
In all	64	11	0

Received this third of March, 1684, of Sir Samuel Grimston,
the sum of sixty-two pounds in full of this bill [signed]

William Russell.

Appendix Four

References to pictures and furniture in Sir Samuel Grimston's Accounts

	£	s	d

1691. Received of Mistress Baker money paid her by John Stephens, cabinet maker, in part for 237 feet of walnut tree at 1s.3d. per foot, the sum £13.0s.0d. which with a guinea my Master [Sir Samuel] received in earnest is £14.01s.0d., so that there remains due 14s.9d.

	£	s	d
1691. Dec. 20. Paid Mr. Arme the upholsterer in full his bill for the damask bed.	48	10	0
1692 March 26. Paid Mr. Baker for furniture, etc.	1	10	0
1692. For lacquering varnish, 1 pint; a book of silver; for two brushes for painting; for oils and colour as by bill.(1)	1	2	1
1693. Mar. Mr. Sparling for *Aesop's Fables*(2)		15	0
1693. April. For black frames, straining frames, cloth, and pasting on the pictures of the Emperor and King of the Romans.		14	0
1693. April. To Mr. Vandest for my Lord and Lady Thanet's pictures.	10	0	0
1693. April. Althorp the potter his bill	8	10	0
1693. July. For a pint of brandy for my Lady's throat		1	4
1694. April 1. To Sir Godfrey Kneller for the picture(3)	22	0	0
1695. May. For the charge of two dozen of plates and engraving		18	6
1695. Dec. 10. To the cabinet maker for tables, stands and glass frames	10	0	0
1696. For a plain table and instruments to measure with	3	15	0
1697. Paid Mr. Meure in full his bill of Delft ware	7	3	0
1697. The glazier's bill for the sashes had to Gorhambury(4)	3	15	8

Notes

(1) Amateur lacquer work was much in vogue as an occupation for ladies at the time.

(2) This may be the copy in the Library, dated 1692.

(3) No mention of which portrait is referred to here.

(4) Mr. J.C. Rogers, writing in *The Manor and Houses of Gorhambury* (1933), regarded the last item as of special interest, as being the earliest record of the new type of wooden sliding sashes coming to Gorhambury. He notes that in a 17th century water colour drawing of the house, most of the south windows 'are changed from the original casements – either in stone or wood frames with lead lights – to sashes divided by stout bars in to rectangular panes, such as all new houses of that time were having throughout; and many old ones, like Gorhambury, were having the windows renewed to comply with the new fashion, but at the expense of a certain incongruity. The Venetian style sash in the central Long Gallery, shown in the painting, is probably not earlier than about 1740. If we may judge by the slight remains, it is probable the windows within the court were not altered, certainly the hall windows and one in the west range still have their 16th century stone frames'.

Appendix Five

Accounts of William Grimston (Luckyn), First Viscount, headed 'Extraordinary Expenses on my Son Grimston's Account, in 1730'

1730	£	s	d
Paid for a silver vestcoat [sic]	15	00	00
Two journeys into Hertfordshire and other expenses	07	08	00
Gave him for his pocket	05	05	00
One piece of fine cambric	02	18	00
Paid Mr. Jacob on account of a new chariot	100	00	00
July the 2nd. Paid the coachman his bill of expenses and horse hire.	02	14	01
Paid for the bob wigs for Sammy	03	03	00
Paid him in money for his pocket	10	10	00
Mrs. Constantine's bill for three pairs of lace ruffles for myself	11	10	00
Mr. Chapman's bill for linen	38	16	02½
August the 3rd. Mr. Arnold's bill for four horses	120	00	00
Gave his servants	02	02	00
5th. Gave him for his pocket	10	10	00
One week's board wages to a servant to the 6th of August		03	00
7th. Paid David's bill of disbursements on Sammy's account with hay and straw	02	14	00
Paid for mending and making some of his linen		14	00
Paid Mrs. Killigrew for all the right and title she has to the personal estate of St Julian's left her by her mother, relict and executrix to Admiral Killigrew	289	10	00
Gave Jemmy towards a suit of clothes	20	00	00
25th. Paid Sammy for his pocket	05	05	00
Expenses in going to St Julian's to view the goods	01	16	00
Paid for a gown and lining for Lady Grimston	24	16	00
September the 2nd. Paid for silk to make Miss a coat	07	10	00
Paid for 4 pairs of new pistols	08	08	00
4th. Paid Sammy for his pocket	10	10	00
Paid David the coachman for straw for his horses		10	00
Paid for fitting up the stables for his horses	03	00	00
Paid for hay for his horses for the whole time	10	00	00
10th. Gave Mr. Piggott two fees for his opinion on the marriage articles	07	07	00
Paid Mr. Car for a new wig for myself	07	07	00
Paid for a pair of leather britches for his postilion	01	01	00
16th. Paid the hatter for livery hats and one for Sammy	05	13	00
Gave Mr. Piggott's clerk		05	00
September 17. Gave Mr. Jacob's letter carrier		10	06
Gave Mr. Piggott for further advice	02	02	00
Gave Walter Cole towards a suit of clothes against the wedding	02	02	00

Paid Sammy for his pocket	10	10	00
Paid for a pair of breeches for the postilion	01	01	00
23rd. Gave Mr. Hendon for his trouble in searching for			
Lady Ann Grimston's marriage settlements	02	02	00
24th. Gave Mr. Piggott another fee	02	02	00
29th. Paid the hosier's bill	08	13	06
October the 2nd. Paid for a chaldron of coals and carriage	02	02	00
5th. Paid for keeping a horse in smithies three weeks		06	00
8th. Paid Sammy for his pocket	10	10	00
Gave Mr. Ward for his opinion and perusing my			
marriage settlements to clear up some obstacles made			
by Mr. Jacob in the settlements of my son	02	02	00
Paid David the coachman for hay and straw and other			
things for Sammy's horses to the 10th of October 1730	01	09	00
20th. Paid for a bob wig for Sammy	01	01	00
24. Paid Mr. Piggott for perusing a marriage settlement	02	02	00
30. Expenses of Mr. Jacob's with coach hire and entertaining			
Mr. Jennings the night he came to town	01	13	00
Paid Sammy for his pocket	15	15	00
31st. Entertaining Mr. Jennings on Sammy's account		19	06
Paid at Doctor's Commons for a faculty and charges	11	16	00
November 4th. Paid Sammy for his pocket	50	00	00
5th. Gave the servants at Miss Lovell's and my son's servants	10	10	00
6th. Gave Mr. Crispin for his expenses on my account	01	01	00
10th. Paid Botty his expenses in attending his brother Grimston		08	06
Expenses at Mr. Thorpes in settling the supper		07	00
Paid Mr. Arnold for one horse for myself	30	00	00
Gave the servant		10	06
Paid Mr. Wildman for a pearl necklace	200	00	00
Paid ditto for a gold equipage set with diamonds	110	00	00
Paid Mr. Wildman for the wedding ring		14	00
Paid Mr. Seymour with the ten guineas I gave Mr. Martin for a			
pair of diamond earrings	1060	10	00
Paid ditto for a watch set with diamonds	285	00	00
Paid ditto for a diamond buckle	130	00	00
Paid ditto for diamond buttons for sleeves	65	00	00
Paid ditto for a large diamond ring	300	00	00
Paid Mr. Barker for a diamond ring	110	00	00
Paid Mr. Martin for a diamond hoop ring	22	10	00
Paid for a gold snuff box	23	12	06
Paid Mr. Vernon for velvet and lining for myself	20	11	06
Paid David for hay for my son's horses		12	06
The value of the hay brought out of the country for my son's horses			
during his stay in Soho Square and straw in London	09	00	00
12th. Paid the fiddlers when I entertained my son and daughter	02	02	00
Expenses at Mr. Thorpe's in settling his accounts		04	00
18th. The saddler's bill for what my son had separate from mine	13	02	00
Mr. Madewell's bill for the glasses used at the supper	12	12	09
Paid Mr. Thorpe bill[sic] for the supper and dessert	40	15	02
For wine brandy and other expenses exclusive of Mr. Thorpe bill	05	00	00
Things had for Sammy's use of Mr. Johnson	14	00	00
Mr. Jacob the coach maker's bill 100 paid before	247	15	00
Paid for buttons for my velvet suit and Botty's	04	19	00
Mr. Barnett the lace man's bill	151	11	06

Mr. Panchard the tailor's bill	26	16	01
Mr. Young the woollen draper's bill	13	03	00
Mr. Alexander's bill	53	04	00
Mr. Chapman's bill for linen	40	00	00
Paid for making Miss coat at her brother's wedding	01	14	00
Paid for a hat and stockings for Botty at the wedding	01	10	00
Paid for a new set of wheels for the chariot	05	05	00
Mr. Constantine's bill	128	04	06
Mr. Elison the woollen draper's bill	47	01	01
Mr. Marriott the tailor's bill	40	10	05
Paid for wax candles at the supper	02	05	00
Paid the corn chandler's bill for my son's horses	12	08	04
Paid for buttons for the liveries and coats	05	02	09
Gave the ringers of St Michael's, the abbey and St. Peters a guinea each, in all	03	03	00
Gave St Albans music		10	06
Paid the harponetts [sic] for seven weeks at Gorhambury and their expenses on the road	07	17	00
Paid Mr. Cowdery the tailor's bill in the city	06	02	06
Paid Mrs. Constantine's bill	158	03	07
Paid Mr. Twinye's bill for tea, etc., in the country	02	02	00
Paid a bill for tea and other things to go into the country	06	17	00
Paid a grocer's bill for things to carry into the country	04	05	01
Paid Mrs. Blythman's bill in the country	44	14	00
Paid Jones her first bill in the country	12	01	00
The sheep venison and pork killed in the country exclusive of the butcher's bills	28	10	00
Paid for oats and hay in the country	20	00	00
Paid for wine in the country	37	10	00
Paid for boar in the country	24	00	00
Cheese and butter, milk and cream with eggs of my own dairy	10	00	00
Paid for wood and cutting with coal	20	00	00
Brandy-arrack [sic] that was in the house exclusive of what was sent down upon the occasion	14	00	00
Paid Mr. Kettle's bill for things in the house	12	00	00
Paid Mr. Paxton's bill	06	09	07
Paid Mr. Hiron's bill		18	00
Paid John Arnotte bill		14	00
Paid Mr. Rud's bill	07	13	05
Paid Mr. Marshall's bill for carriage	03	07	00
Paid for catching larks and paid the errand boy	01	09	00
Paid for midera [sic] sent into the country	02	11	05
Paid Harry Clarke bill for provision bought into the house	05	04	10
Paid the farrier's bill for my son's horse	04	05	04
Paid Mr. Parry the Bishop [sic] of Canterbury's Under Secretary for procuring a licence	02	02	00
Paid Mr. Piggott for his attendance at the signing of the writings and marriage settlements	05	05	00
Gave Mr. Jacob's servants and coach hire		17	00
Paid Mr. Jacob's bill of disbursements	73	14	06
Paid Mr. Jacob's bill for drafts and engrossing	126	09	00
Gave him for his extraordinary trouble	200	00	00
Gave Mr. Jacob's clerk	21	00	00

Paid Mr. Ward's clerk not included in Mr. Jacob's bill as

charged above	01	01	00
Paid Mr. Piggott for making my will to settle my affairs agreeable to my son's marriage ..settlements	10	10	00
Gave his clerk	01	01	00
Paid Mr. Pembroke for adding a codicil to my will upon Mr. Forth's going off to subject my son to pay the arrear due to me of the £2,000 I was to receive upon the estate settled upon him at marriage	04	04	00
Paid off two debts for monies borrowed to clear and discharge in full Lord Bruce's claim upon my estate of £30,000 left his lady by Sir Samuel Grimston's will without which I could not settle my Hertfordshire estate upon my son clear at marriage but must have been subject to this sum then owing	2000	00	00
Total paid upon my son's account	7054	14	00
Received of Mr. Jacob and Mr. Horsey for my daughter Grimston's fortune	20000	00	00
Disbursements as appears by this book	07054	14	00
Received neat but.	12945	06	00
for which I settled for present maintenance out of the Hertfordshire estate	2100 pr. ann.		
more out of Hertfordshire in reversion	2000 pr. ann.		
more out of my Essex estate in revesion	500 pr. ann.		
	4600 pr. ann.		

and a jointure that covers the whole Hertfordshire
estate of £1,600 per annum free from all deductions
whatsoever

Great fortunes know not what to demand and when bought
at so great an expense not worth having

Appendix Six

Epitome of William, First Viscount Grimston's Will

His body to be buried in the family vault at St Michael's Church, with little expense and ceremony. The funeral is to cost no more than £80. 'I have a loving and tender wife and three younger sons, Harbottle, George and Henry'. To his wife for her life in addition to her jointure, the farms Spinnells and Cooke in Bradfield Miseley and Weeks, also all jewels, lockets, watches and rings, 300 ounces of plate to be chosen by her, and a coach or chariot with one pair of horses. She is to receive £200 immediately after her husband's death.

His son James Grimston is to have all plate except that chosen by his mother, linen, stock of cattle, farming utensils, etc., in Gorhambury and Bottom House. Also a close of arable land called Vallence Close, otherwise Highway Close, otherwise Bowl Close, containing seven acres more or less whereon a windmill formerly stood in the parish of Redbourn, which was purchased of Thomas Dagnell. The property is to be settled with the rest of the estate. The pictures, looking glasses, china, statues, lustres, books, and all the furniture are to be heirlooms. Mention of daughter Jane married to Thomas Cape of St Albans. She is to have 'my brilliant diamond ring which I bought of Seymor the goldsmith for £300' and he recommends his son-in-law to let the said ring descend as an heirloom in their family. His sons James and Harbottle are to convey and settle a farm called Fawns Wood and Munckwood or by whatever other name called in St Peter's, lately purchased of Joshua Pembroke. James, Harbottle, George and Henry are each to have £1,000 in South Sea Annuities.

Appendix Seven

Will of Harriot, Third Viscountess Grimston, 4 November 1780

This is my last Will and Testament. Whereas I have a great dislike to all pomp in a funeral ceremony I order mine to be conducted in the following manner. That my body should not be embalmed or opened (unless I should die of some disorder that may make the opening of it useful to mankind) thatit may be conveyed in a hearse to the town of St Albans in the County of Hertford to be laid in the vault of my dear husband's family in the church of St Michael's in the said town, and it is my desire to be attended to the grave by only my housekeeper, my own maid, the house steward and my servant John Dober should be with me at my decease, but if he should have left my service Lord Grimston's *valet de chambre* to go instead of him. And now as to worldly effects and property. I give devise and bequeath in manner following.

To my dear husband James Bucknall, Lord Viscount Grimston, etc., etc., his heirs executors administrators and assigns, I give all my messuages lands tenements and hereditaments whatsoever with their and every of their appurtenances (as well leasehold as copyhold as freehold) situate in counties of Somerset Surrey and elsewhere, to have and to hold to the said James Bucknall Grimston Lord Viscount Grimston his Heirs Executors Administrators and Assigns, and I will that the said Lord Viscount Grimston shall have an absolute power over all my estate both real and personal (trusting to his candour and judgement to make a proper distribution of the said effects to our dear children) subject nevertheless to the following legacies:

To my ever dear and honoured Mother Harriot Walter during her natural life I give and bequeath the rents and profits of my farm called Sondes Place in the parish of Dorking and county of Surrey and all the stock in husbandry therunto belonging.

To my cousin Anna Maria Cockburne one hundred pounds.

To my cousin Edward James, son of Mary James, sister of Dr. John Mervin Nooth, five hundred pounds, the interest of which money the said Mary James shall enjoy during her natural life, after which the principal shall be entirely at the disposal of the said Edward James.

To my father's faithful servants John Dober and David Browne fifty pounds each.

Lastly I do appoint the said James Bucknall Grimston Lord Viscount Grimston the sole Executor of this my last Will and Testament in witness whereof I Harriot Grimston the Testatrix have to this my last Will and Testament set my Hand and Seal this twenty-fourth day of November in the year of our Lord one thousand seven hundred and eighty.

Witnesses Jas. Simkins, Jas. Esternod, and Henry Bateman.

Concise Bibliography

Archaeologia, various volumes
Aubrey, John, *Brief Lives*, ed. Oliver Lawson Dick
Bayley, T.D.S., *Bradfield Church*
Burnet, Gilbert, *History of My Own Times*
Bury, J.P.T., *Address of Thanksgiving* (Corpus Christi College, Cambridge)
Cage, John, *The History and Antiquities of Redgrave in Suffolk*
Chambers Bunten, *Sir Thomas Meautys and his Friends*
The Creevy Papers
Collectanea Topographica, Vol. 5, 'History of de Gorham Family'
Daly Briscoe, A., *A Stuart Benefactress*
Drinker Bowen, Catherine, *The Lion and the Throne*
Erskine Hill, *The Social Milieu of Alexander Pope*
Evelyn, John, *Diary*, ed. E.S. de Beer
Fulford, Roger, *The Royal Dukes*
Gale, Frederick, *Memoirs of Robert Grimston*
Geners, R., *The Complete Book of Herbs*
The Gorhambury Archives
The Historical Manuscripts Commission Publications, various volumes
Kelch, R.A., *Newcastle, A Duke Without Money*
Lodge, E., *The Pedigree of Ireland, 1789*
Luttrell's *Diaries*, 1706
McCutcheon, Elizabeth, *Sir Nicholas Bacon's Great House Sententiae*
Middlesex and Hertfordshire Notes and Queries, Vol. iii, p. 132
Nichols, John, *The Progresses and Public Processions of Queen Elizabeth*
Oman, Carola, *The Gascoyne Heiress*
Rogers, J.C., *The Manor and House of Gorhambury*
Scott, Jonathan, *Piranesi*
Smith, J.T., *Nollekens and His Times*
Spedding, John, (ed.)., *Works of Francis Bacon*
Tittler, Robert, *The Making of a Tudor Statesman*
Walpole, Horace, *Fugitive Pieces by Noble Authors*

Index